D1488725

WITHDRAWN

THE SECTIONAL CRISIS AND NORTHERN METHODISM:

A Study in Piety, Political Ethics and Civil Religion

by

DONALD G. JONES

Jesse Lee Prize Essay of the Commission on Archives and History, The United Methodist Church

The Scarecrow Press, Inc.
Metuchen, N.J. & London
1979

Library of Congress Cataloging in Publication Data

Jones, Donald G
    The sectional crisis and northern Methodism.

    (Jesse Lee Prize essay of the Commission on Archives
and History, the United Methodist Church ;)
    Bibliography: p.
    Includes index.
    1. Methodist Episcopal Church--History. 2. Church
and social problems--Methodist Church. I. Title.
II. Series. United Methodist Church (United States).
Commission on Archives and History. Jesse Lee Prize of
Commission on Archives and History, the United Methodist
Church ; .
BX8381. J66   287'. 632   78-9978
ISBN 0-8108-1175-8

FOR

My Parents

Margaret Venables Jones
Clarence A. Jones

JESSE LEE PRIZE
of
COMMISSION ON ARCHIVES AND HISTORY
The United Methodist Church

1974

The plan for establishing an annual prize for a book-length manuscript on some aspect of the history of American Methodism was developed in connection with the Bicentennial of American Methodism, celebrated at Baltimore, Maryland, in 1966. It was proposed by the Committee on Awards which first met at Garrett Theological Seminary on March 27, 1965. The name honors Jesse Lee (1758-1816), author (1810) of the first history of American Methodism.

Subsequently the program was modified in two ways: the prize was offered biennially instead of annually and the money was committed directly to publication of manuscript.

The first award went to Lewis M. Purifoy in 1967 for "Negro Slavery, the Moral Ordeal of Southern Methodism, 1844-1861." The prize was awarded in 1968 to Lester B. Scherer for "Ezekiel Cooper, An Early American Methodist Leader." The third award went to William B. Gravely in 1970 for "Gilbert Haven, Racial Equalitarian, A Study of His Career in Racial Reform 1850-1880." The 1972 award went to Robert W. Sledge for "Hands on the Ark: The Struggle for Change in the Methodist Episcopal Church, South, 1914-1939." In 1974, the award was conferred upon Donald G. Jones for "The Sectional Crisis and Northern Methodism: A Study in Piety, Politics, Nationalism and Ethics, 1864-1876."

ACKNOWLEDGMENTS

My interest in the era of the Civil War and Reconstruction and specifically the response of Northern Methodism to that sectional crisis began over a decade ago in a seminar at Drew University taught by Gordon Harland. Subsequently, it was my privilege to have Professor Harland as the primary guide of my dissertation on this subject. This book is a refinement and updating of that study.

It is not possible to mention all of those to whom I am indebted for aid in this project, but there are some who stand out. To three diligent academic assistants at Drew-- Nancy Axelrad, Eve Rommel, Julia Shaw Accetola-- who spent many hours in the library searching out primary resources, I express deep gratitude. To my former department chairman, Paul Samply, and Dean Richard Stonesifer, who encouraged me and in important ways provided release time to do this work, I owe a hearty "thank you." To John H. Ness, Jr. of the Commission on Archives and History, The United Methodist Church I offer warm thanks for efforts in arranging the final publication details. I am also very grateful to the staff of the Rose Memorial Library at Drew for their cooperative and expert help on my behalf.

My deepest gratitude goes out to the three most important mentors in my life--Gordon Harland, George Kelsey and Will Herberg. To Gordon Harland with his capacity to stimulate and guide scholarly study; George Kelsey for his superior academic precision and Will Herberg (whose death in 1977 I still mourn) for his penetrating and broad erudition, I owe more than words can say. Their personal encouragement, scholarly instruction, and friendship were of inestimable value to me in the completion of this study.

Finally, I want to express great appreciation to my wife, Karen, who, with her own sense of history and expertise in the English language, read and edited this book with care and intelligence.

Donald G. Jones
The Drew Forest
Madison, New Jersey
1978

TABLE OF CONTENTS

CHAPTER 1

INTRODUCTION

This is a book of dissent. It repudiates and seeks to
correct much of the conventional wisdom about evangelical
Methodism in the third quarter of the nineteenth century.
For instance, it emphatically dissents from the view that the
ethic of the Methodist clergy in the North was expressed exclusively in terms of individual piety. It also dissents from
the commonly held notion that Protestantism during Reconstruction represented "the summit of complacency," a view-
point of Henry F. May which is shared by such scholars as
Robert Handy, Winthrop Hudson and Martin Marty (who discussed Reconstruction under the chapter heading, "The Complacent Era," in The Righteous Empire). The view that social and political quietism prevailed during this period is
belied by the documentation and interpretation in this study.

This book is also a polemic against the "carpetbagger"
interpretation of northern Methodism found in such valuable
studies as Ralph Morrow's Northern Methodism and Reconstruction and Hodding Carter's The Angry Scar. As such,
it should be read as a case study shaped by the multi-faceted
revisionist work of C. Van Woodward, Kenneth Stampp,
James McPherson, Timothy L. Smith, H. Shelton Smith and
William Gravely, among others.

Finally, it is perhaps important to know that this
work represents a scholarly quibble (if not a quarrel) with
my friend William Gravely, who, in his extremely important
book on Gilbert Haven, emphasized the radicalism of Haven
in contrast to the conservatism of northern Methodist leadership. In stressing that Haven was a "prophet without honor,"
Gravely misrepresented, I think, a rather large middle
ground between the poles of radicalism and social conservatism.[1] My point is simply this. Haven was not alone by
far in desiring to mix religion with politics in a prophetic
and redemptive fashion. Figures such as T. M. Eddy, Daniel Curry, Daniel Whedon, James McClintock and Abel Stevens

come to mind as others who shared his dream of racial equality and of a transformed, socially vital Methodism.

If this study does not win the arguments conclusively, I hope it does serve to advance scholarship in nineteenth century studies by illuminating a form of social Christianity antedating the rise of the Social Gospel.

My central thesis is that most of the prominent leaders of northern Methodism in postbellum America understood their denomination to be engaged in an aggressive mission to Christianize every aspect of society, and that the reflection and action they gave to this task was marked by a social ethic and political responsibility going way beyond what is usually indicated by such labels as "frontier religion," "pietistic individualism," and "evangelical moralism." An underlying assumption shaping this thesis is that, more than any other factor, the tragic dimensions of the Civil War and the constellation of issues emerging out of Reconstruction awakened these churchmen to a fresh social awareness while at the same time forcing them to face broader social and political expressions of moral evil and moral good.

In other words, the story of the Methodist Episcopal Church during the period following the Civil War is not the tale of circuit riders ready to dismount in bewilderment and defensiveness in response to the complexities of post-war America. It is not the tale of a "spiritualized" church interested only in fitting born-again Christians for heaven-- though it was surely engaged in that. It is a story of a confident and aggressive form of Christianity engaging American society and political structures with a highly disciplined institution, and with a gospel whose social relevance was assumed. This old-time religion did not proclaim a Christ against culture. Indeed, it was a kind of political religion rooted in a traditional faith vibrating in sympathy with Lincoln's conviction that this nation was "the last best hope of mankind."

This was a Christianity and civil religion that formed a powerful resource and motivation for "meddling" in political endeavors to elect Lincoln, impeach Andrew Johnson, support the fourteenth and fifteenth amendments and join with the radical Reconstruction Congress in the pursuit of justice for free blacks. This is not to deny strong elements of denominational chauvinism and self aggrandisement. It is also not to suggest that northern Methodist leaders had a "social con-

cern" or a program of "social action" after the fashion of
the gospel movement or the bureaucratic approaches of contemporary church groups.

The Methodist Episcopal Church, finding itself at the
center of public life with social and political influence perhaps unsurpassed at any time before or since, understood itself as sent to permeate, evangelize and Christianize American life. Northern Methodists did not engage in "social action" as a special task of the Church. Their mission to
America and to the world was articulated without reference
to fine distinctions between the personal and the social, the
temporal and the spiritual.

How Methodist clergymen saw their providential role
on the new continent was stated clearly during the proceedings of the Christmas Conference in 1784.

Question: What may we reasonably believe to be
God's design in raising up the preachers called
Methodists?

Answer: To reform the Continent and to spread
scriptural Holiness over these lands. [2]

Through the first half of the nineteenth century it was understood that the task of reforming the continent--and, beyond
that, redeeming mankind--was to be accomplished primarily
by evangelical means. As the Church followed the frontier,
going from success to success, the task was generally interpreted in highly individualistic rhetoric. In the antebellum
period, however, a change took place. More and more the
pulpit and the religious press began to wage war on civil
and social problems. The conspicuous part some Methodist
clergymen played in the anti-slavery crusade and the part
most clergymen played in the temperance campaign is well
known. Because both issues involved not only moral dimensions but institutional considerations, Church leaders, around
the 1850s, for the first time took decided stands on political
questions. [3]

For a variety of reasons, which will be examined in
succeeding chapters, the northern connection of Methodism
emerged from the Civil War in a formative period of social
teachings. As will be shown, considerable moral clarity and
social intelligence were evidenced in discussions and official
pronouncements concerning the meaning of the Civil War, the

meaning and destiny of the nation, the role of religion and politics, the relationship of Church and State, color caste, political reconstruction, and the relationship of blacks to the destiny of the nation.

On the other hand, as many scholars have pointed out, northern Methodism scarcely distinguished itself in meeting the issues of the urban-industrial revolution. Clergymen of the Methodist Episcopal Church did indeed suffer from economic myopia, political irrelevance and moral evasion as they met with this new frontier. They made no attempt to speak to, or even for, industrial workers. Moreover, little was done on behalf of women's rights. This has all been well treated and documented in many significant studies.

Nevertheless, northern Methodism cannot be charged with avoidance and withdrawal. Even in the cities, where there was little grasp of the economic, political and social dimensions of certain moral problems, Methodist clerics did attempt to speak to the social and moral questions involved in massive immigration, urban poverty and political corruption. And they did engage in city missions and promoted social services with great vigor, making a substantial contribution to society. It is not, however, the intention in this study to focus on the social ministry of Methodism to the city and the economic order. Historians have persistently emphasized this aspect of Protestantism and the social order after the Civil War. If in this book the stress is on the sectional conflict and Reconstruction, it is primarily in the interest of a more balanced estimate of the social philosophy and particular social teachings of northern Methodism. This study is aimed at a corrective emphasis, not a comprehensive assessment of the social thought and action of the Methodist Episcopal Church during the late Civil War and Reconstruction period.

Any attempt to understand northern Methodism in its corporate relations to society or to interpret its social philosophy, teaching and action requires a consideration of Protestant Christianity in general during this period in American life. Accordingly, Part I proceeds with these two queries: First, what sway did Protestant Christianity have in the social order during the post-Civil War period? As a movement and institution, what influence did Protestantism have in society relative to other institutions? Second, what was the status of Methodism; what unique role did this largest single denomination play in public affairs and the common life of the nation?

While Part I emphasizes external social and historical factors, Part II investigates relevant internal theological and ethical postulates, ecclesiastical tradition, and the self-understanding of the Church in relation to national destiny. The three chapters in this section are designed to illuminate how three interrelated categories provided a basis for Methodist self-understanding and a frame of reference for comprehending the denomination's social attitudes, political involvements, and apparently emerging social ethics. Thus, this second part is focused by the question, "How did northern Methodist leaders see themselves and their Church?"

Part III delineates the social ethic of northern Methodists concerning the relations of Christianity to the social order, the issue of the pulpit and politics, and the role of the Church in society. The final chapter focuses on the issues surrounding political and ecclesiastical Reconstruction and black Freedmen, with special stress on the interpretation of Reconstruction, the teaching about race and the position of the Methodist Episcopal Church on color caste and civil rights.

The denominational approach to American religious studies, long out of vogue among professional historians, is coming back, I believe. It is time, certainly, for historians both secular and religious to shed the faddish prejudice against such studies. It is my hope that, aside from its substantive contribution, this book will illustrate the continued usefulness of "church" histories for an understanding of the American experience.

Many of the issues which confronted religious institutions and the nation in the 1960s and 1870s are yet with us. By examining the response of one segment of Protestant Christianity to questions of racial justice, national destiny and meaning, church and state and social change a century ago, resources, spiritual and rational, might be uncovered that could give nerve and wisdom to a generation deeply involved in the same issues a century later.

Notes

1. William Gravely. Gilbert Haven, Methodist Abolitionist: A Study in Race, Religion, and Reform, 1850-1880. Nashville and New York: Abingdon Press, 1973.
2. Emory Steven Bucke, ed. The History of American Methodism. New York: Abingdon Press, 1964, I, p. 226.

3. Kenneth Edwin Barnhart. "The Evolution of the Social Consciousness in Methodism." Unpublished Ph.D. Dissertation, University of Chicago, 1924, p. 85.

PART I

A SUMMIT OF INSTITUTIONAL
VIGOR AND POWER

CHAPTER 2

THE POWER* AND PRESTIGE OF PROTESTANTISM

In a period when the Protestant Church seems on the defensive; when its bureaucratic spokesmen indulge in self-flagellation; when its voice through resolutions, sermons and the religious press is of little significance to the power centers and decision-making places of our national life; when its professed religious faith has little effect on the common life or the laity, it requires a great deal of historical imagination to grasp the power and prestige of Protestant Christianity in our nation just a century ago. Of the great institutions touching daily life, Protestant Christianity and politics were dominant and most real to Americans of the Civil War and Reconstruction Era and the early part of the Gilded Age.[1] In the 1860s politics and the Churches still offered the best professional opportunities. Consequently the best minds and most prestigious men were found there.[2] For this reason a study of the interactions between clergymen and politicians, and between Church and state, is of especial pertinence. Particularly is this true of the reconstruction period when religio-moral issues seemed to converge with socio-political questions to a greater extent than in other times.

At the close of the Civil War the vast majority of Americans, whether Church members or not, were encompassed in "popular" if not in "Ecclesiastical" Protestantism.[3] While approximately 16% of the population were actual church members, Protestantism's influence far exceeded the constituent strength of the Churches. There is considerable evidence that many non-members were regularly attending church services, public lectures by clergymen, and religious conferences.[4] Ralph Gabriel, in his searching study, American

---

*The word "power" is used in this chapter to denote institutional vigor and influence.

8

Democratic Thought, makes persuasive his assertion that a composite of "the democratic faith" and "Protestant Christianity" permeated the intellectual climate of the mid-nineteenth century. [5] This blend of civil religion and Protestant piety formed the dominant religious experience of the time. [6]

It was a time when men in their secular vocations moved easily from the "secular" to the "religious" realm-- though they would not make that distinction. It was a common occurrence, for instance, for a General to hold prayer meetings with his men during the Civil War. Illustrative of evangelical piety during the war years is a correspondence from a prominent Methodist layman, General Clinton B. Fisk, who in the heat of battle could write to Bishop Matthew B. Simpson:

> I assure you my hands, heart and head are well
> employed day and night, week days and Sunday.
> It would do you good to "drop in" at my Soldier
> meetings. I arrange for Brigade gatherings on the
> Sabbath convening in one place--the Officers, men
> and Chaplains of the entire brigade. I conduct the
> meetings myself and the Lord is with us. We had
> a blessed meeting of this kind in 'Fort Curtis'
> yesterday. [7]

In another letter Fisk assures the Methodist Bishop, "Revival yet in progress."[8]

The significance of religion as news and the Protestant Church as socially important is evidenced by the close coverage newspapers and periodical journals gave to Church activities. In 1866 during the centennial celebration of the Methodist Episcopal Church, virtually every major newspaper carried commendatory articles on the progress of this largest Protestant denomination in America. Typical of the coverage was an article in the New York Tribune lauding the Methodist Episcopal Church for its "great power in the land" and its influence both "temporal" and "spiritual." The secular writer, expressing sentiments that sound strange to the ears a century later, writes, "nothing can be more marvelous than the growth of this Church."[9] Harpers Weekly and The Nation, especially, gave close attention to Church activities during the Civil War and in the two decades following. It was a time when it was not at all unusual for a prominent person to mix religious piety with his everyday business. The editor of the New York Sun in 1861 not only inserted

much about revivals, church meetings and missionary activities in his paper along with war news, crime and stock
market reports, but he also "saw to it that a prayer meeting
was held every day at noon in the Sun editorial rooms; and
after the war had begun, he urged that Union generals should
be instructed not to fight battles on Sundays."[10] George
Crooks records that Bishop Simpson's visits to the war-of-
fice of Secretary Stanton were usually followed "by an invitation to the secretary's private room, where long conferences
were held, ending sometimes in earnest prayer."[11] Daniel
Drew could leave the Stock Exchange and the "scramble for
cash" to attend class-meetings and testimonial meetings in
his church on Mulberry Street where he enjoyed telling "what
the Lord had done" and of wrestling with "other sinners at
the mercy seat until he gets them through."[12] Not to know
how easily one could move from guns to revivals; from statecraft to prayer; from making money to religious exhortation,
is not to know the age.

Protestantism and Education

The cultural dominance of Protestantism can be illustrated in a variety of ways, of which one of the most reveal-
ing is the strong Protestant coloring in public education. It
is true that many of the states during the post-war period
had officially excluded sectarian teaching either by amendment
or by their original constitutions. But it is a mistake to sur-
mise, therefore, that religious teaching or even orthodox
Christianity was excluded. It is to be remembered that Horace Mann, while opposed to "sectarian doctrinal instruction,"
nevertheless argued that "in every course of studies, all the
practical and preceptive parts of the Gospel should have been
sacredly included...."[13] Mann left little doubt concerning
the importance of Bible reading in the public schools and,
at the same time, rejected a sectarian dogmatic theology.
He writes:

> I suppose it to be their belief, as it is mine, that
> the Bible makes known to us the rule of life and
> the means of salvation; and that, in the language
> of the apostle, it is a 'faithful saying, and worthy
> of all acceptance, that Christ Jesus came into the
> world to save sinners'; but still, that it would be
> a flagrant transgression of our duty to select any
> one of those innumerable guide boards ... which
> fallible men have set up along the way, and to pro-

claim that the kingdom of heaven is only to be sought for in that particular direction. [14]

Pointing out the prevalence of Bible reading in Massachusetts' schools and not disapproving of such a practice, Mann argued that

> The use of the Bible in schools is not expressly enjoined by law, but both its letter and spirit are in consonance with that use; and as a matter of fact, I suppose there is not, at the present time, a single town in the commonwealth in whose schools it is not read. ... [15]

On another occasion he said he "regarded hostility to religion in the schools as the greatest crime he could commit." [16]

The religion that was by common consensus permitted in the public schools was a practical Protestant form of morality and piety which received a special encouragement and impetus during the great revivals of 1858. Robert Handy points out that at the close of the Civil War, Protestants were still an "aggressive, self-confident, and surprisingly homogeneous group ..." who saw no reason "why their influence should not continue to grow." [17] The continuance of Bible reading and incorporation of religion in classroom activity was a prime means by which Protestants sought to further their influence with a view to Christianize society. T. M. Eddy, a prominent leader in the Methodist Episcopal Church and editor of the Northwestern Christian Advocate, declared, in 1868, that "education is the handmaid of Christianity and the safeguard of our republican institutions." [18] It was not an uncommon sentiment. To most Protestants at this time religion and education were thought of in Horace Mann's terms, i.e., as integrally related. By the end of the century, however, religion and education, following the secular trend, had become independent concerns. [19]

Despite the agitation on the part of Roman Catholics and liberal secularists, and the impact of "the new geological evidence concerning the origin of the world and the new biological evidence concerning the origin of man," at the close of the war the traditional views of creation and of man's spirituality maintained their hold upon the great majority of people in general, as well as upon those who dominated American schools and colleges." [20] Most teachers during this period would have no qualms in teaching out of Asa

Thomas Mears Eddy (1823-1874), Editor of the <u>Northwestern Christian Advocate</u> in Chicago. He was a zealous advocate of freedman rights and radical reconstruction.

Gray's Lessons in Botany and Vegetable Physiology, published in 1857 and reissued in 1879, which contained the following edifying assertion:

> And the interest will be greatly enhanced as the
> student rising to higher and wider views, begins
> to discern the System of Botany, or, in other
> words, comprehends more and more of the Plan
> of the Creator in the Vegetable Kingdom.
>
> Now this word plan of course supposes a planner,
> an intelligent mind working according to a system;
> it is this system, therefore, which the botanist is
> endeavoring as far as he can to exhibit in a classi-
> fication. In it we humbly attempt to learn some-
> thing of the plan of the Creator in this department
> of Nature. [21]

A book of chemistry, published in 1873, opens with
a perfect illustration of the integral relation between religious
inspiration and academic information:

> Each tiny atom is watched by the Eternal Eye and
> guided by the Eternal Hand. When Christ declared
> the very hairs of our heads to be numbered, he
> intimated a chemical truth which we can now know
> in full to be that the very atoms of which our hair
> is composed are numbered by that same watchful
> providence. [22]

The intentional inculcation of religious piety in the McGuffey
Readers, widely used in the post-war period, is well known.
In the preface of the New Sixth Eclectic Reader it is frankly
stated that articles were selected with a view to "elevating"
the scholar by "purity and delicacy of sentiment, and especially to furnish the mind with valuable information, and
to influence the heart by sound moral and religious instruction."[23]

These few examples are but a small sample of those
that could be cited to support the thesis that students in the
public schools as well as in the numerous sectarian academies, in the decade following the Civil War were being
taught a religious view of the world with a vivid Protestant
coloring, and were taught that the laws of nature and morality rested upon divine sanctions.

This moral-religious approach prevailed for at least

two decades following the war, even though a new "separa-
tionist" mood began to emerge in the mid-seventies and
finally held sway by the end of the century. Already in 1875
President Grant recommended a constitutional amendment
prohibiting the teaching in the public schools of any sectarian
religious tenets. Responding to Grant's recommendation,
James G. Blaine proposed an amendment that would make
separation absolute, carrying provisions explicitly forbidding
the teaching of religion in publicly supported schools. Though
it was overwhelmingly passed by the House (180-7), this
amendment did not obtain the two-thirds majority vote in the
Senate (28-16). [24] What is significant about the vote is that
it followed straight party lines, with the Republicans voting
for it and the Democrats opposing it, a fact which reveals
the growing power of the Roman Catholic population. Protestant Republicans were simply opposed to aid for parochial
education. Thus, conservative Protestants, prompted by an
"anti-Romish" animus, unwittingly joined with religious lib-
erals and secularists to provide the way for complete separation of religion and education.

The factors contributing to the receding influence of
Protestantism in public education are many and complex and
it is not the purpose here to go into that. Suffice it to say
that in the period immediately following the war, Protestantism as a movement continued to move into the sphere of education with remarkable success until towards the end of the
century, when Protestantism met the insurmountable challenge of an increasing population with a non-Protestant orientation and a new secular mood permeating the higher levels
of education.

Protestant domination in the ethos of American life
in the 1860s and 1870s is also reflected in the sphere of
higher education. Most of the colleges in the country at
this time were founded by Protestant denominations and continued to serve the interests of the Church. [25] The Methodists, who, along with the Baptists, accepted as a matter of
course the Presbyterian and Congregational control of higher
education in the early part of the nineteenth century, beginning in the 1830s, "entered upon a period of College-found-
ing unprecedented in the history of denominational activity."[26]
In the thirty years preceding the war the Methodists had
founded thirty-four permanent colleges. This new "mission
endeavor," as they referred to it, was continued with unre-
lenting fervor after the war. [27] From 1865 to 1886 the
Methodist Episcopal Church established twenty-eight colleges

and seminaries, all of which still exist. [28] Among this list
are some of the greatest of American colleges and universities, including such schools as Boston University--1869,
Syracuse University--1870, University of Denver--1880, University of Southern California--1880. Without exception every
institution of higher learning founded by the Methodists--and
it is generally true for all other Protestant denominations at
this time--had a clergyman for President. [29]

The importance of having a prominent "pulpiteer" to
head a university is indicated by a letter to Bishop Matthew
Simpson of the Methodist Episcopal Church upon the founding
of Northwestern University in 1855. Dr. John Evans, a prominent Methodist layman and successful business man, im-
portuning Simpson to accept the presidency of Northwestern
University, articulated the qualifications necessary to properly fill the position:

> We must have a man of learning, eloquence in the
> pulpit, energy of character, and skill in manage-
> ment or we shall not accomplish the great good
> designed in the establishment of an institution of
> the highest order. [30]

There were those who began opting for an undenominational approach in higher education. President Eliot of
Harvard gave the commencement address at Smith College in
1879 and commended Smith College with regard to its approach to religion. He said, "It is entirely undenominational
in its management and instruction," and added that in taking
this position it follows the example of "Harvard, Yale, and
Columbia, which declare their policy to be unsectarian, and
appoint professors from various sects." [31] E. L. Godkin,
in reporting Eliot's statement, was inclined to believe the
assessment inaccurate. "We question very much," he
writes, "whether a member of the Unitarian denomination
would be appointed to a professorship in either Yale or Columbia." [32] He could have added Princeton, Wesleyan, Dartmouth, Boston, Amherst or any number of others. In 1869,
for instance, former president Lord of Dartmouth wrote to
the alumni warning them to "avoid rationalism, the worst
enemy of Christianity, and to submit their reason to the authority of God in the Bible." [33]

Godkin, a keen observer of American institutions,
was convinced that the major universities were still overwhelmingly sectarian and orthodox in makeup. The substance

and tenor of the debate in the next several issues of The Nation, through correspondence and editorial reply, shows that Protestant sectarian dominance of higher education in the late 1870s was no longer taken for granted and, though editor Godkin may have been more accurate in judgment, President Eliot's views represented the new mood and were prophetic of what was happening in higher education.

Prestige of the Clergy

The high prestige of the clergy during the third quarter of the nineteenth century is another gauge of the over-all importance of the Church in the common and official life of the nation. The following remarks of a layman writing for the Atlantic Monthly in 1858 would be unthinkable in twentieth-century America, or, perhaps, anytime after the 1880s:

> There are more than thirty thousand preachers in the United States, whereof twenty-eight thousand are Protestants, the rest are Catholics....
> . . . .
> No class has such opportunities for influence, such means of power; even now the press ranks second to the pulpit.
> . . . .
> What personal means of controlling the public the minister has at his command! Of their own accord, men 'assemble and meet together,' and look up to him. In the country, the town-roads centre at the meeting-house, which is also the terminus a quo, the golden mile-stone, whence distances are measured.
> . . . .
> Other speakers must have some magnetism of personal power or public reputation to attract men; but the minister can dispense with that; to him men answer before he calls, and even when they are not sent by others are drawn by him.... No man of science or letters has such access to men. Besides, he is to speak on the grandest of all themes, --of Man, of God, of Religion, man's deepest desires, his loftiest aspirings. [34]

That this expression captures the truth of the matter for the Civil War period and the immediate post-war period may be

seen in the next chapter, where the influence of the clergy
is treated in greater detail. Patronage during the reconstruction period, distributed from the highest offices in Washington, D. C. , had to take into account the numerical and political strength of particular clergymen and denominations.

Lord Bryce, the well known observer of the American
scene in the post-Civil War period, witnessed to the "built-
in" prestige of the clergyman.

> The position of a minister of the Gospel always
> carries with it some dignity--that is to say, it
> gives a man a certain advantage in the society,
> whatever it may be, to which he naturally belongs
> in respect of his family connections, his means,
> and his education. In the great cities the leading
> ministers ... are among the first citizens, and
> exercise an influence often wider and more power-
> ful than that of any layman. In cities of the second
> order, the clergymen ... move in the best society
> of the place. Similarly in country places the pas-
> tor is better educated and more enlightened than
> the average member of his flock, and becomes a
> leader in works of beneficence. [35]

The conditions following the Civil War favored the
preacher and helped to shape an era in the life of the American Church in which "princes of the pulpit" would reign.
Speaking of this time of rapid population growth concentrated
in the cities, Robert Michaelson reminds us that, "The
spoken word was the chief means of entertainment and education. Any man who could speak well at the popular level
was assured of an audience. "[36]

The great power and popularity of the Protestant
minister makes intelligible the active and effective role of
the Methodist clergy in public affairs during the reconstruction
period. At the same time a change in the character of ministerial influence, when they had popularity but not political
power, helps us to understand the demise in social and political relevance of northern Methodism in the second decade
following the war.

The shift from a strong influential Protestantism during
Reconstruction to a receding significance in the public life of
the nation in the post-reconstruction period is focused and indicated in the loss of ministerial prestige and influence in the

last quarter of the century. Handy notes that "this theme of the loss of ministerial prestige and influence crept frequently into the literature about the ministry in the late nineteenth century. "[37] Not only preachers, editors of the religious press and homiletics professors treated this theme, but men such as Godkin thought it important enough to make comment. In the same article in which he took exception to President Eliot's remarks about non-denominationalism in higher education, he also took exception to Eliot's observation that "it is a common opinion that interest in the great themes of God and immortality, and life and death, has died out." Godkin, with his usual perspicuity, could see that it was not so much a change in religious interest as it was a change in an institution. The office of the clergy, he perceived, had begun to lose ground.

> As far as our observation goes--and each person
> can only base an assertion of this kind of his own
> observation--the 'common opinion' is not that in-
> terest in these great themes has died out, but that
> the belief that anybody can speak about them with
> special authority has greatly declined. The in-
> terest in the themes is as deep as ever, no doubt.
> There is hardly any man who can ever cease to
> regard them as tremendous; but there is a wide-
> spread and growing opinion that no person can
> throw much light upon them, and that no secrets
> about them are communicated in divinity schools
> which are not within the reach of every one who
> walks the highway. It is this belief which is
> weakening the hold of the churches on the educated
> class, of which so much complaint is made, and
> which is diminishing the influence of the clergy,
> and which is doing so much to make a minister's
> success depend on his personal qualities rather
> than on his professional degree. [38]

A. N. Littlejohn, an Episcopalian bishop, delivered a series of lectures on the Christian Ministry in 1884 in which he sought to "give an account of its Stewardship" in the face of its "Alleged Decline of Influence. "[39] Writing as one thoroughly acquainted with Godkin's view of the current prestige of the Sacred Office, he writes:

> Nothing relating to the Christian Religion is more
> characteristic of these closing years of the century
> than the allegation, pressed every day with increas-

ing emphasis, that the influence of the Christian
Priesthood on the thought and life of the time has
not only changed in its form and direction, but
that it has declined in bulk and force. Whatever
the Clergy themselves may think of the question,
it is clear that the world at large has not been
backward in making up or in announcing its verdict. [40]

Underscoring the editor of The Nation's suggestion that re-
placing the prestige of the professional office was an emerging "cult of clerical personality," the Bishop continues:

There was a time when the Priest's position and
influence were accepted as things of course; when
no one dreamed of intruding into functions universally conceded to him and touching some way all
sides of life. But all that is radically changed.
Now the Priest's authority amounts to no more
than the moral power won by force of character,
or the intellectual power created by superior discipline and attainments. [41]

In lamenting the diminishing influence of the clergy in his
day Bishop Littlejohn recalled the powerful influence of ministers on the educated class; the political favors they received; the special immunities that were theirs; the prominence they held "in fashioning the chaotic and reconciling the
conflicting elements of social and political life"; the leadership they exerted in "liberal and popular education"; the em-
ployment of religious press "in the interests of mankind";
and the immense service to "the poor and disinherited by the
pastoral office."[42] This recollection was not of the distant
past, but of the immediate past. The whole tenor of his
discussion and the way he dealt with the allegations of declining ministerial influence--though he himself did not entirely accept them--illustrate the point that Protestant Christianity was going through a radical change in its relations
with society in the period under consideration. The literature on the declining influence of the clergy, taken up increasingly in the late 1870s and onward, shows by inference
the power of the clergy and the Church at the close of the
Civil War.

The Religious Press

No more striking index to the pervasiveness of Protes-

tant influence and religious vitality can be found than in the
role of the religious press. In giving comparative statistics,
compilers of the Tenth U. S. Census note the "successful con-
duct of what is known as the religious press. "43

> In 1850 there were 191 religious newspapers and
> periodicals; in 1860 the number had increased to
> 277, an increase of 57%. No attempt was made
> to estimate the circulation of the religious press
> until the census of 1870, when there were reported
> 407 religious papers, with an aggregate circulation
> of 4, 764, 358. The Tenth Census reveals this num-
> ber increase to 553, with a correspondingly in-
> creased circulation.

> The religious periodicals of the United States com-
> prise among their number many of our oldest and
> most successful journalistic enterprises. 44

The religious group was the largest of all the various classes
of periodicals[45] and was without question one of the most
important institutions in American public life. [46] Editors of
the Methodist press were among the most powerful in the
Church, and it is not without significance that the editorial
office was the main stepping-stone to becoming a Bishop.
Such men as Edward Thompson, Calvin Kingsley, D. W.
Clark, Gilbert Haven, Matthew Simpson, among others, were
all chosen to the episcopal office from editorships in the
Methodist press.

In commenting on the strong appeal of religious journals and papers in the early part of the nineteenth century,
Whitney R. Cross, struggles to make sense out of this phe-
nomenon in the light of our day when "theology is a very
nearly dead subject. "

> The puzzle of such an attraction resolves itself in
> two ways. First, a continuing itineracy often
> accompanied the paper, making local friends who
> in turn urged its support. A train of camp meet-
> ings, revivals, conventions, and quarterly sessions
> also kept adherents in contact. To others beyond
> immediate reach, the magazine, even were its
> heavy doses of theology not read, could be a con-
> stant reminder of intellectual and spiritual ties,
> while some leisurely seepage of doctrine originally
> imbibed by ear might filter into the inner con-

sciousness. But suggestion of such indirect influence begs the major question. It seems an inescapable conclusion that a considerable proportion even of laymen read and relished the theological treatises. [47]

Cross's conclusion about a pre-Civil War era may be drawn for the period following the war. Lord Bryce, with some astonishment, records that in the 1880s "interest in theological questions is ... keener than it has generally been in England since the days of the commonwealth." [48] Relating this theological interest to the medium of the religious press he continues:

> A great deal of the ordinary reading of the average family has a religious tinge, being supplied in religious or semi-religious weekly and monthly magazines to many parts of the West. The old problems of pre-destination, reprobation, and election continue to be discussed by farmers and shopkeepers in their leisure moments with the old eagerness, and give a sombre tinge to their views on religion. [49]

The role of the religious press as a cultural influence in nineteenth-century America has not been adequately assessed, but it is known that as a communications medium, the churches--through tracts, lesson material, magazines, weekly papers, books, pamphlets and scholarly journals-- were unsurpassed. [50] What is the significance of this? The answer is obvious: the churches became the chief dispenser of information and values to the American people. As such, the churches played a key role in interpreting the meaning of grave social and political issues to many people who would not otherwise even know such issues existed. Donald Mathews argues that this is exactly what happened in the antebellum period with regard to the slavery question. Slavery did not touch the vast majority of citizens as an immediate problem, but, because the religious press increasingly took up the topic before the war, "even those localities which did not face the problem directly would be engaged." [51]

Lord Bryce, after a perusal of the literature which the ordinary American educated farmer and worker read, was led to conclude "that the Bible and Christian theology altogether do more in the way of forming the imaginative

background to an average American view of the world of
man and nature than they do in modern Protestant Europe. "52
In exerting such a profound influence on the thought and
imagination, the church, primarily through its press and pulpit, provided special moral-religious categories for viewing
the sectional conflict during and after the war. Thus the
Protestant churches of both sections ideologically transformed
the Civil War from a bloody clash of economic and political
interests into a religious-moral crusade. There is also
strong reason to believe that the impact of the religious
press was a very determinative factor in shaping the humanitarian and religious motivations of those who went South after
the war to help the freedmen.

Church officials and, especially, editors of various
denominational weeklies were quite conscious of the power of
the printed page. This knowledge led them increasingly to
use the periodical press as a means of inculcating political
views and as an instrument for guiding political action. The
editors, being among the most prestigious in a particular
denomination, spoke with an authority going way beyond that
of a local preacher. Indeed, editors of the religious press
saw themselves as "preachers of the printed page. "53 As
preachers to a vast congregation of readers they purposely
helped to form the social conscience of the Church with a
view to influencing the course of public policy.

The increasing concern for social and political issues
in the Methodist Episcopal Church was a result of the increasing power it exercised as a social institution. Before
1850 it had been considered outside the province of the
Church to deal explicitly with most political questions and
to try to influence public opinion on these matters. But, as
the Methodists became more conscious of their status, articles in the various Christian Advocates, with increasing fre-
quency, contained direct political teaching. One editor in
1865 defended his right to go beyond the religious themes in
his editorial sermon:

> The intellectual wants of our readers must not be
> overlooked, and the great moral and practical
> questions of the day must have their place in the
> prompt, full and fair discussions of every live,
> wide-awake religious paper, or the unscrupulous
> demagogues and politicians will not only run away
> with the questions, but will take the people along
> to support them. 54

The dynamic of Protestantism is revealed not only in the number and circulation of the religious press, but in the confident and self-conscious desire on the part of Protestant denominations to use this instrument as a means of permeating the life of the nation with the leaven of Christianity.

In sum it needs to be reiterated and underlined that Protestant Christianity was still the dominant cultural fact of the nation at the close of the Civil War, and that, as a vital religious movement, evangelical Christianity continued with increasing aggressiveness until sometime around the 1880s. The notion of Reinhold Neibuhr that "religious vitality" began to wane after 1850 cannot be sustained on the basis of the evidence. [55] There is evidence that points to a gradual recession in the influence of evangelical Christianity, notably in the field of education and in the declining prestige of clergy--before the advance of the secular spirit in the 1880s and 1890s. In this period Protestant churches were being gradually pushed out from the center to a marginal place in the social life of the nation.

The pervasiveness of religion--especially the Protestant brand--provided a special relevance for the attitudes and actions of the Churches, making them foremost of the social institutions of the day. [56] There is no doubt that issues emerging out of the sectional conflict took on special meanings; understandings were cast in a special language; and responses of the government and citizenry were conditioned by the central place of the churches in the nation's life. [57] On the other hand, the fact that the Churches were at center stage meant that historical forces and events tended to influence their social teachings and actions in a unique way. The next chapter will endeavor to show that, by virtue of its central place in the social structure of American life, the Methodist Episcopal Church came to play a leading role during the reconstruction period in social criticism and social action. The posture of this denomination and its response vis-à-vis the broader social issues was in part shaped by its own inner dynamic, and in part by the prominence it held as a social institution.

Notes

1. Robert T. Handy. The Protestant Quest for a Christian America. Philadelphia: Fortress Press, 1967, 10, 11. Cf. H. Wayne Morgan. The Gilded Age. Syracuse: Syracuse University Press, 1963, p. 5.

2. Lewis G. Vander Velde. The Presbyterian Churches
    and the Federal Union: 1861-1869. Cambridge:
    Harvard University Press, 1932, p. 4.

3. Handy. The Protestant Quest ..., pp. 10, 11.

4. "No Salvation Out of the Church," The Methodist, VI,
    (June 10, 1865), p. 180. The editor wrote that it
    was "a lamentable fact that there are multitudes of
    people ... attending our churches, holding pews in
    them ... who do not belong to the church."

5. Ralph Henry Gabriel. The Course of American Demo-
    cratic Thought. New York: The Ronald Press Com-
    pany, 1940, pp. 14, 15, 170-72.

6. The use of the term civil religion conforms to the
    meaning given it under the category Protestant civic
    piety in the fivefold typology found in American Civil
    Religion, eds., Russell E. Richey and Donald G.
    Jones. New York: Harper and Row, 1974, p. 17.

7. Clinton B. Fisk to Matthew Simpson, February 9, 1863.
    Clinton B. Fisk Papers, Drew.

8. Clinton B. Fisk to Matthew Simpson, February 21,
    1864. Clinton B. Fisk Papers, Drew.

9. "The N. Y. Tribune and the M. E. Church," Christian
    Advocate (New York), XLI, (January 4, 1866), p. 4,
    citing New York Tribune, n. d.

10. Frank Luther Mott. American Journalism: A History:
    1690-1960. 3rd ed. New York: The Macmillan
    Co., 1962, p. 373.

11. George R. Crooks. The Life of Bishop Matthew Simp-
    son. New York: Harper & Brothers, 1890, pp.
    370-71.

12. Bouck White. The Book of Daniel Drew. New York:
    Doubleday, Page & Co., 1913, pp. 125, 126.

13. Raymond B. Culver. Horace Mann and Religion in the
    Massachusetts Public Schools. New Haven: Yale
    University Press, 1929, p. 170.

14. Ibid., p. 193.

15. Donald E. Boles. The Bible, Religion, and the Public Schools. Ames, Iowa: Iowa State University Press, 1961, p. 26.

16. Edwin Scott Gaustad, ed. Religious Issues in American History. New York: Harper & Row, 1968, cited in Chapter 16, B, "Religion and Education in America," Will Herberg, p. 236.

17. Handy, The Protestant Quest ..., p. 11.

18. "1867-8, " Northwestern Christian Advocate, XVI, (January 1, 1968), p. 4.

19. R. Freeman Butts and Lawrence A. Cremin. A History of Education in American Culture. New York: Henry Holt and Co. , 1953, pp. 385, 386. The authors delineate three views that emerge in the very heated debate that began to take place in the 1870s: "(1) the view favoring sectarian religious instruction, taken principally by the Roman Catholics, (2) the view favoring nonsectarian instruction and Bible reading, and (3) the view rejecting both Bible reading and religious instruction per se. " It was the third view that won out, so that by the end of the century virtually a complete extrusion of religious based moral teaching has taken place. This new secularism in education signifies the changing status and erstwhile influence of Protestant Christianity. This shift helps to explain the changing approaches to social issues by northern Methodists at the close of the Reconstruction period. See also the essay by Will Herberg in Gaustad, Religious Issues ... , p. 235, et passim.

20. Butts and Cremin, A History of Education ..., p. 325.

21. Asa Gray. Gray's Lessons in Botany and Vegetable Physiology. 3rd ed. New York: Ivison, Blakeman, Taylor & Co. , 1879, pp. 194, 195.

22. Winfred Ernest Garrison. The March of Faith. New York: Harper and Brothers Publishers, 1933, p. 66, citing Steele's (sic) Fourteen Weeks of Chemistry, 1873, n. p.

23. Wm. H. McGuffey. McGuffey's New Sixth Eclectic Reader. Cincinnati: Sargent, Wilson & Hinkle, 1857, p. 8.

24. Boles, The Bible, Religion ..., p. 31.

25. George P. Schmidt. The Old Time College President.
    New York: Columbia University Press, 1930, p.
    184 et passim.

26. William Warren Sweet. Revivalism in America. New
    York: Abingdon Press, 1944, p. 149.

27. Ibid.

28. A. W. Cummings. The Early Schools of Methodism.
    New York: Phillips & Hunt, 1886, p. 429. The
    information is obtained from Cummings' "Classified
    List of Educational Institutions of the Methodist Epis-
    copal Church Existing in 1886."

29. Ibid., p. 29. See also Schmidt, The Old Time College
    President, in the last two chapters where the author
    discusses the shift from the president as preacher,
    teacher and scholar to the president as the business
    executive, citing the industrial revolution as the
    chief causitive factor contributing to this change.

30. John Evans to Matthew Simpson, April 2, 1855. Mat-
    thew B. Simpson Papers, Drew.

31. "Cultivation of Theology in Colleges," The Nation, XXIX,
    (July 3, 1879), p. 6.

32. Ibid.

33. Schmidt, The Old Time College President, p. 192.

34. "Henry Ward Beecher," Atlantic Monthly, I, No. VII,
    (May 1858), pp. 862-63.

35. James Bryce. The American Commonwealth. New
    York: Macmillan and Co., 1891, pp. 580, 581.

36. Robert Michaelson, "The Protestant Ministry in Amer-
    ica," in The Ministry in Historical Perspectives,
    eds. H. Richard Niebuhr and Daniel D. Williams.
    New York: Harper & Brothers, 1956, p. 281.

37. Robert T. Handy, "The Ministry in American History:
    A Reflection in the Light of Ecumenical Encounter,"
    Mid-Stream, IV, No. 4 (Summer 1965), p. 122.

38. "Cultivation of Theology in Colleges, " The Nation,
    XXXIX, (July 3, 1879), p. 6.

39. A. N. Littlejohn. The Christian Ministry at the Close
    of the Nineteenth Century. New York: Thomas
    Whittaker 2 and 3 Bible House, 1884, p. ix.

40. Ibid. , p. 8.

41. Ibid. , p. 10.

42. Ibid. , pp. 19-21.

43. Ibid. , pp. 19-21.

44. U. S. Bureau of the Census. Tenth Census of the United
    States: 1880. The Newspaper and Periodical Press,
    "The Religious Press, " p. 119.

45. Ibid.

46. Jerald C. Brauer. Protestantism in America. 2nd ed.
    Philadelphia: Westminster Press, 1965, p. 195.

47. Whitney R. Cross. The Burned-over District. Ithaca,
    New York: Cornell University Press, 1950, p. 108.
    See also the discussion by Robert Handy, The Protes-
    tant Quest ..., pp. 8, 9.

48. Bryce, The American Commonwealth, p. 589.

49. Ibid.

50. Donald G. Mathews, "The Methodist Episcopal Church
    and the Antislavery Movements. " Unpublished
    paper, 1966, p. 9.

51. Ibid.

52. Bryce, The American Commonwealth, p. 597.

53. "Declined to Subscribe, " Western Christian Advocate,
    XXXI, (February 10, 1864), p. 14.

54. "A Religious Newspaper, " Zion's Herald, XXXVI, (Feb-
    ruary 15, 1865), p. 26.

55. Reinhold Niebuhr, "The Impact of Protestantism Today,"

Atlantic Monthly, CLXXXI (February 1948), pp. 58,
59. Niebuhr relates the loss of religious vitality
to a decline of "the total impact of Protestant Christianity upon the life of the nation" and suggests two
causes for the loss of Protestant influence: ... first,
the general growth of secularism ..., and secondly,
the increasing tendency of Protestantism to become
middle-class ..., " p. 58. I do not take issue with
the basic thesis, but it would seem that Niebuhr sets
the date marking the advent of decline at least two--
if not three--decades too early.

56. Matthews, "The Methodist Episcopal Church ..., " p. 2.

57. Winthrop S. Hudson. The Great Tradition of the American Churches. New York: Harper & Brothers,
1953, pp. 108, 109. Hudson underscores this thesis
with the suggestion that the "great significance of
Lincoln is that he bears a witness, in his person and
in his faith, to the extent to which the free churches
had shaped American culture.... The ideals, the
convictions, the language, the customs, the institutions of society were so shot through with Christian
presuppositions that the culture itself nurtured and
nourished the Christian faith. So complete was the
penetration of the culture that an Abraham Lincoln--
lacking even a nominal formal relationship to a
church--was enabled to reflect accurately and to
exemplify profoundly the basic insights of the Christian faith. "

CHAPTER 3

METHODISM: THE PREDOMINANT ECCLESIASTICAL
FACT OF THE NATION

At the close of the Civil War the churches of evangelical Protestantism, particularly the larger ones, had a
social and political impact on American life the extent of
which is difficult for a twentieth-century generation to comprehend.   Churches were the main bearers of moral values
and American ideologies.   Indeed, the social and moral disjunction between the North and the South found its clearest
and most potent institutional expression in the larger denominations.

Chief among the denominations, by way of wealth,
strong leadership, total membership, general constituency,
power of its press and national organization, was the Methodist Episcopal Church.   After a slow start in the pre-Revo-
lutionary War period, Methodism gained momentum in the
wake of the Great Revival (1795-1830), becoming in the ante-
bellum period a major force in shaping American life.   Donald G. Mathews asserts that this "influence resulted from a
process enveloping two generations," and granting the social
significance of Methodism during this period, he nevertheless
avers that the influence "was comprised neither of compelling ... nor immense prestige. "   The source of the power
was the undramatic process of organizing "millions of people
into small groups that provided religious fellowship, moral
norms and general values for a life beset by the stresses
and strains of economic growth, political development, and
geographic mobility. "[1]

It is hard to overestimate the importance of the organizational structure of the Methodist Episcopal Church.
Its genius was in conserving the fruits of revivalism through
a disciplined connectional system while not losing evangelical
zeal and passion.   The power of the episcopal office, the
ubiquity of the bishops and traveling preachers, the pervasive-

ness of religious publications, and the ordered government--
from the General Conference down to the class meeting--
created a national system of communications, an institution
providing order in the national life, and strong bonds of unity
for an overgrown new republic. This organizational structure was perhaps the key source of Methodism's influence.
It is the background of a more publicly recognized and sought
for power and prestige during the Civil War and Reconstruction period.

The business of saving souls was the preoccupation of
Methodists in the first half of the nineteenth century. But
this emphasis on personal salvation was altered and supple-
mented by a new social Christianity. Realizing their social
importance, Methodists began to interpret their success,
temporal and spiritual, as a sign of divine favor and as a
call to special responsibility. They also began to identify
the mission of the Church with the destiny of the nation
more closely than before. In short, the northern connection
of Methodism intentionally and actively sought to influence
social and political life. Thus, it is in the third quarter of
the nineteenth century that northern Methodism was tagged
as a "political church." Indeed it was, but they did not
think they were "meddling in politics." Clergymen simply
assumed moral guardianship over public affairs as a task
integral to the mission of the Church.

It is worthy of note, as we attempt to gauge the relative importance of the Methodist Episcopal Church at the
close of the war, that men of affairs and statesmen of re-
nown saw the schism in Methodism in 1844 as a precursor
of the Civil War. It is a recognized thesis that religion can
be one of the strong bonds of national unity. In America
the large denominations that spread out across the land,
combined with the general potency of religion in public life,
made this especially true.

The Schism in Methodism

Henry Clay was one who saw the pernicious influence
of the 1844 cleavage between Northern and Southern Methodism. His prescience and forebodings may be seen in the
following communication written on April 7, 1845:

Dear Sir:

Our mutual friend, Mr. Mitchell, of Frankfort,

delivered to me the day before yesterday your
letter, with several publications under your name
in regard to the unfortunate controversy which has
arisen in the Methodist Episcopal Church of the
United States, all of which I have attentively pe-
rused. . . .

I have long entertained for that church sentiments of profound esteem and regard ... I will
add with great truth that I have witnessed with
much satisfaction the flourishing condition of the
church and the good sense and wisdom which have
generally characterized the administration of its
affairs, as far as I have observed it.

It was, therefore, with the deepest regret that
I heard in the course of the past year of the danger of a division of the church in consequence of
a difference of opinion existing on the delicate and
unhappy subject of slavery. A division for such a
cause would be an event greatly to be deplored,
both on account of the church itself and its political tendency. Indeed, scarcely any public occurrence has happened for a long time that gave me
so much real concern and pain as the menaced
separation of the church by a line throwing all the
free States on one side and all the slave States on
the other.

I will not say that such a separation would necessarily produce a dissolution of the political
union of these States; but the example would be
fraught with imminent danger, and, in cooperation
with other causes unfortunately existing, its tendency on the stability of the confederacy would be
perilous and alarming.

Entertaining these views, it would afford me the
highest satisfaction to hear of an adjustment of the
controversy, a reconciliation between the opposing
parties in the Church, and the preservation of its
unity.

. . . .

With fervent hopes and wishes that some arrange-
ment of the difficulty may be devised and agreed
upon which shall preserve the church in union and
harmony,

I am, respectfully, your obedient servant,
H. Clay[2]

Dr. W. A. Booth

Henry Clay was not to have the satisfaction of hearing about a reconciliation. The resolution by the northern majority in 1844, that "slavery was a moral sin" and that bishops of the church could not be slaveholders, met with the fateful response of the southern church to secede and organize an independent body in 1846. Its secession and independence were justified on the grounds that because slavery was a civil-political question "The Southern Church separated from the Northern that she might keep out of politics."3

Lecturing his fellow congressmen during the great debate on Henry Clay's Compromise measure of 1850, John C. Calhoun viewed the sectional division of American Methodism as an augury of the final dissolution of the Union. Speaking of the "cords that bind the States together," he declaimed that, "Some are spiritual or ecclesiastical; some political; others social.... The strongest of those of a spiritual and ecclesiastical nature consisted in the unity of the great religious denominations, all of which originally embraced the whole Union."4 These strong cords contributed greatly in forming the fabric of national unity. But Calhoun saw already the renting of the cloth as, one by one, first the Methodists, then the Baptists, and soon the Presbyterians, the three largest denominations in the land were unable to "resist the exploding effect of slavery agitation."5

> The first of these cords which snapped, under its [slavery agitation] explosive force, was that of the powerful Methodist Episcopal Church. The numerous and strong ties which held it together are all broke, and its unity gone. They now form separate churches, and, instead of that feeling of attachment and devotion to the interests of the whole church which was formerly felt, they are now arrayed into two hostile bodies, engaged in litigation about what was formerly their common property. 6

In perhaps his greatest speech (March 7, 1850), Daniel Webster expressed the same anguish over the cleavage in the Churches.

> The honorable senator from South Carolina the other day alluded to the separation of that great religious community, the Methodist Episcopal Church. That separation was brought about by differences of opinion upon this particular subject

of slavery. I felt great concern, as that dispute
went on, about the result. I was in hopes that
the differences of opinion might be adjusted, because I looked on that religious denomination as
one of the great props of religion and morals
throughout the whole country, from Maine to Georgia, and westward to our utmost western boundary.
The result was against my wishes and against my
hopes. [7]

There is little doubt that the breaking of ecclesiastical bonds was one of the chief causes of the final sectional
breach. H. Shelton Smith was quite right in observing that
"Ecclesiastical division not only foreshadowed political dis-
union, but actually prepared the moral ground for it. "[8]
Certainly, the moral interpretation of the slavery question,
which was to transform the tragic conflict into a moral crusade for northerners, can be traced in part to ecclesiastical
schisms. And in the South distinguished clergymen called
on the confederate states to follow their suit by seceding on
grounds that it was "the only right and honorable course to
take. "[9]

A study of the two branches of Methodism reveals
that they not only articulated, but embodied the cause of
their respective sections. This zealous identification of the
churches with the causes of their own region is not surprising when it is recognized that both religious bodies contributed greatly to the definition of sectional ideologies and
vocation. Hence, it is essential for historians--religious
and secular--to examine the role of Protestant denominations
in order to view the full drama of the sectional crisis.

Ecclesiastical history in many ways becomes a micro-
cosm of this tragic era in American history. This is especially true of the Methodist Episcopal Church, which was
so intimately woven into the fabric of social life in America.
If this was true for years before and during the war, it was
more true in the case of northern Methodism immediately
following the war. But its relative status in the nation needs
to be established more precisely.

The Status and Vitality of Northern Methodism

What can be said about the status of Protestantism's
most representative and largest denomination--the Methodist

Episcopal Church--on the eve of Appomattox? The familiar
tribute from Lincoln to the northern Methodists in May 1864
serves to indicate the power and influence of this denomination:

> Gentlemen, --In response to your address allow me
> to attest the accuracy of its historical statements,
> endorse the sentiments it expresses, and thank
> you in the nation's name for the sure promise it
> gives.
>
> Nobly sustained as the government has been by
> all the Churches, I would utter nothing which might
> in the least appear invidious against any. Yet
> without this it may fairly be said that the Method-
> ist Episcopal Church, not less devoted than the
> best, is, by its greater numbers, the most im-
> portant of all. It is no fault in others that the
> Methodist Church sends more soldiers to the field,
> more nurses to the hospitals, and more prayers
> to heaven than any. God bless the Methodist
> Church! bless all the Churches! and blessed be
> God! who in this our great trial giveth us the
> Churches. [10]

Two decades after the cleavage between the Methodist
Episcopal Church, North and South, the Northern Church was
greater in membership and property holdings than any other
Protestant denomination in the country. [11] Far from declining in strength as a result of the war, the Northern Church
had actually "gone forward in her legitimate work with little
interruption and with surprising prosperity." [12] The bishops,
in their "address" to a war-weary General Conference in
1864, documented their claim that "in nearly all our leading
interests there has been a most cheering and even wonderful
progress. " The statistics presented showed an increase of:

> 252 local preachers
> 124 churches, and of $2,007,914 in their probable
> value
> 313 parsonages, and of $362,982 in their probable
> value
> $6,859 for Conference claimants
> $150,749 in the amount collected for the Missionary
> Society*

*This represents an increase of 60% in contributions for
mission between 1860 and 1864.

$15, 655 in the amount collected for the American
   Bible Society
1, 253 Sunday Schools
7, 668 officers and teachers
101, 584 scholars[13]

The bishops accounted for the decrease in membership of
sixty-eight thousand during the war years by "the large numbers ... who have fallen in battle, and have died in camps
and hospitals" and by acknowledging the

> secession of ministers and members in the Vir-
> ginia portion of the Baltimore Conference, growing
> out of dissatisfaction with the earnest antislavery
> principles of our Church, and partly from the dis-
> persion of a number of our societies in the Border
> Slave States. [14]

How did they account for their successes? "Whatever
other explanation may be given," the bishops were compelled
to say, "It is the Lord's doing, and it is marvelous in our
eyes. "[15] For most this recognition of providential benefi-
cence would come to be interpreted as a vindication of the
rightness of the Northern cause and as "marching orders"
to go South. However proper it is for bishops to grant
deity the ultimate credit for ecclesiastical success, there
is room for closer scrutiny in the interest of determining
whatever penultimate causes there might be.

The Methodist Episcopal Church was in a uniquely
favorable position to exercise considerable influence on political conditions and was therefore in a position of special
advantage both during and after the Civil War. No one recognized the political importance of Methodist bishops more than
Lincoln.

> The president discovered very quickly that, the
> issues of the war being moral, the support of the
> churches was of the last importance to him. He
> knew well that no men understood the people so
> thoroughly as the Methodist bishops, who, being
> without dioceses, were continually passing over
> the length and breadth of the land. [16]

More important than the moral question for Lincoln and the
Union cause was the convergence of ecclesiastical interest
with the interest of the Union. It was of utmost importance

for the Northern bishops to maintain the unity of the Methodist Episcopal Church in Maryland and in other states below the border. In resisting the secession of parts of the Church and beguiling clergymen and members to stay with the northern Church, Simpson and others no doubt played the chief role in saving Maryland for the Union and succeeded in retaining many congregations in other border states for the Union cause. [17] The northern connection of Methodism did not go unrewarded. Because of the services it had performed for the Union and because Methodists were not bashful about asking for their just deserts, the Methodist Episcopal Church was in a place of especial advantage. This was one of the reasons behind the success story told by the bishops at their 1864 General Conference.

In keeping with the general tone of the times and the toughmindedness of clergymen, Methodists were not chary about engaging in political forays within or without the Church, nor were they faint-hearted in asking for favors in return for services rendered. Bishop Edward Thompson candidly admitted that when army contracts were passed out, Methodist laymen "were not forgotten." An excerpt from his speech in 1866 underscores the point:

> Of the increase of public wealth, which has been
> very large since the war began by reason of the
> stimulus given to manufactures and commerce, the
> increased prices of agricultural products, and the
> opening of new sources of wealth, such as oil wells,
> our Church has had her full share--perhaps more
> than her full share; for no Church has been more
> loyal than she, if any as patriotic, active and
> earnest in suppressing rebellion.... And when
> army contracts have been awarded, and grants to
> purchase cotton in rebellious States have been
> made, our people had not been forgotten or ig-
> nored.... Without unduly or dishonestly seeking
> to profit by the war, the attitude which our Church
> has borne of the Government has naturally and
> necessarily increased her wealth. [18]

Financial gifts for the erection of churches were made frequently by the government during the years following the war. The condition on which this financial aid was given was that those buildings would be used for Freedmen Bureau schools when needed for that purpose. [19] Participating in the general prosperity of the North, receiving special remunerative favors from the government, and becoming partners with the government in common cause placed the Methodist Episcopal Church in a position of great advantage as it penetrated the South with designs of ecclesiastical, social and political reform.

A good index of the institutional health and vitality of northern Methodism at the close of the war may be seen in the response of the churches and people to a call for a "thank offering" as a means of celebrating the "Centenary of American Methodism." During the General Conference of 1864 a "Centenary Committee" was organized to plan the celebration commemorating the completion of the first century of American Methodism in 1866. The committee deemed it proper that this occasion should be observed "with special solemnities and pious offerings, which shall present before God some humble expression of ... gratitude."[20] The "spontaneous" offering asked for was two million dollars, to be used primarily in founding colleges and seminaries and for building and improving church edifices.[21] The response of the Church was more than fourfold greater than the asking, the grand total being over eight million dollars.[22]

The financial success, past accomplishments, and present significance of American Methodism did not go unnoticed in the secular press. In commenting on the gigantic financial projects of the centenary committee, Harper's Weekly noted that the amount of money collected "was the largest amount ever contributed by an American denomination, in one year, for one occasion," and recorded that it was a very significant fact that "Nearly all these funds are to be consecrated to the educational interests of the church."[23]

Harper's Weekly gave almost the entire issue over to coverage of this form of Protestantism. Justifying this rather unusual proceeding, the editorial writer declared that Methodism, "For good or ill, ... has become the predominant ecclesiastical fact of the nation." With extravagant praise the writer asserted that not only was it the largest religious body in America, it was without equal in "robust vigor," and pointed out for special commendation the fact that "it has the most powerful religious press in the world."[24]

Nearly all of the nationally circulated periodicals and many prestigious daily newspapers took notice of the centennial celebration. Typical of the accolades heaped on the Methodists is the following expression from a lengthy article in the New York Tribune:

> The sect can take up the boast of England, that
> the sun does not set on its altars. Its mission-
> aries follow the drum-beat of England in their
> march round the world. Nothing can be more mar-
> velous than the growth of this Church.... Many
> heard the Gospel from faithful lips when they were
> in sin, or were counted among the lowly ones of
> earth. They found religion no less an aid to their
> temporal than their spiritual interest.... They
> have not forgotten the Church of their fathers, and
> have resolved to make it a great power in the land.
> ...
> With undimmed power, with numbers almost untold,
> and with resources that the wealthiest Churches
> among us might envy, it enters on its second cen-
> tury. It still illustrates the motto of its founder,
> 'All at it, and always at it. '25

Denominational spokesmen from other bodies, prominent clergymen and theologians rained abundant praise on the
Methodists. Even Philip Schaff, not known for excessive
praise of American Methodism, commented on their "uncommon energy and activity; and ... their organization eminently fitted for great general enterprises and systematic,
successful cooperation. "26 He admitted to its social force
suggesting that "in the state of Indiana it even controls the
political elections ... and among the negroes, too, both
free and slave, Methodism has most influence. "27

Henry Ward Beecher, responding to a Methodist who
had been chiding him on the looseness of his Calvinism,
said, "Whether this is Calvinism or not, I fully believe that
it is predestined that the Methodist Church shall play a very
important part in the affairs of this world. "28

As the compliments poured down on the denomination,
a Methodist editor, still smarting from the days when they
were the objects of ridicule, hastened to point out that "The
time is now past when sneers and derision are ... a legitimate part of the Christian courtesy to be accorded to the
followers of Wesley. " "Instead of this, " the editor continues,
"we see a tendency ... almost universal, to copy the Methodist style of doing the work of God. "29 But it was not easy
to emulate the Methodists, for their work was accomplished
in part by virtue of their close and cordial relations with
government officials.

Edward Raymond Ames (1806-1879), Bishop of the M. E. Church from 1852. After the Civil War he was active in extending the influence of Northern Methodism to the South. Secretary of War Stanton issued an order permitting him to take over churches of the M. E. Church, South.

Methodism and Political Influence

Bishop Ames, the only Methodist bishop appointed as chaplain of the army, was an intimate personal friend of Secretary of War Stanton. Not only was Bishop Ames very active for the Northern cause in giving patriotic speeches and offering patriotic prayers around the country, but in the capacity of a chaplain he rendered many services for the government at the behest of Stanton. [30] Ames did not fail to take advantage of the debt owed. In November of 1863 Stanton authored a War Department directive placing at the disposal of the bishop "all houses of worship belonging to the Methodist Episcopal Church, South, in which a loyal minister ... appointed by a loyal bishop of said church does not officiate."[31] This right of occupancy among the vanquished was given teeth by the further instruction of the directive to military officials to aid in the execution of the order. Within a month after the issuance of this order the remaining three bishops of the Northern Church, fortified with government credentials and aided by military force, entered upon the new mission field of the South. [32]

Mention has already been made of Bishop Matthew Simpson's relationship to the Secretary of War and President Lincoln. The most prominent of Methodist clergymen, Simpson had an open door to the high courts of the nation, his influence with the president being widely known.

> During the war few men exerted a more powerful influence by public addresses in support of the Union than Bishop Simpson; and though he never turned aside for a day from his sacred calling, he was not unfrequently in counsel with the Administration, whose confidence he had in marked degree. [33]

Whenever he was in Washington and had the opportunity, Simpson did not hesitate to confront the President himself with the claims of the Methodists for political spoils. On one occasion after he had made his appeal on behalf of the "numerically strong" Methodist Church, to the Bishop's astonishment, Lincoln promptly invited him to name the minister to Honduras. [34] Though he declined the offer that time, Simpson returned again and again with appeals for political patronage.

One of the first striking political coups for Simpson

Matthew Simpson (1811-1884), Bishop of the M. E. Church from 1852. As a pastor and friend to Abraham Lincoln, he was deeply involved in Civil War and Reconstruction politics.

and the Methodists was the appointment of John Evans as
Governor of the Colorado Territory. [35] The story of how
his appointment was to be used by the Methodists is illustrative of how political influence and power were exerted in
the interest of the Church. Calling upon their friend, Rev.
J. L. Smith of Indiana, Evans and Simpson offered him a
proposition: the bishop would appoint him superintendent of
missions in the Colorado country, and Evans would name
him Secretary of State for the territory. He was assured
that his evangelistic endeavors in the territory of Colorado
would not be hindered by his political appointment, as a
deputy could be retained to do that work. The tale is instructive notwithstanding the fact that Smith declined the
offer. [36]

Among the many Methodist political triumphs, perhaps
the most significant was the appointment of James Harlan
as Secretary of the Interior. He already had influence with
Lincoln, gained by his opposition to Ben Wade and the Radicals in his role as U. S. Senator from Iowa. Nevertheless,
it took plotting and scheming on the part of Simpson and
his associates to enforce upon the government appropriate
honors for Methodism. [37] While no one can be sure, it
seems reasonable to assume that the great number of Methodist votes for Lincoln in the election of 1864 played an important part in his decision to appoint Harlan to the cabinet
post. There is little doubt that Simpson made Lincoln well
aware of the power of the Methodist ballot. Certainly, Lincoln was not unmindful of the conspicuous part Simpson
played in the election campaign. Bishop Simpson, the most
eloquent orator of northern Methodism, was invited to give
his famous "War Speech" twice that fall. In Pittsburgh in
mid-October he aroused the audience to pandemonium. [38]
Mark Hoyt, a wealthy New York Methodist laymen working
for the election of Lincoln, arranged to have Simpson deliver his famous address in the Academy of Music of New
York City on November 3, five days before the election.
The letter of invitation speaks for itself:

> Office of Hoyt Brothers,
> 28 & 30 Spruce Street
> New York, Oct. 26th, 1864

M. Rev. Bishop Simpson

Dear Sir:

I received a telegram this PM, which I suppose

to have been sent by your good lady intimating
that you could come to New York and deliver your
address on Thursday evening Nov. 3rd. I have
acted upon that intimation and have secured the
academy of music for that evening. It is the only
evening we can have it before the election and all
of your friends here agree that you should speak
before that time. Speaking here at that time with
the full report promised of the speech in the Tribune Times Herald and Evening Post is equivalent
to speaking to the nation and will give ample time
for it (the speech) to produce its result on the
election. (Italics mine) Can't you bring your
family with you? Your friends will be delighted
to see them and have them witness the demonstra-
tions of a lively New York audience. Waiting your
reply and also your response to the Committee's
invitation I remain

> Fraternally yours,
>
> Mark Hoyt[39]

Simpson rose to the occasion on the eve of the election,
which found Lincoln in political difficulty while McClellan
was taking advantage of a disheartened and war-weary citizenry. Many feared that a verdict against Lincoln might be
given by a people whose spirits were downcast.[40] The purpose of the speech was to infuse new faith in the nation, to
elevate spirits by affirming the glory and greatness of the
Union, to assure the audience and the nation that God had
not forsaken America, and to affirm the "providences of
God" in and through the Civil War events.[41] At one point
in the speech, with a high pitch of patriotic piety, he sang
out the words:

> A nation that has in itself the power to elevate its
> own citizens, and to exert a good influence upon
> nations abroad, has the especial favor of God....
> It is certainly not God's plan that we should pass
> away. Then how could the world do without us?
> The people of all nations look to us. If our coun-
> try goes down, one-half of the world would raise
> a wail of woe, and sink lower. God ... cannot
> afford to lose the United States.[42]

According to the various reports of the speech, the

bishop did not make one partisan statement in behalf of Lincoln, but the people could not miss the point. If "God cannot do without the United States," certainly the people were being asked to conclude, "the United States cannot do without Lincoln." And certain Methodists would extend the sentiment, "and Lincoln cannot do without the Methodists," as is evidenced by a letter from General Clinton Fisk to Bishop Ames. Worried that Lincoln might revoke the Stanton order in response to rebel and conservative agitation around his area in St. Louis, Missouri, he writes:

> ... I am suspicious that there will be an effort made by the rebels of the Church South in this City to procure the President's disapproval of the Sec of War's action in this matter and I thought it wise to write you suggesting that you have an early interview with 'Father Abraham.' It would be a terrible blow to Loyalty in the Mississippi Valley and a great encouragement to disloyalty were the President to disavow the bold yet wise action of Mr. Stanton. ... The course pursued by the President in the case of Dr. McPheeters ... has been damaging to the cause of Christian patriotism in St. Louis. McPheeters was and is an out and out disloyalist openly in unmeasured terms the usurpations of the baboon tyrant--[and] insulted his loyal members by baptizing children at his altar, clad in rebel colors--naming them 'Sterling Price' and 'Beauregard'....
>
> ...
> I hope the President will not listen to the clamor which may be raised against Mr. Stanton for the position he has taken with regard to the Church South. ...
>
> ...
> Father Abraham must remember that we Methodist(s) are great voters. [43]

The story of Methodism's involvement in politics and patronage has been well documented and exemplifies beyond a shadow of a doubt the power and influence of the Methodist Episcopal Church. [44] The various positions obtained by Methodist clergymen and laymen ranged from minor clerkships, postmaster positions in small towns and appointments to military academies, to governorships, promotions to the rank of General in the Army, a position in the President's Cabinet and seats on the Supreme Court of the United States. [45]

Clinton Bowen Fisk (1828-1890), Northern Methodist layman, Army officer and businessman. As a member of the Freedman's Bureau and as an acquaintance of Lincoln and Grant he worked to secure economic and social benefits for freedmen.

Typical of the boldness of those Methodists desiring political spoils was Clinton B. Fisk, cited above. Entreating Bishop Simpson to secure for him a promotion to the rank of Brigadier General, he said,

> I wish you would call on Atty. General Bates at your earliest convenience and arrange for a visit to the President for all three of you [Gov. Gamble was the third]--don't let Mr. Lincoln turn you over to Genl. Halleck for I have never been to West Point. Your strong forte will be with 'Father Abraham'; tell him to take me 'on probation' as a Brigadier Genl for six months and if at the end of that time I am deemed unworthy of the position I will return my commission. [46]

His promotion was secured, and, giving Simpson expressions of gratitude, he wrote that he would rather have "him [Simpson] present my 'cause in court' than have one hundred politicians make a raid on the War Department in my behalf."[47] A year later Brigadier General Fisk was inclined to seek another promotion, to Major General. With characteristic brazenness he implored Simpson once again to ask "Father Abraham" to "make me a Major General and give me General Schofield's place." "Why not one Methodist Major General?" he asked. "We furnish the soldiers by the two thousands.... Let the Bishops adjourn and make a raid on the President."[48]

That Methodist prestige and influence was great is further evidenced by the fact that Bishop Simpson was chosen to give the funeral oration over the body of the martyred President at Springfield, Illinois, and that Dr. J. P. Newman, long and close friend of the Grants, baptized the President and received him into membership of the Methodist Episcopal Church.[49] A social note further illustrates the point. A biographer of Simpson records that in their Philadelphia home the Simpsons entertained General and Mrs. Grant and, "a decade later, President and Mrs. Rutherford B. Hayes."[50]

Not only bishops were in a socially and politically advantageous position in the nation, but there is persuasive evidence that ordinary Methodist clergymen were likely to be men of some standing in their communities.[51] One Methodist layman, acknowledging the position of prominence of his Church's clergymen, bemoans the fact and warns them of the consequences:

> The Methodist ministers being supposed to under-
> stand the masses of the people and to have most
> direct access to and influence over them, their
> opinions are used very freely by politicians
> [who] ... make a direct effort to secure Methodist
> ministers as their agents, because on all moral
> and religious questions the clergy are regarded as
> leaders of the people.... [Chagrined, he continues]
> They form a well-known element in political, cal-
> culations, and the church is scarcely aware how
> many yield to the temptation. [52]

Another testimony to the political power of Methodism
in the North came from the Methodist Episcopal Church,
South. In the bill of indictment brought by the Southern bishops against the northern Church at the close of the war was
the charge that they had become a political organization.
The keynote thus given by the bishops, it was taken up and
sounded throughout the southern Church by preacher and
press. Among the northern spokesmen responding to the
accusation, Daniel Curry, editor of the Christian Advocate
(New York), was one of the first in coming to the defense.
Later in the debate, this fiery exponent of a thoroughgoing
Reconstruction policy would vociferously argue the merits
and legitimacy of the church's responsibility in and to the
social order. At this juncture, when Curry and others were
still somewhat hopeful that the southern Church would respond to overtures for fraternal relations and eventually ask
in repentance for re-admission to the "mother church," he
responded modestly, but firmly.

> We have said very little in reply, because we have
> felt the church needs no vindication in that particu-
> lar at our hands; nor do we now propose to either
> deny the charge nor to palliate its atrocity. We
> confess the charge so far as to concede that in
> our church organization is held a very considerable
> amount of political power, which is brought into
> actual exercise, influencing the affairs of the coun-
> try. But we deny that our church has in any proper
> sense become a political body, or that either col-
> lectively or by its individual ministers or mem-
> bers as such, it has anything to do with the de-
> cisions of political parties. [53]

Continuing his discourse, Curry reflected further on the right
of a Church to exert its influence in public issues while

eschewing partisan politics, and in a low key gave warrants for the role the Methodist Episcopal Church had indeed played in such matters. Picking up a theme which would be elaborated in various ways many times during the Reconstruction, Curry then writes:

> Nor is it at all strange that these things should be so. Great political questions usually involve an ethical element which in most cases secures their acceptance or rejection by right-minded people. [54]

Heretofore Methodist spokesmen had not consciously articulated an apologia for social and political responsibility. It did not occur to them. Ecclesiastical motivations were fundamentally religious, and missionary expectations and designs were enunciated without reference to a radical distinction between political and religious or temporal and spiritual spheres. They did not have to talk about "social responsibility" as a special task. Responsibility for society and the nation was assumed as inherent to the mission of the Church and the requirements of the Gospel. Even when an extreme individualistic ethic was preached, the moral values and social ideals were common to religious and secular aspects of life, so that the individual easily played his roles as citizen and Church member, workman and Sunday School leader, college president and clergyman without awareness of mutually exclusive spheres of activity. In many cases the unspoken "social concern" for better laws, fewer taverns, more responsible statesmen and new schools belied the spoken, "individualistic" ethic preached from the pulpit. But not all preaching in the nineteenth century was merely individualistic. Gilbert Haven, preacher, educator, editor and later bishop in the Methodist Episcopal Church, appealed to the Jewish traditions and the Puritan heritage when he declared with approval the faithfulness of the New England ministry in "setting forth the relations of the Gospel to the laws and customs of man."[55] Even Haven, more explicit than most Methodist clergymen, did not expend much energy defending the right of the Protestant pulpit to treat the issues of public life. He simply went ahead in the tradition of New England Puritanism, proclaiming "alarm or the exultation, as national sin or national virtue gave the occasion."[56]

Rather suddenly all of this changed and a raft of articles began appearing in the Methodist press vindicating the right of the Church to speak on political and social issues.

How did it come about that northern Methodists began

to treat more self-consciously and systematically the relations of politics and Christianity? The answer is twofold.
First, because of their institutional prominence in the main-
stream of public life they found themselves, partly by design, but mainly by reason of historical forces, inextricably
involved in the major issues of the national community. Especially was this true when the moral, humanitarian and
evangelical concerns of the Church coincided with practical
social-political questions, prominent among which were
slavery, temperance, national destiny, and the plight of the
freedmen. Because of the institutional nature of these and
other issues, the assumptions of a religious individualism
had to give way to a more rigorously articulated social
teaching as a theoretical justification for a social stance and
for action already taken. Thus, in a characteristically
American way a theology of social responsibility was being
hammered out on the anvil of concrete events. The thought
of the northern Methodist Church was taking shape as churchmen sought to clarify their own involvement in the shatter-
ing events of a fateful period in the American story.

The second reason for setting forth an apologia for
church involvement in social and political affairs has already
been suggested. It was the indictment of southern Methodists
charging their northern brethren with "acquiring the political
habit" that provided the catalyst. A. T. Bledsoe, editor of
the Southern Review and spokesman for southern Methodism,
set the pace in condemning the Methodist "politicos" of the
North by declaring their role in civil affairs an "adulterous
defection" that made them a Church "more deeply stained
with political corruptions than any other in America."[57] In
contrast he states the necessary destiny of the Methodist
Episcopal Church, South as a church

> whose breath shall not smell of the potations of
> Babylon, whose eye shall not be red from the
> vigils of the caucus, whose voice shall not be
> cracked by the mad brawl of the hustings.[58]

In the face of such accusations and in the context of political
and ecclesiastical Reconstruction, leaders in the northern
Methodist Church were driven to justify their ways before
God and men.

The Methodist Episcopal Church was still an evangelical "movement" after Appomattox, exhibiting vigorous
ecclesiastical accomplishments. By virtue of their religious

successes--accounted for in part by their cordial relations with government officials--Methodist leaders were in vital contact with the public affairs of national life. By purposive action and through fortuitous historical circumstances, the Methodist Episcopal Church was the "predominant ecclesiastical fact of the nation," giving this denomination a political influence "perhaps stronger in this period than it had ever been before or since."[59] To know the extent of this influence and how seriously Methodist leaders were taken by politicians and statesmen is to make intelligible the emergence of a social teaching and the concrete social and political involvement during the reconstruction period.

The prominence of northern Methodism in the social and political life of the nation during the immediate post-war period is also necessary background for viewing the changing place of the Protestant churches in the second decade after the war. Through a series of resounding set-backs to their aggressive mission in the South, and in the face of changing cultural and social conditions in the North, the Methodist Episcopal Church became increasingly a marginal force in public life. To the degree that Methodist leaders were chastened by various circumstances and were losing their influence in public affairs, they reverted to a simplistic moralism and social evasion as they faced the problems of an industrial age.

While the attitudes and activities of the Methodist Episcopal Church must be understood in terms of its relative prominence in public life and the pattern of its corporate relations to social institutions, this is not enough to tell the whole story. Northern Methodists must also be understood in terms of their own inner dynamic and self-understanding.

Notes

1. Mathews, The Methodist Episcopal Church ..., p. 3.

2. James M. Buckley. A History of Methodism in the United States. New York: The Christian Literature Co., 1897, pp. 128-30.

3. Albert T. Bledsoe, "The M. E. Churches, North and South," Art VI, The Southern Review, X, No. 21 (January, 1872), p. 408.

4. The Congressional Globe, vol. xxi, part 1, p. 453.

5. Ibid.

6. Ibid. , p. 453.

7. William Warren Sweet. Methodism in American History. New York: Abingdon Press, 1953, p. 277, citing Webster's Works, V, p. 331.

8. H. Shelton Smith, Robert T. Handy, Lefferts A. Loetscher. American Christianity. II. New York: Charles Scribner's Sons, 1963, p. 178. Donald G. Mathews takes a more restrained view in his book, Slavery and Methodism. Princeton: Princeton University Press, 1965, p. 290. He writes: "In the dissolution of a national identity within the churches, the moral disjunction of the United States was institutionalized. This fact did not necessarily portend civil war, but it was a warning sign, a prophecy of the hostility and bitterness which could come were sectional fears and antagonism extended beyond the moral realm into the world of force and power. "

9. Smith, et al. , American Christianity, II, p. 178.

10. Journal of the General Conference of the Methodist Episcopal Church, 1864. New York: Carlton & Porter, 1864, p. 380.

11. The best comparative statistics are found in The American Annual Cyclopaedia and Register of Important Events, 1865; Daniel Dorchester's Christianity in the United States, New York, 1895, and the U. S. Bureau of the Census Reports. In all of these sources the various Methodist Churches lead their nearest competitors the Baptists and Presbyterians (in that order) in total membership and in the aggregate value of church edifices--with the Methodist Episcopal Church leading the particular denominations--in both categories.

12. Journal of the General Conference, 1865, p. 274.

13. Journal of the General Conference, 1864, p. 274.

14. Ibid. , p. 275.

15. Ibid.

16. Crooks, The Life of Bishop Matthew Simpson, p. 368.

17. Ibid., pp. 369-71; Clark, pp. 212-14, 235.

18. Farish, The Circuit Rider Dismounts, p. 35, citing the New Orleans Christian Advocate, February 3, 1866.

19. L. C. Matlack, "The Methodist Episcopal Church in the Southern States," Methodist Quarterly Review, LV, (January, 1872), p. 105.

20. Journal of the General Conference, 1864, p. 445.

21. Ibid., p. 446.

22. Journal of the General Conference, 1868, p. 593.

23. "Centenary of Methodism," Harper's Weekly, X, (October 6, 1866), p. 186.

24. Ibid.

25. "The N. Y. Tribune and the M. E. Church," Christian Advocate and Journal, XLI, (January 4, 1866), p. 4 citing New York Tribune, n. d.

26. Philip Schaff. America. Cambridge, Massachusetts: Harvard University Press, 1961, p. 137.

27. Ibid., p. 138.

28. H. H. Moore, The Republic to Methodism, Dr. New York: Hunt & Eaton, 1891, p. 8.

29. "Methodism and Now," Zion's Herald, XLVI, (June 3, 1869), p. 258.

30. William Warren Sweet. The Methodist Episcopal Church and the Civil War. Cincinnati: Methodist Book Concern Press, 1912, pp. 151, 152.

31. Buckley, A History of Methodism ..., p. 178.

32. Morrow, Northern Methodism and Reconstruction, p. 34. It should be noted in this discussion that the Church was engaged in self-service and was quite

literally an agency in the struggle for power. The
political power of the Church was, however, used
to pressure politicians and statesmen to support such
legislation as the Civil Rights Bill of 1866; to pass
temperance legislation; and to adopt equal suffrage
laws.

33. James Edmund Kirby, Jr. "The Ecclesiastical and
     Social Thought of Matthew Simpson. " Unpublished
     Ph. D. dissertation, Drew University, 1963, p. 221.

34. Matthew Simpson to Simon Cameron, November 27,
     1861. Simpson Papers, Drew. See also Clark, p.
     225.

35. John Evans was a distinguished layman in the Methodist
     Episcopal Church prominent in founding Northwestern
     University located in the village of Evanston which
     was named after him. --Matthew B. Simpson, ed.
     Cyclopaedia of Methodism. Philadelphia: Everts &
     Stewart, 1878, pp. 349-50.

36. Clark, The Life of Matthew Simpson, pp. 227, 228.
     Smith was already serving in the dual capacity of
     collector of internal revenue for the government and
     presiding elder in the Methodist Church and could
     not see any special advantage in going to the frontier
     when he had a good thing going.

37. Ibid., p. 329.

38. Ibid., p. 240. Harper's Weekly carried a report of
     the Pittsburgh address describing the effect it had
     on the audience: "The effect of his discourse is
     described as very remarkable. Toward the close
     an eye-witness says: 'Laying his hand on the torn
     and ball-riddled colors of the Seventy-third Ohio,
     he spoke of the battlefields where they had been
     baptized in blood, and described their beauty as
     some small patch of azure, filled with stars, that
     an angel had snatched from the heavenly canopy to
     set the stripes in blood. With this description be-
     gan a scene that Demosthenes might have envied.
     All over the vast assembly handkerchiefs and hats
     were waved, and before the speaker sat down the
     whole throng arose as if by magic influence, and
     screamed, and shouted, and saluted, and stamped,

and clapped, and wept, and laughed in wild excitement. Colonel Moody sprang to the top of a bench and called for "The Star-Spangled Banner," which was sung, or rather shouted, until the audience dispersed'. "--"Bishop Simpson and the Flag," Harper's Weekly, VIII, (October 15, 1864), p. 659.

39. Mark Hoyt to Matthew Simpson, October 26, 1864. Simpson Papers, Drew.

40. Crooks, The Life of Bishop Matthew Simpson, p. 383.

41. Ibid., p. 382.

42. Kirby, "The Ecclesiastical and Social Thought of Matthew Simpson," p. 305.

43. Clinton B. Fisk to Bishop Ames, February 21, 1864. Clinton B. Fisk Papers, Drew.

44. The best study of this involvement may be found in Chapter VI of James Kirby's dissertation, "The Ecclesiastical and Social Thought of Matthew Simpson," pp. 221-72.

45. Ibid., p. 222.

46. Clinton B. Fisk to Matthew Simpson, November 10, 1862. Clinton B. Fisk Papers, Drew.

47. Kirby, "The Ecclesiastical and Social Thought of Matthew Simpson," p. 249.

48. Clinton B. Fisk to Matthew Simpson, October 29, 1863. Clinton B. Fisk Papers, Drew.

49. William Warren Sweet, "Methodist Church Influence in Southern Politics", Mississippi Valley Historical Review, I, (March 1915), p. 555.

50. Clark, The Life of Matthew Simpson, p. 276.

51. Milton Powell. "The Abolitionist Controversy in The Methodist Episcopal Church." Ph.D. Thesis, University of Iowa, 1963, p. 116.

52. John A. Wright. People and Preachers in The Methodist

Episcopal Church. Philadelphia: J. B. Lippincott Co., 1886, p. 185.

53. "Political Power of Methodism," Christian Advocate (New York), XL, (October 26, 1865), p. 340.

54. Ibid.

55. Gilbert Haven. National Sermons, Sermons, Speeches and Letters on Slavery and its War. New York: Carlton and Lanahan, 1869, p. v.

56. Ibid.

57. Bledsoe, The Southern Review, X, No. 21, p. 404.

58. Ibid.

59. Sweet, Illinois Historical Society Review, pp. 163-64.

PART II

SELF-UNDERSTANDING OF NORTHERN METHODISM

INTRODUCTION (Part II)

The social thought and action of the Methodist Episcopal Church can be understood more fully by inquiring into the self-understanding of Church leaders and official spokesmen with special reference to how they viewed the nature and destiny of their Church in terms of their own ecclesiastical history and the destiny of the nation. While a "common mind" cannot be etched with great precision, considering the size and diversity represented in this denomination, it is possible to discern broad outlines of a corporate personality. Notwithstanding the differences that are sometimes sharp and decisive, there are certain common impulses, themes, perspectives and goals that may be delineated.

Three interrelated categories, forming a focus for Methodist self-understanding, emerge from an investigation of the materials. These categories or frames of reference provided northern Methodists with a basis for social and political involvement of no small degree and became sources of an emerging social ethic. Methodist leaders and spokesmen in the North saw themselves and their Church as: 1) called and directed by Providence; 2) sent on mission; and 3) having a destiny uniquely related to the destiny of the nation. Accordingly, this section will be divided into three chapters suggested by the above categories, with a view to perceiving the inner dynamic of the Methodist Episcopal Church. Such an approach is an attempt to complement the treatment of external relations and status found in the first part of this study.

CHAPTER 4

PROVIDENCE AND HISTORICAL INTERPRETATION

"Methodists have always been trustful believers in divine providence," wrote Abel Stevens, the historian of Methodism in the mid-nineteenth century.[1] "Much of the morale of Methodism," he continues, "has been owing to the prevalent belief of its people that it has been signalized by providence, and that, therefore, extra-ordinary providential designs are to be accomplished by it."[2] This consciously held, though not sharply defined doctrine of Providence was utilized considerably in interpreting the past, present and future of Methodism; in discerning the meaning of the Civil War; in justifying reconstruction activity; and in commenting on social and political issues. Sermons, official resolutions and editorials were filled with allusions to the "providential hand of God." To miss the prominence of this doctrine is to miss the key to the self-image of Methodists, and therefore to miss the basic impulse of their mission in and to the world.[3] "As a philosophy of history," writes Milton Powell, "the doctrine of providence served to give Methodists a feeling of intimate relationship with the events of the past and of their own time."[4] Insofar as this was true, the doctrine of Providence saved Methodists from an other-worldly orthodoxy and a narrow individualistic evangelicalism.

History, for Methodists, was the context of God's activity; thus, according to one editor,

> Devout Christians study not only the word of God, but also his providences. By carefully discerning the 'signs of the times' they learn much of his will in its present application to human affairs.[5]

Moreover, the Church was the chief means by which the providential design of history was being unfolded. True, the task of the Methodist Episcopal Church was to convert sinners, but that was not all. Methodists saw themselves under divine

mandate to shape history itself. Such an understanding lay
back of the words of R. S. Foster, onetime president and
professor at Drew University and bishop, when he said,
"America will determine the future of the world. From her
will emanate the deciding factors. We ought to be chief
among the determining factors of America. "6

Understanding the activity of God and His chief agent,
the Church, in intimate relationship to historical events
meant that preachers of the printed page and pulpit had to
pay close attention to the affairs of life. God's judgment
and promise appeared in ordinary events. Bishop Simpson
said, "I do not expect I shall ever become a Calvinist, but
I believe I am becoming more and more satisfied of the
government of God even in the smallest matters. "7 Consequently, Simpson could admonish his listeners to discern
God's hand in a "business disaster, " in the "loss of property, " even in the passing "thought of [a] dear one. "8 But the
broader movements and events of history were also under the
Providence of God; hence, it was a common practice for
religious journals to cover current events not only to dis-
seminate information (that was important in view of the fact
that many readers did not come into contact with secular
journals), but also as a means of prophetic interpretation
and spiritual uplift. One writer, justifying the practice of
political comment in religious papers, put it this way: "The
true Christian patriot will find much to inspire his gratitude
to the Great Ruler of Nations, in a careful survey of our
foreign relations, especially from a foreign point of view. "9

In an editorial under the title "Religious Not Political,"
appearing in the Zion's Herald, the editor argues that ordination to the ministry carries with it a mandate to don the
robes of Isaiah and that Methodist clergymen ought not hesitate to speak words of judgment concerning all "practical
questions. " Thus, "God made it the duty of his prophets ...
to take a careful over sight of his whole territory. " The
promise of God, following this injunction, was that He would
pour the "light of inspiration upon his perceptive faculties
that he might see more than was visible to common eyes. "10
The "whole territory" included religious and secular spheres
at home and abroad. Whether it was the disaster at Bull Run,
the revolutionary activity of the Fenians, the impeachment
trial of President Andrew Johnson, the unity of Germany
wrought by Bismarck, the corruption of politics in New York
City, or race riots in New Orleans--all of these and com-
parable historical events came under the purview of Methodist

eyes and became a text for proclaiming God's word. Frequently Methodist journals teeming with political discussions were read to congregations from the pulpit. [11]

What was the rationale of churchmen with an admittedly evangelical and conservative theology for taking the social and political order with such seriousness? The answer to that is manifold, but it is a thesis of this study that the doctrine of Providence provided a theological framework and an impulse that made it not only possible, but necessary to treat social and political issues as an inherent part of the Church's mission to the world. Because history was viewed in the context of the Providences of God it was possible for most of the leading clergymen of northern Methodism to treat, as a matter of course, "worldly" events with a holy seriousness.

The teaching of God's Providence saved Methodists not only from an other-worldly orthodoxy, but from a narrow individualism as well. The eyes of most historians of the American Church have focused too exclusively on the frontier and the defensive reaction of Protestantism to the issues of the Gilded Age, and not enough on the reaction of the Churches to the Civil War and Reconstruction. For this reason the social dimension of religious expression during and after the Civil War has not been appreciated. It is true that pervading the revivalist tradition of Methodism in the nineteenth century was a strong emphasis on the immediate confrontation between the individual and God, and a stress on personal piety as the fruit of salvation. But just as the individual was seen as standing before God in terms of guilt and forgiveness, sin and sanctification, so the Church, the nation and various communities of men were viewed as objects of divine judgment and mercy. Just as individuals had a providential vocation to fulfill, so Churches had a mission, and the nation had a destiny. "What is true of an individual," writes a Methodist editor, "in a very important sense, is true of a nation. The nation has a life, interests and destiny, and is as dependent upon God for prosperity, as is the individual."[12] This capacity to see the nation as a complete organic entity, and not simply as an aggregate of individuals, allowed Methodists individually and corporately in official pronouncements to speak of "national sins." Gilbert Haven, the most consistent prophetic voice of Methodism, could refer to "the American heart" and the evil of color caste that still possessed it after the Emancipation Proclamation. [13] Even the conservative and "so called" individualistic doctrine of sanctification became a resource for broader social judgments from Haven's pulpit. Condemning the "social slavery" and "political slavery" that still prevailed in American society during the post Civil War years, Haven declared:

> The victims of our contempt feel the yoke of bondage with which we still burden their souls. The liberties they have won only make these chains the more galling. Not until every such fetter is broken will God's controversy with America come to an end. . . . They (Americans) only need to conquer this prejudice, to become the model and the inspiration of all the nations of the earth. May Church, State, and Society, in all their life, speedily reveal the perfect cleansing of the American heart from the unbrotherly distinction of man from man. 14

Calling the nation to accountability for "social sins" and recalling the nation to its responsibilities on the part of Methodist clergymen was not motivated by the kind of humanistic spirit that animated New England transcendentalists or Unitarians. Virtue, whether individual or national, was a part of religion. At the heart of social concerns was the evangelical task. An individual could not effectively witness for Christ if he manifested an impure life. America could not be a model of Christian civilization and an agent in the Providential hand of God for Christianizing the world with a national heart defiled by the sin of color caste.

It was this profound conviction that churches, nations and individuals had destinies to fulfill in the order of Providence that enabled the Methodist Episcopal Church in the third quarter of the nineteenth century to approach critical and perplexing social problems with a sense of moral urgency while at the same time holding firmly to a transcendent religious perspective rooted in a traditional orthodoxy. In fact, Gilbert Haven represented a most conservative theological stance--including faith in a personal Sovereign God, a firm belief in the inerrancy of the scriptures, a belief in the Methodist doctrine of "holiness, " a strong support of revivals and camp meetings--and at the same time was regarded as radical in his social thought and actions. His theological conservatism was intimately related--indeed, was the source-- of a social liberalism. The key to how this wedding of conservatism and liberalism cohered can be understood in terms of Haven's vision of a Christian Commonwealth which had its roots in New England Puritanism. An example of how an incredibly liberal position concerning women's suffrage was based on this vision will suffice to demonstrate this point:

> She is of the Commonwealth, having equal rights with every other member. She is bone of our bone and flesh of our flesh. Surely, all enforced exclusion of her from her just claims is the greatest injustice. If we pre-eminently despise the man who strikes a woman, how should we feel toward the State which thus strikes down all its women, and robs them of all power of defence from its blows?
>
> Above all, we need her help. Christ is seeking to establish his empire in the earth. It is an empire of peace, of unity, of righteousness, of love. It is to be established in good-willing men, in holy laws, in sacred institutions, in purified society. How can this be done except by the cooperation of the best and most numerous members of that society? Only by woman's vote can the kingdom of God be completely established. Only thus can we save the State from debauchery and utter demoralization. [15]

While one of the practical outworkings of the doctrine of Providence was the vision of a Christian commonwealth, it was not the only use to which this teaching was put. The point to be underscored before turning to a more complete treatment of how this teaching was applied is that far from being exclusively individualistic in ethical considerations, most of the prominent and powerful Methodist leaders became almost excessively concerned with the forms of collective life and their relations to a faith understanding. This is not to say that all were as socially liberal as Haven, nor did all interpret the providential designs of God in the same way. What is manifestly clear and will be demonstrated with greater precision in succeeding chapters is that the judgment, often made by Social Gospel and even post-Niebuhrian theologians, to the effect that evangelical Protestantism in the mid-nineteenth century reflected an individualistic ethic, is simply not true. Charles H. Hopkins, one of the purveyors of this view, has written, "The characteristic religion of mid-nineteenth century America comprised a well-articulated body of doctrines and doctrinaires ... that resulted in a smug preoccupation with the salvation and perfection of the individual."[16] Conveniently ignoring certain men in the largest and most powerful denomination in the country, in favor of invoking the more dramatic if not the more crass pronouncements of Henry Ward Beecher, and also ignoring the Church's response to the sectional conflict, Hopkins can say of Protestant conservatism that "It devoted itself to the reformation of the individual, leaving social consequences to take care of themselves."[17] This assessment is refuted by the record. Seeing the rule of God over such corporate forms as the Church and nations became the perspective which enabled Methodist clergymen to view sin in its corporate manifestations and actively engage in political means of bringing the national life into greater harmony with "republican principles" and the "designs of God." The prophetic criticism of slavery as an evil institution; the official Methodist support of the Thirteenth, Fourteenth, and Fifteenth Amendments, the active agitation for laws granting suffrage to freedmen; the pleas and active efforts for temperance reform; the use of Methodist power to elect the "right" politicians to office; the discussions of war and peace and official action supporting Lincoln's war policy; the massive efforts in the field of education--all of these and more cannot be understood simply in terms of an individualistic ethic or what has been called an "ethic of conversionism."

Two events, the Centenary celebration of American Methodism and the end of the Civil War, provided occasion for reflection on the providential activity of God and, correlatively on what that activity meant in assessing the nature and destiny of the Methodist Episcopal Church. The effort to explicate various interpretations of these two events and to discern the meanings they held for Methodists is intended to set the stage for understanding the manner in which Methodists related the mission of the Church to the destiny of the nation, and how this understanding provided the basic motivation for social concern and action.

The Doctrine of Providence and the Centenary of American Methodism

Northern Methodists were infused with the conviction that their denomination had been uniquely called by Providence to effectuate God's purposes in America and in the world. This was not simply pious exuberance or a characteristically American expression of denominational pride. For Methodists celebrating their one hundredth anniversary in 1866 there was concrete evidence that God had an agenda for his-

tory and that the Methodist Episcopal Church had been selected to play a major role in carrying out that providential
plan. The evidence was their remarkable growth in the
first half of the nineteenth century and the increasing wealth
and national prestige of the denomination in the third quarter
of the century. These historical occurrences were clear
manifestations of divine favor and as such implied special
responsibility.

All of the sermons, editorials, articles and official
statements relating to the Centenary celebration extolled
Methodism's success in terms of God's special favor. The
Methodist historian Abel Stevens was commissioned to write
the official history of the first century of American Methodism. In a moving and romantic narrative with Horatio
Alger overtones Stevens views the "progress" of American
Methodism from its humble origins to the "chief religious
embodiment of the common people" as the most remarkable
ecclesiastical movement of this country. [18] Most Methodists
were quick to agree. However, more important than the
boldness of Methodist self-adulation is the interpretation
they gave as to what this remarkable success meant. The
evidence of God's special call to Methodists to be one of the
chief agents for the achievement of his purposes was real
and concrete. Equally important in discerning the meaning
of this special history was the framework in which this history was viewed. The philosophy of history provided by the
doctrine of Providence became that frame of reference and
was employed as a means of Methodist self-understanding.

The providential view of history commonly held contained a distinct scheme of periodization. Reviewing books
by Herder, Hegel and Schlegel in the Methodist Quarterly
Review, a Methodist writer rejected both the schemes of
Herder and Hegel. Schlegel, however, represented a point
of view that could be incorporated into a Christian understanding of Providence. The Methodist reviewer focused on
Schlegel's formula, "the restoration in man of the lost image
of God," or "the return of the race to that original state of
perfection from which it had fallen." [19] The theory conceived
of the race after the fall "degenerating age after age until
about the Christian era: since that time the process is supposed to be one of recovery and return...." [20] It was the
turning point, the advent of Christianity, that interested this
Methodist and provided him with a scheme that was widely
accepted among Methodists as a view of "providential process." The Old Testament represented a period of continual

falling away from God and was regarded as preparatory to the new period in history inaugurated by Christ.

Three periods comprised the scheme of history as developed by this reviewer. The first and central point "is the cross of Christ--the great central fact, the manifestation of God in the flesh. "[21] This event marked the beginning of the first period of the Apostolic Church when "Christianity rose majestic from the ashes (of a degenerate Judaism), soaring on loftier pinions, and bearing in her bosom the elements of a greater melioration and advancement, than the world had ever before seen. "[22] The second period begins with Constantine and "the hopeless reaction of the dark ages." This period of fall and decline came about through the corrupting influence of the Roman civilization. [23] The third phase began with the Reformation, when the "pure spirit of Christianity, after having groaned for ages under the increasing burden of ... errors and corruptions" finally broke through like water from a decaying dyke. [24] What was significant about this third period was the concurrence between the true English Reformation in the seventeenth century and the discovery of America. This history of redemption would culminate when the entire world was converted to Christianity. By Christianity, Methodists meant "Protestant Christianity, " and the means by which world conversion would come about was "evangelical effort, "[25] of which Methodism was the chief instrument.

Abel Stevens, in a history of American Methodism, written after the Centenary Celebration, sought to explain the chief causes of the success of Methodism. He gave one primary cause and a variety of proximate causes. The primary cause was that Methodism "was a necessity of the times, a providential provision for the times. "[26] In articulating what he meant, Stevens put forth the same threefold periodic scheme outlined above:

> History, if not as much under the sway of laws as physics, is nevertheless a providential process. The Apostolic ministry founded the kingdom of Christ in the world, but the apostles themselves predicted the rise of Antichrist and the great 'falling away. ' The medieval night, a thousand years long, followed; the Renaissance, with the Reformation, began the modern history of the world. [27]

Stevens went on to describe how the "progressive power" of

Abel Stevens (1815-1897), Editor of Zion's Herald and The
Methodist. He was a moderate on issues concerning Southern
Methodism, but a proponent of Freedman rights and a defender
of the right of preachers to engage political issues.

the Reformation was about to be exhausted in the eighteenth
century when, as a "providential necessity," God called
forth the Methodist Church and the New Republic as new
agents of his redemptive plan. [28]   In an earlier article in
the Methodist Quarterly Review Stevens enunciated a more
refined periodization within the third phase of history as a
means of providing a meaningful context in which the present
could be understood:

> The first is comprised of the period of Wesley's
> personal ministry, in which it began, extended in
> both hemispheres, and was at last more or less
> consolidated into an organic system.   The second
> was its testing period, its great seven years' war
> of 'fiery trial,' from the death of Wesley to near
> the beginning of the nineteenth century.
>
> At the conclusion of this probation its fidelity was
> rewarded by remarkable prosperity, and by the
> sudden appearance in its ranks of men of extra-
> ordinary capacity, who quickly elevated its intel-
> lectual character, confirmed its system, and de-
> veloped its energy in plans for universal mission-
> ary conquest.   The missionary development may
> be considered its third and, it is to be hoped, its
> permanent stage; permanent at least till the evan-
> gelization of the world. [29]

That which gave evidence of providential favor was the "remarkable prosperity."   The tabulation of successes in 1866
became more than a routine exercise in bookkeeping.   It
was understood as a call to "heroic purpose" rooted in the
knowledge of unparalleled "historical achievement for more
than a hundred years."[30]   There was a sense in which
Methodists became heady over their successes as they basked
in the Favor of God.   One Methodist clergyman unashamedly
remarked, "Our righteousness hath been rewarded by the
fruits of the earth."[31]   The official addresses and articles,
however, always contained admonitions not to glory in man.
Typical are the words of a Methodist editor at the close of
an enthusiastic Centennial narrative devoted to the "wonderful
history of American Methodism":

> God forbid that on this celebration we should glory
> in man.   The view of methodism and its success ...
> is not written, nor intended, to inspire pride and
> vainglory, but to exhibit the extent of the benefits

and mercies for which our united thanks should be
presented to the God of our fathers and our God.
His hand is in all of this, for he is 'great in counsel and mighty in work, ' and the entire glory must
be given to his infinite mercy and goodness. [32]

The Central Committee of the Centenary Celebration
struck this basic theme in their first official proclamation
when they reminded Methodists of the obligation implied in
the recollection of great events and heroes of the past. In
declaring that they were the "heirs" and the "trustees" of
the great legacy of Methodism, they insisted that Providence
had equipped and called her for a "grand mission to the
world. "[33] As both heirs and agents of Providence the Church
was enjoined to use its legacy well. For conservatives during this period this meant expanding denominational strength;
for the more progressive churchmen it also meant that; but
in addition it indicated a call to guardianship of the manners,
morals and civil life of the nation to the end that the "Great
Republic" might be the model Christian nation in the world.
The latter group interpreted providential stewardship as a
demand to translate spiritual liberty into social and political
freedom. A Methodist professor asked, "Have we not rather
forgotten the universal law of moral compensation, as appli-
cable to nations as to individuals, that the richer the blessings the higher the duty; ... Have we not forgotten that, in
making us ' the heirs of the ages, ' God intended to exact of
us in return the most heroic performance and the most generous sacrifice for the principles of eternal right and justice that any nation was ever required to pay?"[34]

The doctrine of Providence provided a perspective
for a philosophy of history which was interpreted in such a
way as to give Methodists a sense of sublime destiny. That
which made it sublime was the special role Methodism was
playing in this third and final phase of historical development. And this sense of providential destiny provided the
impulse for an aggressive social mission both for the individual Methodist leader and the Church in its official capacity. Not all bishops, editors and leading clergymen interpreted the task of the Church in terms of social reform and
social justice, but great numbers did.

Milton Powell has made a strong case for his thesis
that before the abolitionist crusade in the antebellum period,
the doctrine of Providence was used to provide a conservative approach to social and civil affairs. [35] The belief that

the designs of Providence were unfolding in history according
to God's own timing suggested to Methodists a rather limited
role for the Church in structural change and limited human
responsibility in civil affairs. Certainly Methodists in the
antebellum days thought of the Church as the chief means by
which the divine scheme of history was being unfolded, but
its effect on social and civil life was indirect; that is,
through the individual fruits of evangelicalism. "Throughout
most of the half-century prior to the Civil War," Powell
asserts, "American Methodists were able to believe that the
acts and policies of the Republic could be accepted as satisfactory progress."[36] Increasingly, however, Powell notes
that some Methodist clergymen began to discern the "failure
of slavery to correspond to the general improvement of society," which was "compounded by the ostensible growth of a
slave power with great influence...."[37] It was during this
period when Gilbert Haven, LaRoy Sunderland, Orange Scott
and Hiram Mattison, among other northern Methodists, were
agitating for a stronger anti-slavery position by the Methodist Episcopal Church, that many Methodists began to re-
evaluate the role of their denomination in the divine order
of history. But it was not until the Civil War that the majority of Methodists heard the call for a more active and
aggressive approach to social and political matters.

The Doctrine of Providence and the Civil War

It is not the purpose here to discuss in any detail
either the role of the Methodist Episcopal Church in the Civil
War or Methodist interpretation of specific events, but rather
to demonstrate how the doctrine of Providence was used to
make sense out of that fierce and bloody fraternal conflict
and how interpretations of the war came to inform the mission of the Church during Reconstruction. Once the war
was over, Methodist clergymen, convinced that God had
spoken, sought to discern the sovereign voice. This was
not the "still small voice." It was the God who thundered
from the "brazen throat of the cannon" and by the "flashes
of the lightning that gleams from this fearful thunder-cloud
of war" as a generation looked "shuddering into the abyss of
utter ruin."[38]

Out of the crisis and tragedy of this savage war came
the best of Methodist theological reflection. This confessional
theology was at once more vital, touching the depths of life,
and more profound than the attempts at doing theology sys-

tematically during this period. Of course, as Methodists
spelled out the meaning of Providence, they demonstrated
not only their profundity, but also a weakness in relating
an overruling Providence to history. On the one hand, many
Methodist interpreters did see that God was judge of both
sides; that the "sins of the fathers" and their own sins were
being visited upon them; that the nation was going through
times of needed purgation; and that northern Methodists were
being called to reassess their own history, not from the
mountain peaks of success, but from the valleys of humiliation where they can "look back over the slimy path of compromise and concession...."[39] For instance, there could
be no smug self-satisfaction when northern Methodists examined their own relations to the slavery issue, especially in
the excruciating knowledge that not until after the Emancipation Proclamation of Lincoln did the General Conference re-
vise the General Rule on Slavery to include a ban on "slaveholding" within the Church.[40]

During the war and immediately upon its end, northern Methodists were able to plead self-guilt in the mirror
of God's providential judgments. Herein were seeds of theological richness, and a politics of repentance. On the other
hand, Methodists were too confident and exact in their readings of Providence. For Lincoln the "almighty had his own
purposes," and His ways were inscrutable. For Methodists,
"The hand of God in history is plainly discernible by all
those who receive the doctrine of the Divine interposition in
human affairs."[41] This presumption eventually led northern
Methodists to express the moral meaning of the war in black
and white terms, especially as Reconstruction plans met
with increasing Southern intractability. Identifying the purposes of Providence too specifically, Methodists failed to
plumb the depths of moral ambiguity which could have been
a source of greater wisdom as they endeavored to be faithful in their mission.

Disentangling the various motifs, meanings, and lessons is difficult indeed. There were differences; there was
hysteria and sober reflection; there was profundity and
banality, but whatever else may be said, Methodists had a
transcendent frame of reference that would not allow them to
admit that there was no meaning to the dramatic historical
tragedy through which they had just lived. It was not a
"needless war." One writer for the Christian Advocate
spoke for Methodists when he declared that "the voice of the
war is the voice of God."[42] But what was being spoken in

and through this great cosmic drama being played out beneath the passing of temporal events? If God's Providence was unfolding in the third, and many believed, final, phase of history, what then was the meaning of this bleak dramatic episode intimately seen and felt?

It has already been noted that Methodist interpretations of the war were not transparently uniform. Nevertheless, an investigation of the literature of the times reveals at least four common themes more or less consistently enunciated. The war was:

> 1) a providential judgment on the Church and nation both North and South for being unfaithful to the designs of God; in consequence, therefore, a call to penitence;
>
> 2) a means of producing a new birth of nationhood and of securing national goals of freedom and equality through chastisement and baptism by fire;
>
> 3) a calling of churches to be conscious agents of Providence on a new and grand mission;
>
> 4) a vindication of the Northern cause.

The procedure will be to take each interpretive theme in order, with a view to showing how the war provided a mirror for self-reflection; became a fundamental source of Methodist self-understanding; and provided the basis for interpreting their future role in history.

Before the attack on Fort Sumter editors of the Northern Methodist journals uniformly predicted war. Editor Eddy of the Northwestern Christian Advocate regarded "civil war as inevitable and close at hand."[43] After all, was this not portended in the secession of southern Methodists from the mother church in 1844? The general uneasiness and quiet excitement preceding the fall of Sumter had the effect of shifting evangelical concerns from the individual to the nation. One report from Brighton, Michigan told of a three weeks protracted meeting during which time only a few sinners were "powerfully convicted." It was "almost impossible these troublesome times to persuade men to believe to the saving of the soul."[44] Illustrative of the ominous mood which turned hearts and minds from the individual before God to a nation confronting a terrible judgment were the many calls for a day of fasting and prayer for "our sins as a nation."45

Bishop Simpson struck the common theme of divine judgment at the outset of the war. In an address in Chicago he developed the idea that God was the great director and disposer of history whose hand could now be seen in terrible judgment on a nation that had sinned. First, the nation was to have been a "pattern of piety to bear the truth abroad through the nations of the world," but it had failed to give of its wealth "for the dissemination of the gospel." Secondly, Bishop Simpson referred to the great "national sin itself"--slavery--which thwarted God's justice and the very purpose for which he had raised up the nation. 46 The editor of the most conservative of northern Methodist journals, The Methodist of New York, admitted that "Politics would seldom have admission to the pulpit," but he thought that in "times like these the pulpit should speak as the oracle of the God of nations...." In advising clergymen as to appropriate texts, he suggested, "The scathing terms of the 'imprecatory' Psalms may be relevantly used ..." to sound forth the message, which was twofold. "God has been chastening us," was the first part. The Second was the word of judgment on "the unparalleled crime of this rebellion."47

A common interpretation of the national sin was in terms of "forgetfulness of God." An editorial on Lincoln's Thanksgiving Day Proclamation expresses this theme:

> As a nation until the breaking out of this rebellion, we have enjoyed unparalleled prosperity; but unmindful of the source whence the prosperity came, we have been ungrateful, neglectful and forgetful even of God. Out of that prolific soil the most gigantic sins have sprung up and luxuriantly flourished, until the wrath of God burst forth upon us in a most terrific storm of war. How long insulted Heaven will suffer that awful tempest to rage around us, and pour its bloody torrents through our valleys and over our plains, we cannot tell. 48

An indication of the nation's dereliction was the Constitution with, appallingly, no mention of God. One prominent Methodist traced the nation's "forgetfulness of God" back to the Constitutional Convention, noting that "many of the framers

of the Constitution of the United States were deeply imbued
with the ideas of the French atheistical school. " Moreover,
when Ben Franklin suggested that they have a chaplain "engaged to implore the Divine blessing and guidance, each
morning during the remaining of the session, " the issue was
briefly discussed and dropped, with "not a single prayer
offered in the entire session of the convention which framed
our national Constitution. " "Is it strange, " inquired this
Methodist, "that a convention which allowed no recognition
of God in its deliberations, should have framed an instrument in which God is not acknowledged?"[49]

Expressing the same theme more substantively, another prominent Ohio Methodist pointed to the meaning of the
sectional conflict in terms of God's judgment on "Our Apostacy as a Nation. "[50] The apostacy was seen "as a failure
to carry out the Divine purpose for which we were raised
up as a nation, " and that purpose was articulated in the national covenant--The Declaration of Independence. [51] He
wrote:

> The design of our planting as a nation is clearly
> set forth in the nation's 'Life Covenant, ' which
> bears date July 4, 1776, and contains these ever-
> memorable words, then first in the providential
> unfolding of the ages made audible to the ears of
> mankind: 'All men are created equal, endowed by
> their Creator with certain inalienable rights,
> among which are life, liberty, and the pursuit of
> happiness. '[52]

The requirements of the second party of the covenant--the
nation--included the active embodiment of those great principles to the end that the United States would be a "model"
and a living "demonstration" to all people and to extend the
covenant to all peoples. [53] "It was the Divine will that the
new nationality should keep its life covenant by expanding,
by growing, in accordance with the law of its own organic
life. ... Our mission in this respect was important, for it
was worldwide as that of the Church. "[54] The "covenant of
life" had been broken, and the symbol of the apostacy was
slavery. Not just a Southern sin, slavery "received that
sanction of the Government, and brought the whole power of
the nation to aid in perpetuating those deeds of darkness
which were fast making our national life and history 'a devil's
chaos' instead of God's cosmos. "[55]

At stake in the slavery question was always the broader

issue of a grand mission that was being hampered by the
existence of the "peculiar institution." The fundamental sin
was breaking the covenant, the chief expression of which was
slavery. Other wrongs mentioned by this writer and representing the views of many northern Methodists were:

> ... a national irreverence for God and his laws,
> a disregard of the Christian Sabbath and the insti-
> tutions of religion; a want of national integrity, and
> a vast system of demagogism, intemperance, pro-
> fanity, and licentiousness. [56]

Gilbert Haven, that fiery prophet from New England,
could also register the national sins for which the country
was being punished. Yet, he was more inclined to see the
purpose of God in the war as primarily a judgment on the
sin of slavery. The war was a providential revelation of,
"the righteous judgment of God."[57] The following excerpt
from a sermon delivered on the occasion of the National
Fast in 1864 is representative of his position:

> He saw His children writhing under the lash, and
> the lust of their oppressors, under the neglect,
> and scorn, and contumely of the whole nation. He
> has meted out a measure according to our sins.
> 'There are four millions crowded into that black
> hole America,' He says-- 'four millions of my dear,
> desposed children. Thirty millions walk proudly
> the upper deck, lift up haughty eyes to heaven, and
> present a daily prayer that My soul hateth. "Lord
> I thank Thee that I am not as this negro." The
> four millions of their brethren also, daily, from
> the depths of their darkness and distress, cry to
> Me.' And the Lord harkened and heard. He de-
> scended from heaven. He set the battle in array.
> He made brother spring at the throat of brother,
> until, to the number of the enslaved, including even
> their wives and little ones, the mighty men are set
> against the mighty, while death and mourning fill
> all the land. [58]

For Haven it was emphatically not a war in which God was
on the side of the North. The heart of his message was
that because the North was not on God's side, "our just
punishment grows and grows."[59] Noteworthy is Haven's use
of first person plural in his homily on sin.

We almost begin to confess our sins.... We bow

Gilbert Haven (1821-1880), Northern Methodist radical abolitionist editor of <u>Zion's Herald</u> and Reconstruction Bishop.
He was an intrepid defender of civil rights and advocate of
social equality and racial integration.

> the head, but not yet the knee. The nation has
> never yet broken forth in the penitential cries of
> David.... We have been guilty of the enslavement
> and murder of multitudes of Uriahs. We have been
> guilty of the ruin of millions of Bathshebas....
> We have never acknowledged the greatness of our
> sin. We have never cried, 'Against <u>Thee</u>, Thee
> only, have we sinned, and done this <u>evil</u> in Thy
> sight. '60

While the purpose of God in the war was primarily a judgment on slavery, it was not exclusively a Southern sin.
Haven always insisted on Northern culpability. Again, he
spoke for not a few when he said,

> We have been partaker of their sins, and the
> measure of the judgment we have meted out to our
> enslaved brethren shall be measured to us again.
> We must suffer in our hearts, in our anxiety for
> those who go out from us to keep the foe from
> ravaging our firesides, in the dreadful griefs of
> wife, and mother, and child, over those who shall
> return no more. 61

Under the harsh chastisements of a providential God,
Haven could rejoice that the North was being led to repentance. Thus, the proper response to God's judgment was
"not only fasting before Him, but doing as He requires. "62
George Peck, a distinguished Methodist clergyman and editor,
writing in the final days of the war, saw the spectacle of the
fraternal conflict as one of the means "which God in his
Providence sees proper to employ for the punishment of the
nation for her sins. "63 As with Haven, this punishment was
intended to produce penitence, but he feared "that as a nation we are not penitent. "64 A hearty contrition would be
manifested in "works of repentance, " and "productive of the
fruits described by the holy prophet. Isaiah lvii, 3, 5, 6. "65
Repentance meant direct and concrete action in the body politic. Godly sorrow was to be translated into Congressional
and legislative action. In discussing the meaning of repentance as God's means of preparing to "break every yoke, and
let [ting] the oppressed go free, " Haven went on to say,
"Then, after due infliction, after the godly sorrow has
wrought its perfect work, after Congress and the legislatures
of the guilty States shall cooperate in this divine work, or
the President shall himself decree liberty, and shall with his
own hand break the shackles from every limb, then, as He

has promised, He will surely perform...."[66] For Haven
repentance meant holding one's history--personal, ecclesiastical and national--before God's judgment; it meant reflecting
on "what might have been and lamenting on what is. " And
yet, finally, "it is useless to dwell on the past, " remarked
Haven, "... the future is yet before us. "[67] Repentance,
born out of a deep sense of guilt, meant a future-oriented
stance with a new vision, a new strategy, a determination
to right wrongs.

While the phrase, "politics of repentance, " was not
used as such by northern Methodists during this period, it
is an apt phrase for describing an interpretation of the Civil
War in terms of judgment and penitence. Repentance was
assumed to have direct consequences on the social and political order. It meant a moral cleansing and was a pre-
condition for new moral vision and courage. An editor for
the Zion's Herald said,

> As a nation there is evidently something demanded
> of us more than humiliation for sin, more than
> thanksgiving for mercies received; or perhaps we
> should say, that something more is needed to make
> our humility and gratitude perfect and acceptable
> to God. We should cheerfully receive and adopt
> the new ideas which the providence of God is illus-
> trating and urging on our attention. [68]

These "new ideas" came to mean for most Methodists a new
constitutional amendment prohibiting slavery, a new constitutional amendment in which God would be officially acknowledged, and a vigorous reconstruction policy politically and
ecclesiastically conceived.

The point is belabored because it has usually been
missed by interpreters of northern Methodism during the reconstruction period. Ralph Morrow, in his very able book,
Northern Methodism and Reconstruction, missed the point
altogether when he wrote that the Methodist reading of God's
mind in the Civil War meant that "The North had been selected as the executor of a divine judgment against the 'man-
buying, woman whipping, maiden-debauching, children-selling
South. '"[69] While the sentiment just quoted is fair in expressing attitudes of some northern Churchmen, it does not
do justice to many of the major spokesmen for the Methodist Episcopal Church. The dimension of guilt in the self-
understanding of Methodists is clearly a dominant impulse
for religious and social action following the war. [70]

Typical of the way a combination of humility and re-
solve issued forth from this sense of guilt is a statement
appearing in the Christian Advocate of New York in 1866:

> Our course respecting the duty of the Methodist
> Episcopal Church to the emancipated colored people
> of the South has been moderate and conservative;
> quite as much so as our judgment and conscience
> approve. Nor do we now propose to change that
> course, though we think the time has fully come
> both for a more definite policy to be adopted, and
> for a vigorous prosecution of our Southern work to
> be inaugurated. . . .
>
> These colored people are destined to constitute a
> very considerable element in our population, and
> the future of American Society, both politically and
> morally, must largely depend on their condition.
> We believe that a great guilt rests upon our Church
> for its disregard of the claims of the colored people
> of the free states, before the rebellion. (emphasis
> mine) Our censure of our Southern brethren for
> their pro-slaverism is just, and well deserved by
> them; and yet we suspect that had the Saviour's in-
> junction been observed that only the innocent should
> cast the first stone, or utter the first censure, we
> should have been silent. Nor are we as a Church
> doing much better now than formerly, and there is
> great force in the retort given by the South to our
> expressions of interest in the Freedmen, telling us
> to look at home, and take care of our own negro
> population. . . .
>
> We repeat what we have before said, the negro is
> the coming man for whom all who care for the fu-
> ture of society should make way. 71

Or again, the fruits of repentance before the providential judgments of God are evidenced in the "Fourth Annual
Report" of the Freedman's Aid Society in these words:

> Let us atone for our sins, as much as possible, by
> furnishing schools and the means of improvement
> for the children, upon whose parents we have in-
> flicted such fearful evils. Let us lend a helping
> hand in their escape from the degradation into
> which we have forced them by our complicity with

oppressors. Justice, stern justice, demands this
at our hands. Let us pay the debt we owe this
race before we complain of weariness in the tri-
fling sums we have given for schools and churches.
We may longer evade this claim, and turn a deaf
ear to their cry for help, but He who holds the
scales of justice weights our guilt, rejects our hypocritical apologies, and demands that justice be
rendered to this race before we congratulate our-
selves in the mere pittance contributed to this
cause. [72]

The sense of God's judgment on the Church, coupled
with a deep conviction that grievances must be redressed,
suggests a rather sound basis for a social ethic. Indeed,
the acknowledgment of offenses at their hands, which in the
Providence of God must now be removed, is an echo of Lincoln's Second Inaugural, the great text for a religious social
ethic. This is not to say that Methodists exhibited the depth
of meaning expressed in Lincoln's grasp of the inscrutable
workings of Providence. Lincoln believed, as did Methodist
clergymen, that the drama of history was shot through with
moral meaning, that "the judgments of the Lord are true
and righteous all together." Methodists, however, were too
inclined to moralize the workings of Providence by identifying
too exactly the punishments and imperatives of the Almighty. [73]
Reinhold Niebuhr helps to sharpen the crucial difference between the Methodists and Lincoln, as they spelled out the
workings of Providence, when he states that for the President, "while the drama of history is shot through with moral
meaning, the meaning is never exact. Sin and punishment,
virtue and reward are never precisely proportioned."[74] Having said that, it is nevertheless true that the doctrine of the
Providence of God became the source of an ethical style
superior to the revivalistic ethic which characterized Protestantism during the antebellum period. Humility and resolution became the fruits of a self-understanding rooted in an
overpowering persuasion that they were called to account before the judgment of God. An official resolution presented
and approved at the General Conference of the Methodist
Episcopal Church in 1864 underscores this judgment. It
reads as follows:

> 3. Resolved, That we regard our calamities as
> resulting from our forgetfulness of God, and from
> slavery, so long our nation's reproach, and that
> it becomes us to humble ourselves and forsake

our sins as a people, and hereafter, in all our
laws and acts, to honor God.

4. Resolved, That we will use our efforts to secure such a change in the Constitution of our country as shall recognize the being of God, our de-
pendence on him for prosperity, and also his word
as the foundation of civil law.

5. Resolved, That we regard slavery as abhorrent
to the principles of our holy religion, humanity,
and civilization, and that we are decidedly in favor
of such an amendment to the Constitution and such
legislation on the part of the states as shall prohibit slavery or involuntary servitude, except for
crime, throughout all the states and territories of
the country.

6. Resolved, That while we deplore the evils of
war that has filled our land with mourning we rejoice in the sublime manifestations of benevolence
it has developed, as seen in the Sanitary and
Christian Commissions, and in the associations
formed to aid the vast multitudes who have recently become freemen, and that we pledge to these
institutions our hearty co-operation and support.

Respectfully submitted, Joseph Cummings, Chairman. [75]

The second theme that may be discerned from various
interpretations of God's providential purposes in the war may
be put this way: the Civil War was a means of saving the
nation and securing national goals. The majority of Methodist interpreters of the war agreed with Lincoln that the
primary purpose of God was to test "whether the nation could
long endure. " Thus, it was for northern Methodists a "War
of Rebellion. " This theme pervades Methodist literature of
the times. However culpable the North was before the God
of nations, the particular and chief cause of the war was the
conviction that Southerners had assaulted the nation at Fort
Sumter and in so doing had become traitors and rebels. Rebellion was a high political crime, but, more than that, it
was a sin against God. Perhaps the most worked over and
worn text of the Bible was Romans thirteen.

The Civil War became an occasion for serious study

of the origin and authority of civil government, and Paul's
text, "The powers that be are ordained of God, " became
the point of departure from which northern Methodists
leveled their indictment. "Subjection or obedience to law is
necessary to the existence of Government, " writes George
Peck, "and it is but reasonable that we should be subject to
the power that gives us protection.... 'Resisting the power'
is 'resisting the ordinance of God.' Rebellion against a
legitimate government is rebellion against God, and a high
crime."[76] Peck also invokes the traditional "just War
theory" in justifying the use of the "sword" by the civil power to save the nation.

> It is strictly a defensive war. It is for the de-
> fense of the public property, the defense of the
> capital, the defense of the Constitution and the
> laws, the defense of the rights of the people, the
> defense of our nationality. It is a war for a gov-
> ernment against anarchy; a war for freedom against
> usurpation and despotism.... If ever the sword
> was drawn in a holy cause, it is so in the present
> war of the United States government against the
> great southern rebellion.[77]

The continual references to the war as "rebellion" and
the enemy as a "traitor" are indications that for Methodists
it was first of all a defensive war. Grounding the theological rationale for a vigorous support of the war effort in
Romans thirteen, Methodists added to this meaning a punitive
dimension. Daniel Whedon, in a discourse on the meaning
of a nation, set forth a traditional Christian view of the
state as the wielder of the sword. In words representative
of the majority of Methodists he said:

> As our Creator has organized man to be controlled
> by his own will, so he has instituted national gov-
> ernment as divinely authorized controller of a na-
> tions actions. 'The powers that' legitimately 'be, '
> the Apostle assures us, 'are ordained of God'; and
> resistance to their authority is not only political,
> but moral treason.... And as the national govern-
> ment has not, like the individual, a legal magis-
> tracy over and above itself to protect its rights,
> and arbitrate its disputes, so it must, responsi-
> bility to the Almighty Ruler of all, possess the
> power to protect itself, and secure justice in inter-
> national dealing. Hence the magistrate is armed

with the 'sword,' to execute even capital penalty
upon the domestic foe, or prosecute war upon a
foreign aggressor. These two exercises of the
power of the 'sword' stand upon precisely the
same basis; a power not always or often necessary
to be used, but always to be used when necessary.[78]

Daniel Curry, in a similar discourse on "the American Nation," makes the same point; because, "Civil Government is
of God," insists Curry, "it should be obeyed as a religious
duty."[79] Drawing upon the Tory legacy of John Wesley and
an orthodox understanding of Christianity, Methodists set
forth fundamentally conservative arguments--especially against
the pacifists--for prosecuting the war, and conservative ideas
in interpreting the meaning of the war.[80]

     In the eyes of northern Methodists, it was a defense
against rebellion; a punishment of traitors; and a securing
of national unity that gave the war its significance and broad
meaning.[81] So overwhelming was this conviction that an
erstwhile evangelical individualism gave way to corporate
understandings and approaches. A writer in The Methodist
stressed the preference for the corporate over individual
considerations by declaring that

          The roused conscience of the Church resists sin
          in the aggregate; her heart goes out after our
          armies, and though anxious for their individual
          salvation, still, in the nature of the case, she is
          more anxious for their victory over the rebel-
          lion.[82]

Summing up God's purpose in the war, the writer contended
that, "The direct object of the war is not to save men's souls,
but to crush the rebellion and save the nation."[83]

     That Methodists interpreted the war in terms of na-
tional preservation is expressed in the following excerpt from
a resolution passed by the Pittsburgh Annual Conference in
1865:

          This unholy rebellion, we believe, should be
          crushed out at all hazards, and at any cost. If
          this cannot be done without crushing out slavery,
          let slavery be crushed; but, by all means, save
          the Union.[84]

This statement would suggest a closer affinity to Lincoln and

his priorities than to the northern abolitionists. As a matter
of fact, it is almost a direct echo of Lincoln's well known
statement to Horace Greeley--"My paramount object in this
struggle is to save the Union, and is not either to save or
to destroy slavery. "[85] The action of the Confederates was
clearly rebellion against legitimate government. The Southern
states had not revolted against the acts of a tyrant or tyrannical government; rather, they had rebelled because of a perfectly constitutional election and against "the best government
that ever was constituted since the world began. "[86]

Interpretations of the meaning of the war, especially
in the early phases of the struggle, invariably centered
around legal questions, based on constitutional interpretations, and around the authority of government, based on
theological considerations. Preservation of the Union, not
the abolition of slavery, was the predominant view early in
the war. Dr. Edward Thompson, before he became bishop
and while he was editor of the influential Christian Advocate
of New York, expressed this view: "Slavery, though certainly indirectly and primarily, is not directly in question. "[87]
For Thompson, as for most moderate and conservative Methodists, the issue was "government or no government. " He
writes, "So little has slavery had to do directly with the
matter that the abolition agitations have tended to postpone
the issue by causing the majority of the North to side with
the South. "[88]

In the scale of ethical norms, Methodists affirmed,
almost uniformly, the priority of order over justice. Indeed,
a close investigation of sermons, articles and official statements reveals a political position not unlike the one articulated a century later by Reinhold Niebuhr when he said, "In
the political order, the value of justice takes an uneasy
second place behind that of internal order. "[89] But, as with
Niebuhr, many northern Methodists knew that order and justice are intimately related. The Methodists at the General
Conference in 1864 urged all to pray for peace, but warned
"against a false and hollow peace, gained by the sacrifice
of moral principles. "[90] Thompson, who said, "the country
takes the sword not for the extermination of slavery, but
for the upholding of the constitution, " did prophesy that by
the end of the struggle, "the war which we began for the
Constitution may lead to a new edition of the document which
will be read and heard by thousands this day with an emphasis unknown since it was proclaimed--the Declaration of
Independence. "[91]

In the march of events Methodists came to see emancipation of the slaves as an essential ingredient in preserving the nation. The Civil War, which had started out as a struggle to preserve the union, finally became understood as a struggle for the truths of the Declaration of Independence. Union and liberty were inseparable. An editor for The Methodist summed up the meaning of the Fourth of July holiday by declaring that it signified two things: "First, national unity; and secondly, universal liberty. "[92] The North was fighting for both. In a statement issued by the Rock River Conference, Methodists of the Illinois area declared that in the war, "... Right, Truth and Justice are equally involved with the national honor and existence. "[93] Gilbert Haven could not talk about the survival or meaning of the nation apart from the question of slavery. He was convinced that the nation had "never been, in reality, one people, " and that it could never be a unified Republic, "til slavery is abolished. "[94] The abolition of slavery was the means by which the nation could be saved.

The way the ethical norms of order and justice were related in Methodist interpretations of the Civil War may be seen in the attempts to relate the question of national unity and survival to the issue of slavery. By the end of the war northern Methodists generally agreed that in the war God was working out two things: first, the preservation of the union; secondly, the destruction of slavery. The war had taught the nation the importance of social justice and social order. A General Conference report declared faith in "the overruling providence of Almighty God, " under whose "control the nation has been led to abolish slavery and reinvest the emancipated with every civil and political right"; and under whose "restraints" the people learned to pay "respect to authority and obedience to law. "[95] The way these two goals were related varied, but they were invariably set in the context of a vigorous republicanism or "democratic faith" characteristic of the mid-nineteenth century, and in an overwhelming sense of national destiny. It was not simply national survival nor abolition of an evil institution at stake in the war. The very definition and destiny of the nation was being determined. This was the overriding issue. What Thomas Pressly said concerning the context out of which the Unionist historians wrote is apt for understanding northern Methodist reflections as well:

> The Unionist historians had reached maturity in an era in which periodic rebukes had been administered

to the 'emperors and priests' of Europe in the
name of American ideals and institutions. In their
ardent republicanism, they pictured the United
States as an experiment, surrounded by a hostile
world, in constitutional government by majority
rule, the inspiration and hope of forward looking
men all over the earth. Thus in assaulting the
nation, the Confederates seemed to most of the
Unionist historians to be attacking the principles
of representative government upon which the United
States was founded, seemed to be traitors attempting to overthrow from within the world's one constitutional republic. [96]

An anonymous Methodist, reviewing a book on the
meaning of the war, wrote approvingly of the author's thesis
that the war was "an essential conflict between the historic
democracy of the country and the oligarchical tendencies of
the South, founded in the barbarism of slavery."[97] It was
a common view that democracy would inevitably win out and
that all over the world monarchies would give way to the
form of democracy practiced in America. The wave of the
future was signaled in the outcome of the war. [98] Thus, the
war provided the nation with the possibility of achieving true
nationhood. And true nationhood meant that the grand experiment of democracy could be exported for the sake of all men.
This was the central meaning of the Civil War. Sometimes
this theme was discussed in terms of a "restoration" to the
intent of the founding fathers--a "new birth, " a "second
chance" because of the abortive nature of the first birth of
freedom. Therefore, when some Methodists sought to find
the cause of the war, they were plumbing at what was thought
to be a deeper level than the issue of slavery.

James Rusling, a prominent Methodist professor of
law and a Civil War general, represented this view when he
suggested that while slavery focused the issue, "the real
cause of the rebellion lies deeper."[99] He believed that for
the South slavery had become the common platform, the bond
of union through extensive propaganda measures, but that it
was "after all, only a condition of the rebellion; a necessary
condition, we grant; a condition which we would be blind not
to see and allow for. " The vital question being decided by
the war was the vexatious problem that dated back to the
Hamiltonian and Jeffersonian debates on the role of Federal
government. [100]

But our real struggle, as a nation, to the calm

> eye of history, rises higher than the question of
> slavery, and is rather an armed resolve of the
> national government to assert for itself, at last
> authority and power. The rebellion under the
> form of secession, is simply Jeffersonianism
> pushed to its logical results; the war for the
> Union, waged under the form of coercion, is
> merely the healthy return of the government to
> the sounder doctrines of Washington and Hamil-
> ton. 101

The new nation was conceived during the Revolution in the
period of Hamilton and Washington, but the embryo was
stunted by the malignant doctrine of decentralization--which
held sway during the first century of the "fair experiment."102

The Civil War was viewed by Rusling as an obstetric
operation allowing a second and normal birth of the nation.
The suggestion in the article being quoted is that the nation
was not quite a nation prior to the war. Concluding his discourse, he writes:

> With the war once over, we shall have no more
> squabbles about state Rights.... With the only
> stain upon our escutcheon blotted out, with justice
> and liberty established as the corner-stones of the
> Republic, with the reign of law and order made
> sure and absolute ... Then at last become the
> true pride of mankind, and the just hope of the
> world, it is not too much to believe, that our
> career as a nation will only just begin. 103

Called to be a nation in the eighteenth century, this Methodist,
among others, believed that through the loud voice of God in
the war the people of the nineteenth century had heard and
answered the summons.

In a similar vein, Gilbert Haven expressed the meaning of the 1864 election as deciding once and for all the
question of Union. Prior to "The Great Election," the fact
and future of nationhood had always been problematic. In
fact, the first century of the national life was regarded as a
kind of pre-history, an experiment--none too successful--in
embodying republican principles and achieving national unity.
Believing that with the election of Lincoln in 1864 the question
of Union was a settled fact, Haven wrote:

> No longer will we foolishly say, 'our system is an

experiment.' It has ceased to occupy that place
in human affairs. Once the press was an experiment; so was the railroad, so the steamship, so
ocean steam-navigation, so the telegraph, so Protestantism, so Christianity. But they have ceased
to hold such positions. The American Union has
likewise; it stands forth before the world the most
triumphant form of government that exists among
men. [104]

Daniel Curry repeated the same theme when he said,
"Before the war of the Rebellion there was room for a question whether the 'many' or the 'one,' named in the country's escutcheon, should predominate; but that is now settled. "[105] For both Haven and Curry, however, as crucial
as national unity was, it was a formal issue that had no
meaning apart from the material issue of justice for all men.
In discoursing on the meaning of the new American nation,
Curry is absolutely clear that the pervading elements of the
nation must be "equality before the law" and "liberty among
common people. "[106] Haven saw the substantive issue facing
the country in the theme "justice for all men, " especially
"the freedman. "[107]

The doctrine of Providence was used in ante-bellum
days to support a rather conservative approach to social
problems by most Methodists. Northern Methodists who
opposed the radical program of "anti-slavery agitators"--
and they represented the majority--did believe that God, in
his own time and manner, would dispose of the "peculiar institution. " With the Civil War, this view began to be altered, but it was not until the Emancipation Proclamation
that a decisive shift in understanding prevailed. The war
was no longer waged simply for the restoration of the Constitution, but also for the destruction of slavery. Commenting on the meaning of the Proclamation, one Methodist clergyman said, "The providence of God in the war began to be
seen at this juncture in a most striking aspect. "[108] The
signs of Providence were a whole succession of victories.
The war was seen as working a great moral revolution in
the North and in "nothing was the providence of God more
marked than in the moral change wrought in the national
mind" the year of the Emancipation Proclamation. [109]

The great truth that liberty is indivisible was gradually taught to the officialdom of the Methodist Episcopal
Church, a denomination that had been relatively silent on

the institution of slavery, even censorious to anti-slavery clergymen, up until the beginning of the war. They had learned what Lincoln knew well--that granting freedom was an opportunity to preserve freedom and therefore the Republic. This political and moral insight is acknowledged and clearly stated in the Minutes of the New York East Annual Conference during the 1864 session at Hartford. The Committee on the State of the Country reported as follows:

> As Christians and as patriots we cannot but recognize, in the events of our Civil War, the guiding hand of a Divine Providence, our nation has been led by a way it had not known. God has taught us by our sufferings and our sorrows that we cannot preserve our Union except by securing freedom to all. It is a consolation to us that 'He who doeth all things well' is making the war the means of solving the problems of the Nation's destiny. [110]

Methodists firmly believed that God, through His providential chastisements, and through the "sufferings and sorrows" of the people, was recalling the nation to its proper vocation. No Methodist articulated this theme with the depth of meaning and eloquence that marked Bushnell's interpretation of the war as a "sacrificial and cleansing tragedy." No single address had the power or penetration of Bushnell's celebrated oration, "Our Obligations to the Dead," in which he set forth the theme that through the "tragic blood of the war" was born "a full historic consciousness."[111] And yet, the theme is present in the words of Methodists as they attempted to make sense out of the war. Chester F. Dunham has documented the fact that many northern Methodist sermons were constructed around the theme that the war was "punitive and purgative in its design."[112] Bishop Simpson referred to the war as a "baptism of blood" in which the nation's sin would be cast away and the nation would "stand once more, united pure and eloquent, a source of hope to the struggling peoples of Europe."[113] Clergymen did see a process of purification through trial by fire. "God means to save us;" declared one Methodist, "but he means to try us by fire."[114] Haven invited a Boston congregation to draw near to the "mount that burneth with fire" as he preached on the occasion of the Fall of Charleston. Concomitant with the "dread vision of a sovereign God, exercising His power" in punishing judgment, Haven viewed the dread scene as pointing to the "regeneration of the earth."[115] George Peck, sermonizing on the Exodus text, "The bush burneth with fire, and the bush was not consumed," expresses the same theme.

> Still the nation is in the fire, but is not likely to
> be consumed, for God is in the fire. Under his
> supervision the fire is melting away the chains of
> slavery, humbling and purifying the nation, and
> preparing her for a glorious future. [116]

Methodists were probably more superficial in their
treatment of this theme than a Bushnell, a Schaff or a Lincoln, primarily because of a penchant to evade prolonged
theological reflection and a desire to be about the business
of doing God's work. The inclination to moralize God's
workings led them to pass over lightly the theological meaning of providential judgments and redemption in history in
the interest of interpreting the moral imperative. The
question, "What needs be done?" took precedence over all
other questions.

This leads to the third theme. The war was seen as
a means of awakening to consciousness a sense of responsibility and mission. The Almighty was Judge and Redeemer,
but he was also Lord calling the Church to faithfulness.
Acknowledging the hand of an overruling Providence in guiding the nation through a "baptism of fire and blood," members of the New York East Conference interpreted the fiery
ordeal as solving "the great problem of her history in the
destruction of slavery."[117] Quick to find the mandate implied in the act of slavery abolition, this body of churchmen
acknowledged that as agents of Providence at least three
things were required. First, the Church had been tried and
found wanting on the slavery question. The General Conference had not altered the rule prohibiting the holding of
slaves during the last session in 1860. Instructing their
delegates to the General Conference to vote for a change in
the General Rules, they declared "that the time has arrived
when the great body of our church can agree in expunging
all tolerance of slavery from her Constitution."[118] Secondly,
they perceived in the divine orders a call to engage in what
was the most important immediate work, throwing their
strength to the support of a Constitutional Amendment "forever forbidding slavery in every State and Territory of our
domain."[119] Finally, they acknowledged to having been
awakened to the "prospect of reconstruction of the Union on
the firm foundation of freedom."[120]

The Conferences and editors uniformly called for the
enactment of the Thirteenth Amendment. Editors of The
Methodist contended that "The Amendment to the Constitution

of the United States, forever abolishing and prohibiting slavery" was the "order of God, " and not the "logic merely, but in the very destiny of events. "[121] Methodists were concrete and specific in their readings of Providence. Some, "under guidance of Providence, " instructed President Johnson to follow the policy of his predecessor, "who felt that an act of general amnesty should be accompanied by the bestowment of universal suffrage. "[122]

Methodists believed that one of the great lessons in the war had to do with a new understanding of the relation between politics and the Church. The issues of the war resulted in a serious study of church-state relations, of the meaning and role of civil government, and the relations between Church and society. This study led to vigorous justifications by preachers of pulpit and press for engaging in political discussions and delivering political sermons. In the heat of the war an editor argued, because "God established the civil government and made it subject to his laws ... Political Science is intimately related to both theology and ethics. "[123] Believing that religion involved worldly tasks, the editor wrote in another issue,

> We have been told to limit ourselves to religion, as though religion were a thing of empty sounds and imposing forms and spiritual epicurism. ... It accompanies man through all duty, regulating, sustaining, animating him; it attends him in all trial and woe, sweetening sorrow, allaying pain and conquering temptation; it goes through all social institutions, opposing castes, subduing prejudices, counting nothing unworthy of its notice which can promote the welfare, the happiness or improvement of mankind. ... One of the great benefits of the war consists in the emancipation of the pulpit. [124]

Because the above subject matter forms the basis of succeeding chapters, further treatment is not necessary at this point. Suffice it to say that if in the Providence of God the Church saw itself being instructed in the matter of social relations, this marks a radical shift from former understandings informed by a revivalist form of Christianity.

Finally, while the war was an instructor of the Church in social and political matters, it was equally pedagogic in teaching Methodists that they had a great ecclesiastical mission to be fulfilled. More than any other denomination Methodists had been successful in bringing the gospel to frontier America. Now, when the danger of settling down and con-solidating the fruits of the revival appeared, God had signaled a new awakening to mission through the sounds of the war and the "glorious victory." It was a signal "for the initia-tion of a great moral regeneration."[125] The eyes of the Church were turned to the future--and that meant southward. Over and over again the declaration was made that, "A more promising missionary field than this Southern country God never opened for the church."[126]

The exuberance for a southern mission resulted in part from the belief that war had been an instructor in liber-ality and that material resources would be available for such a task. Tallying up the statistics in 1864, Methodists in the North were pleased to report that all benevolent enter-prises of the Methodist Episcopal Church showed a steady increase throughout the war years. Far from setting the benevolent and philanthropic enterprises back, the Civil War period saw the rise of charities and benevolent activity. One Methodist concluded, "... while war has been a strange instructor of our people in deeds of lavish benevolent liber-ality, peace has returned...."[127] It was a "rich augury" of increasing liberality--the wherewithal to accomplish the grand mission set before the Church.

The fourth major theme to be perceived among the various interpretations northern Methodists gave to the Civil War had to do with the providential vindication of the Nor-thern cause and the rightness of the Methodist Episcopal Church as over against the Southern connection. The God of battles had arbitrated the question at issue in the war and decided that the North was right.[128] A writer for the Zion's Herald undoubtedly spoke the sentiments of most Methodists in the North when, in instructing President Johnson on the "Benevolent Purposes of God," he said:

> No one, unless under the influence of the most in-veterate prejudice, doubts concerning the side, in our late civil war, on which God was ready to be-stow his blessing, and with which his purposes harmonized. A year ago the side of God most signally triumphed in the fearful contest which the forces of the rebellion inaugurated and sustained.[129]

Early in the war when the Union army suffered many defeats, Methodist divines preached on the needed "reverses" as the way of Providence in effecting chastisement on the North and awakening the North to the evil of slavery. But the admonition that God had been chastening the North through defeats was invariably tied to the affirmation, "whom he loveth he chasteneth."[130] Bishop Simpson, in assuring Simon Cameron that "God was with our country" after the disaster at Bull Run, queried, "Did not God chasten his own before he redeemed them?"[131] If defeats became evidence that God was on the side of the North, successes were more so. With victories in late 1863 the Christian Advocate asked, "Is not the Lord on our side?"[132] Quotations similar to the ones just cited could be multiplied many times to document the fact that the majority of Northern Methodist clergymen believed their cause to have been vindicated by the God of Righteousness. Such citations are, however, unnecessary. The fanaticism with which this "self righteous" attitude was expressed by northern Protestants is a common theme in histories of the sectional conflict. Indeed, it is a theme that has perhaps been greatly overdrawn. Certainly, all northern Methodist clergymen believed the North had been right, that God had vindicated their cause. But this did not mean that all were vindictive. Usually missing in the histories of the churches during the sectional conflict are the many expressions of self-guilt and magnanimity toward the South. While much of the rhetoric following the war would support the view indicated by Ralph Morrow, that Methodists in the North thought they "had been selected as the executor of divine judgment" against the South, this was not the only view expressed.[133]

As a matter of record many opinion makers and leaders of the Church counseled leniency and charity toward the South at the close of the war.[134] The Methodist Quarterly Review edited by Daniel Whedon took a conciliatory stand toward the Southern Church in editorials in the July and October issues of 1865. In the former issue the editorial writer called on his Church to "Offer, without any airs of our cwn superiority ... the hand of recognition and fellowship." He admonished northerners not to require apologies for slavery nor to interfere with her legitimate rights; rather, "let us avoid seeking to weaken her where she has just posession." Assuring the brethren of the South that "little but tenderness was felt toward them" the writer concluded by declaring, "God is their and our judge."[135] The editorial in the October issue advised earnest anti-slavery men to show a spirit of "magnanimity" toward the southern Methodists and to have a "due appreciation of the wounded

spirit of a proud but self-supposed 'subjected' people. "[136]
Speaking for many in the North the writer said, "We would
not spend one flourish of our pen to prove either side right
or wrong.... Let us patiently and firmly offer to them a
free, equal, brotherly alliance, and so take a first step to
a renovated Union, a regenerated Nation. "[137]

The Western Christian Advocate, speaking to Methodism of the Middle West, doubtless spoke sentiments of many
readers when it said: "A united Church extending from the
Lakes to the Gulf will be the strongest bond of a restored
Nationality and the truest cement of the Federal Union. "[138]
Offering invitations for a reunion, it expressed hope for good
feeling on both sides. [139] Editorial policy in The Methodist
was conciliatory right after the war, with Abel Stevens foremost in advocating lenient treatment. Even the Christian
Advocate of New York, not noted for conciliatory statements,
carried an editorial which exclaimed: "we of the loyal states
are not altogether guiltless. "[140]

William Russ, Jr., who engaged in a study of the
Methodist press during Reconstruction, concluded that at the
end of the war the Methodist press counseled leniency toward
the Confederates. He explained, "for it was felt that both
sides were partly to blame. "[141] Notwithstanding some evidence to the contrary, in general this conclusion seems to
be sustained. After such a bitter partisan war touching the
deepest reaches of the human spirit, it seems incredible that
there would be any expressions of good will. What was the
source of northern Methodist expressions of generosity and
good will? Partly they arose from the pervasive belief that
most Southerners were not really for slavery and had been
led into rebellion against their will by military officers, pro-
slavery propagandists and "aristocratic slave-owners. "[142]
In part they arose from the belief that slavery, the cause
of the rebellion and the cause of the Methodist schism, had
been removed; thus there was no need to "fight over the
dead past. "[143] Partly they issued forth from a very pragmatic belief that expressions of generosity would result in
a great influx into the Methodist Episcopal Church of supposed
pro-unionist Methodists in the South. [144] There are no doubt
other reasons, but the most compelling explanation has already been given in the discussion above of the first theme.
However right northern Methodists felt themselves to be,
there was still a sense in which the war rendered a terrible
judgment on their own sins. This sense of guilt before the
Providence of God was expressed dramatically and boldly in
the Zion's Herald in the following words:

It was not sympathy with the crushed and fallen,
not hatred of wrong, or love of right that produced
emancipation. We have no right to stand up, like
the Pharisee, and say of our Southern brother,
'God I thank thee that I am not as this man--a
thief, a kidnapper, a merchant in human flesh.'
Slaves would have swarmed before our eyes on
these New England Hills, if slavery would pay.
Not our Puritan ancestry, not our church and
schools would have saved us from this curse, had
not God by the laws of nature made it unprofitable.
If cotton could have been made to grow in the Connecticut valley, cotton fields would have been
watered there by the tears of the slave. Would a
state that disfranchises the negro hesitate from
any sense of justice at enslaving him? Alas, how
humiliating is the confession with which we must,
if sincere, appear before God! It is not the stern
integrity and farseeing wisdom of American statesmen that have given us emancipation; not the lofty
faith and self denying zeal of the American Church,
but it is the resistless providence of God. 'Not
unto us, not unto us, but unto thy name.' 145

The depth of this sense of contrition and recognition
of the contingency of northern claims to righteousness in the
corporate body of the Methodist Episcopal Church is difficult
to assess with any degree of accuracy. But that it was
there at all is noteworthy. Northern Methodists did believe
that their cause was right, as vindicated by the results of
the war, but most of them also believed in northern culpability for evils that caused the war. Contra the judgment of
Franklin Littell, there were others besides Lincoln who saw
ambiguity, sinfulness and tragedy in the Civil War. God, to
the leading figures in northern Methodism, was not the "do-
mesticated household god of private persons." He was the
God of nations who required not only mercy but justice. 146

Soon after the closing months of the war the spirit
of magnanimity gave way to a vigorous pursuit of justice
embodied in programs of social, political and ecclesiastical
reconstruction. It is not to be wondered at, that after three
years of engaging in so solemn a business as killing people,
some northerners would not settle for peace at any price.
A Church that supported the war with the strong sense of
providential guidance must seek to preserve the fruits of
victory. "We love magnanimity," declared an official com-

mittee, "but with the heritage of Christ, so far committed to us, we dare not be profligate."[147] What was offered the South was not simply a "magnanimous" peace; rather it was a "just" peace. To the Southerners the words struck their ears as a call for a "victors" peace.[148] A great gulf remained. And soon after the assassination of Lincoln; after the news of the Black Codes; after the disappointment in President Johnson's Reconstruction policy; after southern harassments of northern Methodist missionaries in the South-- magnanimity was transformed into vindictiveness. The yawning gulf between the two Methodisms widened.

In sum, it may be said that the Civil War not only had a profound effect on the outward life of the Methodist Episcopal Church, but that it also exerted considerable influence on the self-understanding of the Church. The war caused a rigorous self-examination of Methodism's own historical tradition and became a source of self-criticism for an erstwhile lack of social concern. In an effort to make sense out of the great conflict and to answer questions raised in the conflict, Methodists made use of the doctrine of Providence. The way Providence was seen in the war may be summed up briefly. Providence was seen as present in the war in three ways. The war came as judgment on the sin of the nation; the failure of the Church; and, specifically, on the slaveholding South. But Providence was also present as redemption and the possibility of new life for the nation and the Church. At moments of deepest despair, Methodists were able to see, through eyes of faith, that a "nation's extremity was God's opportunity."[149] This theme was interpreted both in terms of political and spiritual renewal. Thirdly, Providence was present in the war as a call to responsibility. Providence was judgment and redemption, but it was also a stimulus to action. Methodists were quick to discern the moral and social mandate and were constantly admonished to "heed the call of Providence."[150]

Finally, the purpose of this chapter has been to present typical theological interpretations of the Civil War by the Methodist leadership in the North. The results are intended to show: 1) that northern Methodists were more than partisan Republicans in their support and understanding of the war; 2) that the dimension of judgment in their interpretation of Providence in the war saved them from self-righteous pretentions and a crusading moralism; 3) that the doctrine of Providence, in providing them with an historical consciousness and a means of prophetic interpretation, enabled them to see that in the war the nation did indeed have a new historical birth; 4) that they were genuinely awakened to the cruciality of slavery and color caste as national problems; 5) that the war had the effect of awakening the leadership of the Church to the social dimensions of sin and renewal; and 6) that the war became a determinative influence and resource for understanding the nature and the mission of the Church.

Notes

1. Abel Stevens, "Methodism After Wesley's Death," Methodist Quarterly Review, XLIII (Januaey, 1861), p. 5.

2. Ibid.

3. According to Leland Scott, the key doctrine for Methodists in this period was the doctrine of free will. This is no doubt true inasmuchas "free will" was subject to greater systematic treatment. But I would suggest that even the doctrine of free will was overborne by the more practical doctrine of Providence. See, Leland Scott, "Methodist Theology in America in the Nineteenth Century," Religion in Life, Winter 1955-56, p. 92.

4. Milton Bryan Powell. "The Abolitionist Controversy in the Methodist Episcopal Church." Unpublished Ph. D. Dissertation, University of Iowa, 1963, p. 61.

5. "Our Foreign Relations," Zion's Herald, XXXVI, (March 29, 1865), p. 50.

6. Randolph S. Foster. Centenary Thoughts For the Pew and Pulpit of Methodism. New York: Phillips & Hunt, 1884, p. 68.

7. Mathew Simpson to Uncle Matthew, July 9, 1835. Simpson Papers, cited by Kirby, "The Ecclesiastical and Social Thought of Matthew Simpson," p. 61.

8. George R. Crooks, ed. Sermons By Bishop Matthew Simpson. New York: Harper & Brothers, 1885, p. 51.

9. "Our Foreign Relations," Zion's Herald, XXXVI, (March 29, 1865), p. 50.

10. "Religious Not Political," Zion's Herald, XXXV, (February 17, 1864), p. 26.

11. "Miscellaneous Notes," Christian Advocate (New York), XLIII, (March 12, 1868), p. 85.

12. "Our National Thanksgiving," Zion's Herald, XXXIV, (November 25, 1863), p. 186.

13. Gilbert Haven. Sermons, Speeches and Letters on Slavery and Its War. New York: Carlton and Lanahan, 1869, p. xii.

14. Ibid.

15. W. H. Daniels, ed. Memorials of Gilbert Haven, Bishop of the Methodist Episcopal Church. Boston: B. B. Russell & Co., 1880, p. 343.

16. Charles Howard Hopkins. The Rise of the Social Gospel in American Protestantism, 1865-1915. New Haven: Yale University Press, 1940, pp. 14, 15.

17. Ibid., p. 16.

18. Abel Stevens. The Centenary of American Methodism. New York: Carlton & Porter, 1865, p. 210.

19. "Philosophy of History," Methodist Quarterly Review, XXIV, (July 1842), p. 404.

20. Ibid., p. 405.

21. Ibid., p. 408.

22. Ibid., p. 411.

23. Ibid., pp. 411, 412.

24. Ibid., p. 412.

25. Ibid., pp. 403f.

26. Abel Stevens. A Compendious History of American Methodism. New York: Carlton & Porter, 1868, p. 578.

27. Ibid.

28. Ibid., pp. 578, 579.

29. Stevens, "Methodism After Wesley's Death," Methodist
     Quarterly Review, XLIII, pp. 5, 6. For a similar
     statement see, "Methodism and Now," Zion's Herald,
     XLVI, (June 3, 1869), p. 258.

30. Abel Stevens. Supplementary History of American Meth-
     odism. New York: Eaton & Mains, 1899, p. 40.

31. Northern Christian Advocate, XIII, (April 26, 1865),
     cited by Ralph Morrow, Northern Methodism and Re-
     construction, p. 4.

32. "Our Centenary," The Ladies Repository, XXVI, (July,
     1866), p. 443.

33. "The Centenary Celebration," The Ladies Repository,
     XXVI, (November, 1866), p. 701.

34. Professor Wilson, "Our Historical Position as Indicated
     by Nature and Philosophy," Methodist Quarterly Re-
     view, XLVIII, (January 1866), p. 19. The following
     words indicate the author's line of reasoning con-
     cerning the relationship between spiritual and politi-
     cal freedom: "It was only when, through, religious
     freedom, the masses of the people were taught to
     comprehend fully the meaning of this great central
     idea of Christianity, the union of the divine and the
     human perfection, and consequently the true dignity
     and immortal destiny of man, that a government
     based on the essential equality of all men, and their
     inherent right, in virtue alone of their manhood and
     their responsibility to God, to be free, became pos-
     sible. Thus we find that spiritual freedom always
     precedes and begets social and political freedom."

35. Powell, "The Abolitionist Controversy ...," pp. 50-61.

36. Ibid.

37. Ibid.

38. Wilson, "Our Historical Position ...," Methodist Quar-
     terly Review, XLVIII, pp. 19, 20.

39. Ibid., p. 20.

40. *Journal of the General Conference of the Methodist Episcopal Church, 1864.* New York: Carlton & Porter, 1864, p. 376.

41. "The Providence in the War," *Western Christian Advocate*, XXXI (December 14, 1864), p. 393.

42. "The Methodist Episcopal Church in the South," *Christian Advocate* (New York), XLI, (December 6, 1866), p. 386.

43. *Northwestern Christian Advocate*, January 30, 1861 (n. p.), cited by Margaret Burnham Macmillan, *The Methodist Episcopal Church in Michigan During the Civil War.* Lansing, Michigan: Publication Committee of Michigan Civil War Centennial Observance Commission, 1965, p. 16.

44. Macmillan, *The Methodist Episcopal Church ...*, p. 16.

45. *Ibid.*

46. *Northwestern Christian Advocate*, May 1, 1861 (n. p.), cited by Clark, *The Life of Mathew Simpson*, p. 219.

47. "Sentiments Appropriate to the Times," *The Methodist*, III, (March 1, 1862), p. 60.

48. "Our National Thanksgiving," *Zion's Herald*, XXXIV, (November 25, 1863), p. 186.

49. Daniel Dorchester. *Christianity in the United States From the First Settlement Down to the Present Time.* Rev. ed. New York: Hunt & Eaton, 1895. First ed., 1887, pp. 317, 318.

50. George S. Phillips. *The American Republic and Human Liberty Forshadowed in Scripture.* Cincinnati: Poe & Hitchcock, 1864, p. 174.

51. *Ibid.*

52. *Ibid.*, p. 156.

53. *Ibid.*, pp. 170-71.

54. *Ibid.*

55. Ibid., pp. 174-77.

56. Ibid., p. 177. See also George Peck. Our Country: Its Trial and Its Triumph. New York: Carlton & Porter, 1865, pp. 104-21. Peck saw the war as court action, a "trial" in which God had allowed an indictment to be filed against the nation. To Peck there was no doubt but the charge is fully sustained and what God required was "humiliation, confession, and forgiveness" (p. 104). The whole chapter is devoted to considering the "grounds" of the "Lord's Controversy" with his people.

57. Haven, Sermons ..., p. 42.

58. Ibid.

59. Ibid., p. 423.

60. Ibid.

61. Ibid., pp. 288-29.

62. Ibid., p. 289. See also pp. 430-34 where he rendered concretely what it meant to repent and forsake sins.

63. Peck, Our Country ..., p. 117.

64. Ibid., p. 116.

65. Ibid., p. 117.

66. Haven, Sermons, p. 289.

67. Gilbert Haven, "The Church and the Negro," Zion's Herald, XXXIV, (June 10, 1863), p. 89.

68. "Our National Thanksgiving," Zion's Herald, XXXIV, (November 25, 1863), p. 186. See also, "Punishment," Western Christian Advocate, XXXI, (March 2, 1864), p. 68.

69. Ralph E. Morrow, Northern Methodism and Reconstruction, p. 18.

70. This is not to deny that guilt may become a source of vindictiveness. While there is evidence that it did,

there is more evidence that guilt issued forth in penitential works. What measure of vindictiveness there was on the part of northerners in the south during Reconstruction was more a response to a sense of frustration that things were not working out as planned.

71. "The Church and the Freedmen," Christian Advocate (New York), XLI, (November 8, 1866), p. 356.

72. Reports of the Freedmen's Aid Society, 1869, p. 15.

73. An example of this rather parochial way of reading the workings of Providence may be seen in "Religion and the War," The Methodist, III, (April 19, 1862), p. 116. The writer notes that "military attacks, begun on Sunday ... have almost, if not quite invariably been attended with defeats."

74. Reinhold Niebuhr, "The Religion of Abraham Lincoln," The Christian Century, (February 10, 1965), p. 172.

75. Journal of the General Conference ..., 1864, p. 383.

76. Peck, Our Country ..., p. 23. For a typical official response see Philadelphia Conference Minutes, 1864, p. 44.

77. Ibid., p. 32.

78. Daniel Whedon. Public Addresses. Boston: John P. Jewett & Co., 1852, p. 84.

79. Daniel Curry. Platform Papers: Addresses, Discussions, and Essays on Social, Moral, and Religious Subjects. Cincinnati: Hitchcock and Walden, 1880, p. 132.

80. The war had suggested to many Methodists the necessity of inquiring into the lawfulness and morality of war. A very good example of such an inquiry was an article written by Joseph Horner, Secretary of the Committee on the State of the Church in 1868 and 1876. In an attempt to prove that Christianity had not abrogated the "war power," he showed, with considerable scholarship, that Christians in the early church did take "part in all the affairs of the Empire,"

116. Peck, Our Country ..., p. 88. See also Peck's dis-
     cussion of how "great national reforms are preceded
     by a baptism of blood, " p. 136.

117. New York East Conference Minutes, 1864, p. 40.

118. New York East Conference Minutes, p. 40.

119. Ibid., p. 42.

120. Ibid.

121. "Passing the Amendment, " The Methodist, VI, (Feb-
     ruary 11, 1865), p. 44.

122. Rock River Conference Minutes, 1865, p. 29.

123. "Respect for Government, " Christian Advocate (New
     York, XXXVIII, (March 5, 1863), p. 76.

124. "Divine Law Above Human, " Christian Advocate (New
     York), XXXVIII, (March 12, 1863), p. 84. See
     Minutes of New York East Conference, State of the
     Country Report, 1866, where the committee made a
     point of recording thankfulness that the pulpit had
     "been outspoken on the great questions of the times,
     and has been true to humanity, to constitutional
     liberty, and to God. " As they had been awakened to
     a new freedom of the pulpit, they urged that it
     "must be held sacred. " p. 24.

125. "Editors Study, " The Ladies Repository, XXVI, (Janu-
     ary 1866), p. 127. The editor, I. W. Wiley, ex-
     pressed a nearly universal sentiment in the church
     when he affirmed, "it remains for God and the
     Church to eradicate from the nation the seeds of
     moral and social evil, " which had engendered both
     "slavery and rebellion. " "All at once, " he wrote,
     "... a new and wonderful missionary field is thrown
     upon the Church. " p. 127.

126. Lucius Hawkins, "Methodism in the South, " Christian
     Advocate (New York), XL, (June 22, 1865), p. 194.
         That the war was a means of opening up mis-
     sionary opportunities for the Church became a com-
     mon theme in sermons, articles, and statements.
     Many evidences of this theme could be adduced, but

it is such a commonplace theme that one more typical quote will suffice to make the point. From the
Freedman's Aid and Southern Educational Society Reports, May 1, 1867, p. 1, are these words from
the President, D. W. Clark: "In the providence of
God the South has been thrown open before the
Church by the recent war, and beyond all question,
is the most inviting field of our day for missionary
and kindred beneficent labors. The deliverance of
the colored race from bondage, the peculiarities of
their past and present condition, the gladness with
which they receive the Gospel, and their eagerness
for the essential means of improvement, render them
the most hopeful and interesting class to be reached
by the agencies of a Christian civilization. "

127. "Review of the Minutes of the Committee on the Centennial of Methodism, " Methodist Quarterly Review,
XLVII, (October, 1865), p. 613. See also, General
Conference Journal ... , 1864, p. 383; and Peck, p.
256f. , for further treatment of this theme. Methodists liked to cite the success of both the Sanitary
and the Christian Commissions as illustrations of
how the war taught liberality.

128. "The Methodists, " M. E. Church General Conference,
The Daily Christian Advocate, (May 2, 1868), p. 7,
citing the Chicago Evening Post, (April 30, 1868),
(n. p.).

129. "The President Opposes the Benevolent Purposes of
God, " Zion's Herald, XXXVII, (April 25, 1866), p.
65.

130. "Sentiments Appropriate to the Times, " The Methodist,
III, (March 1, 1862), p. 60.

131. Clark, The Life of Matthew Simpson, p. 219.

132. "Victories, " Christian Advocate (New York), XXXVIII,
(December 3, 1863), p. 388.

133. Morrow, Northern Methodism and Reconstruction, p.
18.

134. For an official expression calling for liberality in
spirit and wealth to alleviate suffering of "the enemy,"

see Philadelphia Conference Minutes, Report on the State of the Country, 1865, pp. 49, 50. See also the conciliatory report in the Journal of the General Conference, 1872, pp. 402, 403.

135. "Report of the New England Annual Conference for 1865 on Church Reconstruction," Methodist Quarterly Review, XLVII, (July 1865), p. 481.

136. "Methodist Churches, North and South," Methodist Quarterly Review, XLVII, (October 1865), p. 634.

137. Ibid., pp. 635-36.

138. "The Work of Missions," Western Christian Advocate, XXXII, (May 24, 1865), p. 164. For a similar expression of good will see "The Spirit of the South," Western Christian Advocate, XXXII, (April 19, 1865), p. 124.

139. "Another Theory of Ecclesiastical Reconstruction," Western Christian Advocate, XXXII, (June 7, 1865), p. 180.

140. "Our Next Duty," Christian Advocate, (New York), XL, (April 13, 1865), p. 116.

141. William A. Russ, Jr., "The Influence of the Methodist Press Upon Radical Reconstruction (1865-68)," Susquehanna University Studies, I, (January 1937), p. 52.

142. H. S. Foote, "Review of War of the Rebellion," Methodist Quarterly Review, XLVIII, (April 1866), pp. 306-07.

143. "Methodist Churches, North and South," Methodist Quarterly Review, XLVIII, (October 1865), p. 635.

144. They seriously overestimated pro-unionist sentiment in the South and thus were genuinely surprised when they received a cool reception.

145. "Freedman and Freeman," Zion's Herald, XXXVII, (January 3, 1866), p. 1.

146. Franklin Hamlin Littell. From State Church to

Pluralism. Garden City, New York: Doubleday & Co., 1962, p. 69.

147. New England Conference Minutes, Report of the Committee on Reconstruction, 1866, p. 42.

148. For an excellent treatment of this problem see Paul Buck. The Road to Reunion, 1865-1900. New York: Vintage Books, 1959, pp. 3-26. See especially p. 8.

149. "Freedman and Freeman," Zion's Herald, XXXVII, (January 3, 1866), p. 1.

150. Freedman's Aid Society Reports, 1869, p. 16.

CHAPTER 5

ON MISSION SENT

Methodists have prided themselves on having a social awareness and social concern. In demonstrating this alleged unique heritage they have usually gone back to 1908 when the Methodist Episcopal Church officially adopted the "Methodist Social Creed." As evidence of the "unique" influence of Methodism in this regard it is proudly noted that this document became the basis of the "Social Creed" of the Federal Council of the Churches of Christ in America in 1909. [1] Bishop Gerald Kennedy in commenting on this fact remarked, in typical Methodist fashion, "If you ask a man who knows the Protestant Churches to define a distinguishing mark of Methodism, he will likely speak of its social concern."[2] Nils Ehrenstrom, in his introduction to Volume I of Methodism and Society in Historical Perspective, developed the theme that since 1908 the Church, particularly the Methodist Church, has assumed a new "acceptance of social responsibility," and that there has been "an almost miraculous upsurge of social concern...."[3]

The implication in most of these discussions is that the sense of responsibility for the public realm sat very lightly on the conscience of the Church in the period preceding the Social Gospel movement. Richard Cameron, in his discussion of Methodism during the Civil War and Reconstruction, allows that social and political questions came to the attention of churchmen but that they were viewed in terms of "religion and morality."[4] The tenor of his remarks reveals a slight condescension with which he views nineteenth century Methodists in comparison to the twentieth century experience of social activism. Bishop Lloyd C. Wicke, speaking before the annual meeting of the Board of Missions of the United Methodist Church, revealed the same condescending attitude toward the Methodist fathers of a bygone era when he declared that "the insulated compartmentalism" of the former missionary effort was a thing of the past and that "Poverty, health, race relations, peace--you name it, these are the concerns of the whole church; these are the gospel's concern, the concern of the entire family of man. "[5] Implicit in this declaration is the notion that these "concerns" are something new in the history of the Church.

Whatever the merits of the social criticism and the concrete efforts to reform society, the Methodist Episcopal Church at the close of the Civil War cannot be faulted for lacking vigor and a sense of responsibility in the way they conceived their mission to the world. Their grand mission was nothing less than reshaping history itself by Christianizing the whole of society. Neither the evangelical rhetoric of nineteenth-century Methodists nor the condescending writing of twentieth-century Methodists ought to obscure the aggressiveness and inclusiveness that characterized the mission of post-Civil War Methodism in its efforts to bring all life into harmony with the providential will of God. Jaroslav Pelikan makes much the same point in emphasizing the significance of

> the Christian zeal and idealism of the Methodist crusaders who believed that it was possible for man to progress morally and to do something about his condition on earth. The Methodist Social Creed of 1908, which was so decisive in the whole history of social Christianity in America, came from such zeal and idealism. [6]

It could be argued that northern Methodism during and after the war exerted a greater influence on the social order than any time before or since. Chapter 3 was designed to show that, because the Methodist Episcopal Church was organically related to the public domain as a powerful and prestigious social institution, it had a profound effect on the public sector in contrast to the marginal position of the Church in twentieth-century society and its consequent failure to be a decisive influence at the vital centers of American life. While much of the influence was indirect and not informed by "social creeds, " there was a conscious mission, notwithstanding its frontier religion orientation, that expressed itself in terms of "social deeds. " The role frontier religion played in stimulating education, both public and religious, and providing an impetus to reform movements and social causes cannot be underestimated. [7] It may well be the case that with the loss of the frontier spirit the actual social relevance of Protestantism was lost. Pelikan, in the following statement, points in this direction:

Like their brethren in faith across the Atlantic, American Methodists concerned themselves for the silent in the land. The American proletariat and the American Negro, both before and after emancipation, were still on the frontier long after urbanization and industrialization had begun to reshape American Society. If anything, it was the loss of the frontier spirit rather than its retention that gradually alienated Methodism from elements of American society that had been its traditional concern, and caused the Methodist Church to be replaced in their loyalties by forms of Christian witness and obedience that seemed to breathe more of a Wesleyan spirit than the respectable Wesleyans did. [8]

Sociologists of religion have described the transformation of Protestantism from a frontier religion of the common man, when revivals produced significant social fruits, to a middle-class, conventional denominationalism. Such a description is germane to the present study, but does not take into account a factor that bridges the movement of revivalism to denominationalism. What is missing in the analysis is that at the very time of denominational consolidation, Protestantism was being awakened to a larger sense of aggressive mission. [9] Nowhere is this to be seen with greater clarity than in the self-understanding of Methodists. The occasion of the Methodist Centennial celebration and the tragic years of the war had the effect of transforming the narrow focus of the evangelical task into a broad vision of national and world conquest. With a new understanding that society and not just the individual came under the providential rule of God, the aggressive Methodist movement did not stop after the war. It was just better organized and financed. A sense that the Methodist Episcopal Church was by special Providence mission sent into the world delayed for a time the inevitable accommodation to middle class culture. How this sense of mission was conceived becomes a question of considerable importance in understanding northern Methodism and the social task.

Methodism Is Missionism

From its inception the Methodist Church has understood itself as providentially called to be mission to the world. Wade Barclay, the historian of Methodist Missions, expressed the conviction that "The Methodist movement as a whole was missionary in conception, in motivation, and in method."[10] Unlike the classical Reformation doctrine of the Church, which was an articulation of the "marks" of the true Church in terms of its gathered visibility, where " the pure word of God is preached and the sacraments duly administered according to the ordinance of Christ, " mission was the central "mark" for Methodists.[11] Identifying themselves with the "Apostolic Church, " which they thought of as essentially missionary in spirit, Methodists during the post-Civil War period were convinced that they had recovered what the Reformers had failed to see as the essential "mark" of the Church.[12] Daniel Dorchester expressed this familiar conviction by declaring that the "Reformation of the sixteenth century fought the outward battle, " which was "merely" an effort to "reform the Church from corrupt doctrines."[13] "Methodism, " on the other hand, was an expression of Apostolic Christianity because it "was essentially missionary from the beginning."[14] What was the symbol of the Methodist Church? Dorchester proudly proclaimed that it was "a missionary map" representative of "the new Christianity--or rather of the old Christianity revived and restored."[15] In a prize-winning essay another Methodist divine gave expression to the same attitude in allowing that with Luther there appeared to be a restoration of the Bible and a lost Christianity; however, the Reformation did not "restore the spirituality and aggressive activity of the primitive Church."[16] For him, as for many other contemporaries, the Reformation was "an ecclesiastical and theological reform. ... It did not awaken the missionary spirit which characterized the early Church. ... "[17]

Reflecting accurately the self-consciousness of Methodists in the previous generation, John Wesley Johnston, in a message to the Board of Home Missions in 1908, stated that, "Methodism is missionism."[18] The year of this statement is important because it marked a transition. With the adoption of the Social Creed, and under the sway of a liberal theology and the Social Gospel movement, Methodists in the twentieth century no longer used such terms as the Methodist "missionary spirit" to distinguish their denomination. The unique distinguishing mark of Methodism came to be expressed in such terms as "social concern" or "social rightousness."[19] When they read Wesley, they found in his writings support for their stress on "social holiness."[20] In contrast, Methodists in the nineteenth century referred to Wesley's writings and efforts as a call to mission. "The world is my

Parish, " said John Wesley. A century after these words were uttered Wesley's American progeny understood that proposition as a mandate to embody its intention and to be a "missionary Methodism. "21

It would be a mistake to think that when these early Methodists spoke of the missionary task they thought of sending missionaries out West or out of the country or into the city. On the contrary, the Church was understood to be essentially mission. It was the Church on mission sent that founded schools and colleges; that sought to implant morality throughout the nation; that fought for the social elevation of women; that agitated for the emancipation of slaves; that endeavored to civilize and Christianize native Africans; that labored for temperance reform--in a word, the Methodist Episcopal Church was thought to have been a movement that did not have, but was mission. The evangelical task was integral to the social task, both of which were viewed in the context of mission. Hence, when northern Methodists organized to move South at the close of the Civil War to aid the Freedmen, they justified such an action by an appeal to the Missionary nature of their Church. They believed that their Church was called by Providence and by her "essential Missionary spirit" to aid the Freedman. 22 Not to go South would be to deny a heritage and a reason for being. Moreover, the various tasks that were delineated as "aid" to the Freedman did not reflect "compartmentalization. " They were viewed as a whole, unified in the context of one total mission. First and foremost was the necessity to preach the gospel and build churches, but along with the evangelical witness, it was simply assumed that the mission South would be expressed in efforts to educate and to elevate the Freedman politically, economically and socially.

The prompting that led northern Methodists to penetrate the South can be understood only to the degree that this constant and central theme of "grand mission" is understood. The rationale for a mission to the South was similar to the justifications for mission endeavors in the West or in foreign countries. A writer in the Zion's Herald in 1863 called for aggressive missionary advances in the South by citing the frontier experience. Against the more conservative brethren who thought northern Methodism should await an invitation, he noted the essential missionary nature of the Methodist Episcopal Church and advised,

With it her spirit and her life should always cor-

respond. She has been the pioneer in the West,
following the new settlements into the wilderness
far in advance of other denominations. She does
not wait for an invitation, but with her ministry of
love goes unsolicited to the needy and the poor....
A new field of labor is opening before her eyes....
Will she dare to be true to her antecedents and
occupy it in the name of the Lord?[23]

The writer then turned to eighteenth-century antecedents and
cited the well-known Wesley dictum: "Go not only to those
who need you, but to those who need you most." This, he
said, "was the motto, and the advice of John Wesley....
This by inheritance is the motto of Methodism."[24]

Just as it is a mistake to assume that missions was a
special activity of the Church, so is it an error to think
that they conceived of their task in an exclusively evangelistic mode. The Reverend Jacob Todd, speaking before the
Church Extension Annual Board meeting in 1874 contrasted
the current Methodist vision of its task with the eighteenth-
century effort, which was "exclusively evangelistic."[35] He
stated that in his time,

Every Church which fulfills its mission, passes
through four successive stages: First it is evangelistic; then it is constructive; next it is educational; and lastly, it is charitable. [26]

This no doubt expressed the prevailing view. The extra-
evangelistic task was usually put in terms of social and
charitable service. But for those deeply involved in the
Southern question, the social dimension of the mission of the
Church took shape around political, economic and social problems in such a way as to go beyond just a "charitable" fulfillment of its mission. In a review of a pamphlet reporting
on the proceedings of the New England Annual Conference
which contained a summons to political involvement in the
South, the more moderate reviewer, while critical of some
of the New Englander's priorities, nevertheless proposed
his own priorities, which were highly political in nature.
Setting forth guidelines for the northern Methodist Mission
to the South, he offered the following advice:

The true order of things, in order that the public
mind may in due time be brought right, we think,
is successively, emancipation, enfranchisement,

education, and finally the political, ecclesiastical,
and social treatment of every man according to his
qualifications, and social intercourse precisely
according to our individual tastes. [27]

As to the special role of the northern Church to "colored
Methodism," this same writer set forth three broad responsibilities: "... it is clearly our duty to stand in such pro-
tective and nurturing relations to all colored Methodism as
shall make it an object of liberal benefaction, advocacy, and
education."[28] The second duty--advocacy--meant for him,
" the duty to assert unceasingly and unanimously the right
of the negro to citizenship and suffrage."[29] There is ample
evidence to substantiate the point of view that in the period
after the Civil War, what was later to be called "social
action" emerged. It should, however, be emphasized that
northern Methodists during this time did not think in such
terms. To exercise what social and political power the
Church had, and to use her resources in advocating the
realization of political rights for her own brethren, was one
dimension of a total mission.

It has been suggested that the missionary zeal was
motivated by a pervasive belief that Methodism was mission
in its very conception, and ideological appeals for missionary
activity were made by reference to the early American frontier experience and eighteenth-century Wesleyanism in England. Among the appeals for strenuous duty there was a
constant theme. Methodists were entreated to engage in
vigorous, even militant, missionary activity by reference to
the tide of history itself as they understood it unfolding under
God's Providence.

Methodism and Historic Parallels

Northern Methodism in the years following the Civil
War was part and parcel of the religious drive to Christianize America that was "a phase of the energy that characterized American life in general."[30] They represented the
same missionary and evangelical fervor that marked most of
the Protestant denominations of the time. But Methodists,
not known for ecclesiastical modesty, saw themselves as
something special. For all the diversity in thought and belief
concerning the social dimension of the Church's mission, there
was, notwithstanding, a common mind when it came to affirming a signal and distinct calling.

The Methodist Episcopal Church understood itself to be standing in the great tradition of those special moments in the history of the Church when true Christianity burst forth. Methodists identified themselves variously with the Reformers of the sixteenth century, the American Puritans and sometimes the Jesuits, and uniformly proclaimed the analogy with the Apostolic Church. Accepting the common nineteenth-century view that primitive Christianity in all of its alleged purity and missionary zeal declined with Constantine and emerged again after the long dark night of the Middle Ages with the dawn of the Reformation, Methodists were inclined to believe that the sun didn't really come up until the eighteenth century with the rise of Methodism. [31] American Methodists in the mid-nineteenth century saw themselves as standing before the high noon of Christianity's recovery. [32] Daniel Dorchester, in describing the character of Methodism as the reproduction of Apostolic Christianity, put it this way:

> It is not a new thing to characterize Methodism as a revival of apostolic Christianity, But it is more: it is a reproduction; still more, it is the propagation of the recovered ideal. [33]

This was not, as Dorchester was pleased to inform, a new theme. Nathan Bangs, the predecessor to Abel Stevens as the principal Methodist historian in the pre-Civil War era, wrote a long book showing that the Methodist Episcopal Church, with special regard to ministerial orders and functions, was the true representation of the "Original Church of Christ. "[34] He concluded that, "... no people, since the apostolic days, have been blessed with such clear expositions of gospel truth as we have been. "[35] Bishop Randolph Foster, writing on the occasion of the 1884 Centennial of Methodism, could say of the first century of Methodism, "Never before since apostolic times was Christ so preached. "[36] The span of time bridging these two quotations represents nearly a half century. It is during this period that the self-understanding of Methodism as the revived embodiment of primitive Christianity reached its most extravagant expression. Thus, this theme becomes a crucial category for understanding the emotional and ideological context out of which post-Civil War northern Methodist leaders thought, spoke and acted.

The 1866 Centenary celebration provided an opportunity for an intensification of this motif that was to arouse fervor and provide much of the inner dynamic of Methodist activity. The theme was struck in a typical Centenary hymn:

> The Apostolic spirit
>   Had come to earth again,
> Men not in churchly "orders"
>   Were preaching Christ to men;
> Glad heralds of salvation,
>   The seeds of life they sow,
> And plead as their commission,
>   "The Master bade me go. "[37]

Abel Stevens saw the Methodist story as a parallel to the history of the Apostolic Church in that both movements had lowly origins and were objects of derision in their respective cultures. In summing up his history of the Methodist Episcopal Church he wrote:

> This lowly Methodist story is but the reproduction, in substance, of the apostolic history; and presents, in full vitality, that original, that only, example of evangelical propagandism, which, when all dogmatic conflicts and hierarchical pretensions, with their wasted passions and pomps, are recorded as historical failures, will bear forward to universal triumph the ensign of the Cross by a catholic, living, working Church of the common people. [38]

A full elaboration of this same idea appeared in an article by Jesse T. Peck. Noting that the early Methodists were just "a handful of the poor and despised amid countless numbers of enemies," and how "by all laws of human forces, we should have been overwhelmed and annihilated," the Methodist Church nevertheless, "grew rapidly ... and multitudes were won by it." "It was," he said, "again the marvel of apostolic times."[39] Methodists believed that they were living witnesses to the truth that "As in the early apostolic Church ... 'God hath chosen the foolish things of the world to confound the wise'."[40]

Viewing the demise of early Christianity as taking place when piety was sacrificed for creedal formulations, one Methodist contended that it was the combination of piety, which was a genuine appropriation of the love commandment, and religious liberty that demonstrated the apostolic character of Methodism.

> This flag, indeed, for the first time raised and
> maintained since the days of the apostles, holds up
> before us the true ideal of original Christianity,
> of vital piety united with intellectual liberty--and
> this is Methodism![41]

After tedious argument for his thesis, he thought the facts of
the matter warranted the conclusion

> that there is no other religious body in the world
> possessing and exerting so manifest and direct a
> tendency toward the preservation, as well as the
> production, of original, genuine, apostolic Chris-
> tianity. [42]

Bishop Janes, to his satisfaction, validated the proposition that the Methodist Church was the true representation
of New Testament Christianity by testing the life and mission of Methodism by the standards of the Corinthian Church.
Ignoring the problematic moral condition, the theological
chaos and the absence of church discipline, he could focus on
the fact that the Corinthians were compelled to "work with
their own hands to obtain bread for themselves and families,"
and also make reference to "the labor, sacrifice and suffering of the apostles who were their ministers."[43]   He then
asked whether the ministry of the Methodist Church was not
the same.   Answering the question in the affirmative, he
exclaimed:

> Certainly more heroic devotion, more patient en-
> durance, and more earnest labor have not been
> displayed by any ministry since the example of in-
> spired Apostles.   Well may the Church which has
> such a ministry rejoice in it. [44]

The religious and moral heroism that Methodists understood
themselves to exhibit became the chief characteristic by
which they vindicated the parallel with the early Church.   As
with "apostolic Christianity which Methodism revived ... her
genius and life, was an aggressive missionary spirit."[45]
Methodism was "an attacking force," said Daniel Curry,
"perfectly mobilized and ready to carry the Gospel to the
most distant outposts."[46]

Believing that in the first stages of the Church, pure
living was the test and not right belief, Methodists, with
their emphasis on holiness, found another characteristic

John McClintock, Jr. (1814-1870), the first President of Drew Theological Seminary and corresponding editor of The Methodist during the Civil War. He effectively represented Northern interests during the sectional crisis.

which made the historic parallels compelling.   John McClintock speaking for this idea exclaimed:

> ... we are the only Church in history, from apostolic time until now, that has put forward as its very elemental thought--the great central pervading idea of the whole book of God from beginning to end--the holiness of the human soul, heart, mind, and will.   Go through all the confessions of all the Churches and you will find even some of them that blame us....   It may be called fanaticism; but, dear friends, that is our mission.   If we keep to that, the triumphs of the next century shall throw those that are past far in the shade. Our work is a moral work; that is to say, the work of making men holy....   There is our mission.... [47]

Another writer emphasizing the same point said, "... Methodism, like primitive Christianity, has been continually elevating its people...."[48] This self-understanding as a holy and missionary people gave impetus and content to a crusade of moral reformation starting with the Methodist Episcopal Church itself and extending to the borders of the continent. Some Methodist leaders, such as Gilbert Haven, could see the social and ecclesiastical implications of spiritual and moral purity with regard to the existing color caste in the Church and society.   Putting first things first, i. e. , bringing judgment to the house of God, Haven averred that if the Church were to throw "her mighty influence against this cruel and a false prejudice, and drive it from the land, " the Methodist Church should be a model of purity, love and equality.[49]   And that meant the Church

> should abolish the iniquity known only to Protestant America, the colored Church.   She should invite all those whom God has called to serve at her altars, which are not hers, but his.[50]

The significance of such a statement as this ought not be underestimated, for it leads to, perhaps, the essential understanding of the role of the Church in society by northern Methodists during the Reconstruction period.   While this subject will be examined in a later chapter, a few words are in order in the present context.   Although Haven is clearly more oriented to the practical and broader social implications of the Church's role in society, his statement does represent,

in a formal manner, a familiar approach to the problem.
In a word, Methodists saw the Church as a model of what
society ought to be, and in their exuberance about the course
of history, what it could be.   As a model it could reduplicate
in visible form the requirements of the gospel, and then
press for the same kind of reduplication in society as a
whole.   That is to say, the Church was seen as an institution where equality before God could be practiced.   Following the demonstration that color caste can be abolished from
within the Church, it could then rightly advocate the same
for society.   Along these lines Professor Hillman, a Methodist clergyman who taught at Dickinson College, thought that
the religious toleration and personal freedom allowed in the
Methodist Church could have salutary effects for the nation.[51]
Alluding to Abel Stevens' judgment that in no "religious society, either ancient or modern ... such liberty of conscience
is now allowed or has been since the days of the apostles, "
Hillman went on to draw the analogy with "political toleration
or liberalism. "[52] Methodism, in exhibiting catholicity, which
for him meant tolerance and liberty, could directly influence
the body politic.   To the degree that Methodism was true to
its own origins, "Methodist catholicity is at one with the
political liberalism of the nation. "[53]

Closely related to, and in part issuing from, the ardent belief that they were the authentic reproduction of apostolic Christianity, Methodists reflected a burning conviction
that they were a providentially called agent of reform.   As
a reformatory agent, the Methodist Episcopal Church had to
bring its life into correspondence with its mission, according
to most of the official spokesmen.   By becoming a model
society, the Church could have a profound effect as a social
and political force in the nation.   As the early Church stood
for religious and moral purity, so Methodists and cathedrals
of Methodism were to represent in their life and mission true
morality, and thus influence and protect the morals of society.

The sort of social responsibility expressed by Methodists was as much rooted in an emphasis on the Church as
an organic unit as in the individual.   Men like Bishop Simpson tended to put stress on the individual, while Haven emphasized the ecclesiastical pole.   Similarly, the Church Extension Society expressed narrower and more moralistic
attitudes toward the moral mission of Methodism than did
the Freedman's Aid Society, which always couched moral
meanings in concrete social, political and economic terms.

Granting the diversity in expressions and points of view, the
evidence demonstrates a more profound grasp of the Church's
social responsibility than recent historiography has indicated.
Perhaps what has not been seen is the significance of church-
manship. Daniel Curry expressed the responsibility of the
Church to society far more than he discussed the individual's
responsibility. It was the "moral power of the Church" that
became a guardian of "public morality" and appealed to the
"public conscience" and became a "conservative influence"
in society. [54] During the days of the Civil War it was the
Church that was called upon by its leaders to repent as a
step towards inner renewal, but also to repent on behalf of
the nation. [55]

What has been important in the preceding discussion
is not whether the Methodist Episcopal Church did bear an
historical likeness to the early Church; rather, it is that
Methodists thought they did. The very claim that Methodism
represented apostolic Christianity as no other Church had
ever done rested upon them as a mandate. The more extravagant the claim, the more aggressive the mission.

Another historic parallel drawn by Methodists focused
on the relationship between the Puritan tradition and Methodism. Here again, it should be said that it is not particularly important for present purposes to assess the validity of
the claims. But the fact that now and then the analogy is
made becomes important for an understanding of what motivated and shaped the vocation of the Church as Methodists
perceived it.

In the period following the Civil War, the American
Puritan tradition was in disrepute in large sections of the
country, especially the South, Central and Western states.
Though written at a later date, William Reed Huntington's
chapter on "Puritanism: The Idea Diminished" perhaps reflected a common criticism of Puritanism among many denominations outside of New England. [56] The conservative
editor of The Methodist, George R. Crooks, remarked that
"all the baser natures in our nation have been stirred to a
ferocious attack upon New England, the home of Puritanism,
as a part of the nation."[57] The charge, according to Crooks,
is that

> ... Puritanism is, both in the old world and the
> new, essentially pharisaical, egotistic, selfish,
> and intolerant, that it has no correct ideas of

civil liberty, that it mischievously mixes politics
and morals, that it is an intermeddler, troubler,
and generally a disturber of the peace.... 58

In the face of such criticism, Crooks, in this rather remarkable article, came to the defense of the Puritan tradition. Because the defense is made by one of the major
figures in Methodism and because it sets forth certain ideas
that are germane to an understanding of Methodist thought,
a cursory examination of this piece would seem useful.

Editor Crooks remarked at the outset that "Like the
Methodists, the Puritans were in their early days first hated,
then ridiculed, but finally recognized as a power in the world,
and accorded their due meed of honor."59 He chose not to
engage in a systematic defense of Puritanism--though he did
cite Hume's admission that English liberty owed its grandest
achievements to the Puritans. Rather, Crooks made reference
to an article that appeared in the Revue Nationale written by
a pro-Union, French Protestant, Professor Laboulaye of the
College of France, who was a close personal friend of John
McClintock, pastor of the Protestant Church in Paris during
the war and frequent contributor to The Methodist. The following quote goes to the heart of the issue:

> We have referred frequently to the noble defence of
> the Union by Professor Laboulaye ... who has
> studied our institutions more carefully, perhaps,
> than any other public man of Europe. To him the
> chief point of interest in our present struggle is
> that it has arisen from the action of the moral
> sense of the nation upon the facts of its political
> condition. And this is, we may say, the chief
> point of interest with the friends of the Union all
> over the world. 'America,' says Laboulaye very
> finely, 'so badly judged in France, gives us the
> spectacle of a fruitful democracy that holds fast to
> the Gospel, and makes Christianity the essential
> condition of liberty. A people risking its fortunes
> upon the exorcism of slavery is the grandest sight
> that this nineteenth century has seen.
>
> ....
>
> The Americans have for a long time known the
> secret of their greatness, for they brought it with
> them from England. From the time of Louis XIV
> they have clearly seen, what we are beginning to
> suspect, that liberty is a force and nothing more,

a force indifferent in its nature, and which may
lead either to evil or to good.... The direction
to be given to it was found by Americans on the
day when they learned that the problem to be resolved is the same in the case of a nation as in
that of each individual, and that political liberty
must be treated just like natural liberty, since it
is the same liberty.... Those two sisters, religion and education, are the guardians of the freedom in America.'60

Commenting on this extended quote, the Methodist editor noted
that this Frenchman comprehended the great "conservative"
elements of American civilization better than some Americans.
Assuming the importance with which religion and education
were held by Methodists, Crooks pointed to the source of what
was to be the essence and goal of the Methodist mission in
the subsequent decades.

The supreme regard for religion and education, to
which he pays a just tribute, is the high distinction
of Puritanism. Its means have not always been
wise, its spirit has often been narrow, but its end,
the realization of the idea of a Christian commonwealth, is the noblest that can present itself to the
mind of man. The manifest destiny of this nation
is to be a Christian nation; our democracy will be
a democracy of churches and schoolhouses. And
so long as church and schoolhouse, religion and
education, are cherished, so long shall we be bound
by indissoluble ties to the spirit of Puritanism. 61

This Methodist writer accurately stated the theme of
the Christian society, which was indeed the legacy of Puritanism, and however transformed, was received by American
Protestantism in the nineteenth century. Methodists defined
their mission as an attempt to educate, emancipate, and permeate society with religion, and finally to convert the world. 62
If this involved interfering in the political order, it was justified by an appeal to the heritage of Puritanism. As one
writer put it, defending northern Methodist political activity,
"Puritanism in politics means conscience or the fear of God
in civil affairs."63 Stating that this form of Christianity was
truly conservative, he said it is "the only salt that can preserve the state from despotism, anarchy, and ruin."64

Gilbert Haven justified his political sermons by reference to the history of the province of Massachusetts Bay in the days of Governor Winthrop when there was a furious pulpit war upon questions of civil and social import. 65 In the introduction to his volume of sermons he wrote,

> These discourses have, therefore, a natural origin. They are of the root of the fathers, alike of the oldest and the youngest of the churches of New England. 66

Haven carried on the Puritan-New England tradition of delivering an election-day sermon, Fast and Thanksgiving Day sermons, and sermons on the "days appointed by the State or National government, for the consideration of State and National duties. "67 His purpose in the sermon was to commend or condemn civil authority as virtue or sin gave occasion. Bringing the pulpit into the very center of public affairs, his sermons became explanations of what God was doing, what He was requiring, what He was promising in the political and military events which, to Haven, represented "the mightiest movements of God in this generation. "68 Daniel Boorstin's discussion of the Puritan sermon could, with few changes, apply to Gilbert Haven's understanding of the responsibility of the pulpit. During the war especially, not only Haven but most Methodist pulpiteers and editors saw the sermon in true Puritan fashion as an occasion "to explain to the people why God was humbling or rewarding them. "69 Most New England Methodists were closer to the Puritan tradition of practical Christianity that included political expression than they were to John Wesley's "no politics rule. " "You have nothing to do but save souls, " Wesley told his preachers. 70 He, the staunch Tory, would have been appalled by the democratic faith that found expression in Christian sermons delivered by his American descendents, and not a little surprised that so much energy and time was spent by Methodist preachers on political matters. But American Methodists, notwithstanding a certain moralism, even sentimentalism, about the progress of history, were too rooted in the Puritan tradition to abandon the belief that "the wholesome laws" of God needed to be enacted and maintained. 71 The tradition reflected in sermons which dealt with such practical matters as "The Fugitive Slave Bill, " "The Nebraska Bill, " "The Church and the Negro, "72 and the tradition reflected in the aggressive effort to enact prohibition, prison reform, educational, and suffrage laws is not a heritage imported from Wesley's England. Thus, when Haven called Methodism the "purer Puritanism, " as opposed

to the later generations of Puritans, he had some foundation
in fact for the assertion. [73]

Northern Methodists might not have been so eager to
trace their roots to Puritanism had not Jefferson Davis,
among other Southerners, attacked the North with pejorative
references to New England Puritanism. [74] George Peck, the
New York clergyman and prolific writer, noted that in certain quarters it is alleged that "Puritanism is fanaticism,
cant, and hypocrisy."[75] "No greater slander was ever uttered," said Peck. Puritanism was for him the purest form
of New Testament order and the gospel. It represented the
spirit of rational liberty and natural equality of man. Acknowledging Puritanism as the great resource of the Church's
love of liberty and equality, he remarked:

> The fact that the men of the Puritan stock hate
> slavery, and pray for universal emancipation, has
> brought this form of faith into great contempt at
> [sic] the South. No form of Christianity will pass
> current there but that which holds in fellowship
> 'the peculiar institution.'[76]

Another writer identified the place of American Methodists with reference to Puritanism. "Each had its distinctive
traits," he said, but "both are outgrowths of English Protestantism, though belonging to different periods of history."[77]
The significance of these two traditions, according to the
writer, is expressed in these words:

> The two moral forces which are most potential in
> the education of the American people are Puritan-
> ism and Methodism. [78]

By moral education he meant that Puritanism, like Methodism,
denied the binding power of human authority and ever sought
for a divine sanction of civil and ecclesiastical functions. He
saw Puritanism as an instructor in the proper exercises of
both authorities while at the same time attempting to build
a pure Christian commonwealth. "Hence the Puritan clergy
have, from time immemorial, had much to do with the political affairs of the Commonwealth."[79]

Surely this Methodist thought of Puritanism as a fount
for Methodism's understanding of its own mission to America
is evidenced in the following statement:

> The common school system, the temperance and

> the anti-slavery movements ... have sprung from
> the exuberant Puritanic life of New England. With
> almost irresistible prenetrative power Puritanism
> leavened the mass of the nation.... 80

Interesting is the fact that Methodists were prone to
look to the Puritan tradition as the source of their democratic social ideology more than to the French Enlightenment.
Daniel Curry could even say that liberty, equality and fraternity were the essential elements of social and political institutions in the American Republic without ever mentioning the
French. Admitting that these essential elements, including
the whole of the Declaration of Independence were not distinctively American, he confessed his nation's debt to "The
deep religiousness of the English Puritans."[81] The battles
of the American Revolution had begun and its earliest victories were in "the debates of the Long Parliament," and at
"Naseby and Marston Moor."[32] The claims of the American
Revolution were "embodied in the 'Petition of Rights'," and
the earliest soldiers, teachers and laborers were the Hamp-
dens and Cromwells, the Sidneys and Russells who "bled and
died, not only, nor indeed chiefly, for English liberty, but
still more for that of the then almost unknown land beyond
the sea." Curry saw America as the scion of the original
stock which grew out of the English Revolution of 1688.
Transplanted into a soil more favorable, with an atmosphere
more congenial, it was "capable of a more rapid and a
larger development."[83]

Northern Methodists distinguished themselves by the
richness and perspicuity with which they identified the source
of their own moral postulates and social ideals. The firm
belief that Methodists were being true to their heritage when
they incorporated into their mission a social dimension should
be reason enough to distinguish even the most radical Methodists from humanistic and principled abolitionists. Bishop
Baker could pass over lightly and even scoff at those who
talked as though the idea of human equality was original with
Thomas Jefferson. Jefferson, he said, "took it from the old
text book; there it is said by the Apostle: 'God hath made
of one blood all nations of men, for to dwell on all the face
of the earth'."[84] At the close of the speech from which
this quote was taken is the Bishop's cry, "Liberty and Union,
now and forever, one and inseparable."[85] There is nothing
special about the thought. The same sentiment was felt and
expressed many times over during the war years. What is
important, so it seems, is the context in which it is said.

Grounded in biblical thought and rooted in tradition with a
remarkable degree of historical consciousness, northern
Methodists, themselves, in the third quarter of the nineteenth
century, represent a heritage of great strength. Compared
to generations of Methodists who came after, who ostensibly
were more conscious of social matters, they come off well.

In commenting on the way in which the large denominations approached the solution to social problems in the
1940s, Paul Hanly Furfey makes this judgment:

> There is often less contrast than one might expect
> between the attack on social problems by the large
> religious agencies and the attack by secular agen-
> cies.... In their official pronouncements religious
> bodies often take a position parallel to that of
> liberal groups, without stating explicitly their own
> distinct basis for their convictions. Social work-
> ers move without difficulty from religious to secu-
> lar agencies and back again as employment oppor-
> tunities arise. [86]

Furfey quite rightly points to a major problem that has never
been completely overcome by the large liberal denominations
in their official social action, social thought and social service. [87] For all of the gains of the social gospel movement
and the contribution of Protestant liberalism in emphasizing
the humane virtues, a grave defect remains. And that is a
failure to honor the past and to articulate the grounds of a
social ministry from the distinct and unique perspective of
biblical faith. The greatness of such men as Haven, Curry,
Crooks, Stevens, Peck, et al. is seen in their capacity to
affirm and work for humane causes without ignoring the biblical and historical origins of the humane virtues. By honor-
ing such traditions as Puritanism, they were provided with
motivation, social ideals and a comprehensive vision of a
Christian society. By relating themselves to apostolic
Christianity, however inordinate in expression, they received
a dynamism at the heart of their activities rarely duplicated
in the history of the Church.

Their successes in building the largest denomination
in the land; the vindication of their moral and religious ideals
in the outcome of the Civil War; and the challenge of new
frontiers and new perils provided Methodists with the energy
to emulate the early Church missionaries and to reclaim the
Puritan vision of a Christian commonwealth. Here it needs

to be said that much more went into the shaping of the
Methodist response to the world after 1865 than has been
often assumed. It is a common notion that the evangelical
denominations in the mid-nineteenth century are to be understood as products of the frontier. What is overlooked in
such an assumption is the transforming influence of the Civil
War, and the ongoing battle of Reconstruction facing the
churches and the nation. Certainly for Methodists the war
had the effect of turning eyes back to New England to gain
perspective on the meaning of the conflict, of national destiny and of the mission of the Church. The motivation,
goals and hopes of Methodism were as much formed by New
England Puritanism as by Western revivalism. The issues
of the new southern frontier even turned some Methodists
back to seventeenth-century England for perspective and understanding. In a word, an understanding of Methodist modes of
thought and action is something deeper and more complex
than much of the current writing on the subject would indicate. The preceding discussion has been intended to show
just that.

Although Methodists did not think of themselves as the
exclusive bearers of the apostolic and true Protestant tradition, they did believe that by virtue of special providential
favor they possessed a more practical and earnest ministry,
a more powerful press, a higher degree of organizational
efficiency, a more vital worship, a purer and more scriptural
theology and a more militant missionary thrust. Rarely dif-
fident in extolling any of their own felt ecclesiastical virtues,
Methodists were most enamored by their militant character.
The boundless use of the military metaphor seems significant
enough for grasping their own self-understanding as mission
sent to justify the inclusion of a few illustrations.

Methodism and the Military Metaphor

"Methodism moves in the van of this noble army of
religious liberty," said Jesse T. Peck, "and the decisive
victory is already historically indicated. " The enemy was
American slavery, that "monster despotism" which was the
"final form in which personal rights were antagonized. "
Recognizing the noble heroism of "brother warriors of every
Church, " Peck was pleased to exclaim that Methodism "had
its just position at the front in the last great conflict, when
the monster fell to rise no more. "[88]

Another Methodist referring to the militancy and

mobility of Methodism as the special genius of a denomination that could push civilization "along the frontiers into the wilderness, " there where "Methodism was at Home, " found the military figure useful in stating his case.

> If we regard the whole Christian Church as an army
> (leaving the Baptists out, who go by water, and
> constitute the navy) then the peculiar organization
> of Methodism will assign her the place of the flying
> artillery.   The cannons and ordinances of the
> Protestant Episcopal Church, are siege guns, which
> do good execution when once they get in position,
> but which are too heavy for field work.   Our Church
> is so flexible that she can limber and unlimber in
> a few moments, and long before the solid columns
> of infantry, or cavalry, or heavy artillery can reach
> the spot, she is throwing solid shot, generally red
> hot, right into the camp of the enemy.   Let the foe
> be defeated, and sound a retreat, and the rumbling
> wheels of Methodism will be heard in hot pursuit,
> while the balance of the army are counting the spoils,
> and reorganizing for a new campaign.   As a matter
> of fact, she is always in the advance, and where
> the battle is the hottest; and if she don't [sic] get
> as much of the spoils, nor take as many distin-
> guished captives as the rest, it is because she is
> too intent upon victory to encumber herself with
> trophies.   Her genius and her equipment both fit
> her for the advanced post in every forward move-
> ment. [89]

In the same idiom Abel Stevens found it not surprising that the Methodist Church manual was called the "Book of Discipline. "   Reiterating the prevalent assumption of Methodists that "their cause has a special vocation; that it is essentially ... aggressive, militant, throughout the land...," he notes:

> Its ecclesiastical system is confessedly a species
> of military regime.   It is designedly such, and for
> an heroic purpose; and that purpose has been
> realized as historical achievement for more than a
> hundred years. [90]

For Matthew Simpson it was Christ "the Captain" or Christ "the Commander" who gave the marching orders, "Go ye into all the world. "[91]   The duty of Methodism as an

"Army of God" was to convert the world. In a moment rare
for Methodists, Simpson found inspiration in a recollection of
Constantine. The reference offers no surprise.

> If Constantine, when he was in the field and his
> enemies were pressing him, seemed to see the
> Cross in the heavens, and on its written, 'By
> this conquer, ' so the Church sees that Cross; it
> is on high, all radiant with light, and the voice
> sounds: 'By this the world shall be conquered. ' 92

Methodists were doing battle against the devil and all
of his evil works. Members of the Church Extension were
convinced that the most effective means of defeating the arch-
enemy was to build chapels and saturate the land with these
"fortresses. " Ira G. Bidwell lectured that each time the
Church casts up a new chapel, she "mounts a new gun a
little nearer the citadel of the Prince of darkness. "93 A
Reverend J. O. Peck, not to be outdone by his brethren in
the use of military rhetoric, sermonized on the necessity of
extending the lines of fortification by building more fortresses
in the enemy's country. "We build and garrison these forts
to expedite the capture of the land. " Seeing the Methodist
chapel as the arsenal of God's Vigilance committed by vocation to protect society, he asserted:

> We have our Krupp guns and mount them in our
> pulpits. Sin and Satan hate the multiplication of
> churches. It means overthrow. It asserts the
> rights of our Redeemer. It proclaims him to be
> the rightful Lord and Sovereign. ... The Church
> is an organization to hunt down the arch-outlaw
> and break up his marauding band. ... The house
> of God, erected anywhere, declares that the world
> belongs to Christ, and this his army is coming. 94

In this highly militant language, the Church was cast
in the light of an aggressive army pounding away at those
forces that would prevent the American Republic from becoming what it was providentially intended to be--a civilized and
Christian nation. What were the specific aims of such an
operation? They were stated over and over again, always
with some variation, but invariably on the same theme. The
following quote is as representative and as comprehensive as
any catalogue of aims:

> Law and order are promoted. Life is more secure.

Property appreciates. Society is elevated. Intelligence increases and education thrives. The rights
of mankind are more justly recognized and maintained. Home is ennobled and emparadised. In-
nocense is protected and helplessness is surrounded
by bulwarks. Temperance is reinforced, philan-
thropy inspired, and benevolence quickened. Vice
is exposed and crime is punished. The individual
is enfranchised in higher manhood, and the commonwealth is environed with new security. [95]

Not to be missed in this listing is the whole range of life
that is represented. From law and order to the rights of
mankind; from national security to the protection of the help-
less; from the elevation of society to the enhancement of the
individual; from economic life to the domestic realm--all of
this and more became part of the Church's strategic aim.

The perils and evils were many. The Western Circuit Rider battered away at the brothels, the gambling dens,
the saloons and the theaters, and frequently entered into
skirmishes with the Baptists and Presbyterians. All Methodists saw in Romanism and infidelity, major enemies. Both
opponents, infidelity and Romanism, posed a threat to the
faith and were of critical theological importance. But the
battle was perceived in broader terms. Along with the theological and ecclesiastical implications of a possible rise in
infidelity were the social and political dangers. It would be
superficial to suggest that Methodist sensibilities were shocked
merely by the religious promiscuity and impious invective of
Ingersol and the "free thinkers." More shocking and threaten-
ing was the peril to the social order if atheism or agnosticism
should win out. Chaplain C. C. McCabe, that indomitable
warrior of the Church Extension Society, gave as a dream,
a picture of Ingersolville, a city of man from which God was
excluded.

Lust and profanity and crime and robbery and vio-
lence and disorder prevailed, until the better class
of atheists themselves fled from it in dismay, as
they would from a pest-house. Infidels can not
deny the existence in our world of death and grief
and tears and disappointment. What remedy do
they propose for the sorrows of earth, which,
sooner or later, come to all? What alleviation
does atheism or agnosticism offer?[96]

Not only the social order, but the political order

which sustains human life would be endangered if "the powers
that be" did not acknowledge that legitimate government was
derivative of "Divine Providence." The viability of America's judicial system was at stake in the battle with infidels.
The Rev. T. H. Pearne argued that historical candor compelled the acknowledgment that "The common law of England ... is the foundation of our judicial system."[97] Not to
recognize that Christianity was an essential element in English common law was to misread history, according to
Pearne. Quoting Blackstone to the effect that all human
laws depend on two foundations, "the law of nature and the
law of revelation," he concluded that "there is not a civilized
nation on the face of the earth that does not recognize God
in its laws."[98] The urgency and militancy that characterized
the Methodist war against infidelity can be understood only
by taking seriously what Methodists themselves meant when
they declared they were God's agents for the protection and
deliverance of the nation. To them Christianity was a good
thing, because by it and through the activity of the Church,
the true political traditions and institutions could be preserved and enhanced.

John P. Newman, elected three times as the Chaplain
of the United States Senate and a close friend of President
Grant, protested against infidelity by centering his main arguments around the social consequences of such a position.
For him it was the Jesuits, not the French philosophers,
who cared for humanity. It was Luther, not Voltaire, who
stood for liberty. It was Lord Bacon and not Diderot who
laid the foundation for education. It was Wesley and Burke,
not Thomas Paine, who stood for true liberty, equality and
fraternity. Closing his argument, Newman queried,

> Nay, who would not proudly claim companionship
> with William Wilberforce and Abraham Lincoln in
> striking off the last manacle from the forms of
> our fellow beings who had been enslaved.[99]

If the social dimension was present in the fight against
infidelity, it was equally so as Methodists confronted Roman
Catholicism. Methodists were not a little disturbed about
the Sabbath pleasures of immigrant Catholics. The force of
the Methodist attack on Romanism is indicated by the following quotations from Roman Catholic periodicals:

> The real enemies to us are the Methodists, ad-
> mirably organized for aggression, and who in their

appeals to the animal nature and sensible devotion, acquire no little power over the sensitive, the ignorant, and the superstitious. 100

In the Catholic Tablet Protestants were taunted for their "airs of superiority" and it was added that Catholicism "is joy, and worship is a perpetual feast.... You can never make them accept the Puritanic gloom ... and whip the beer-barrel if it works on Sunday. "101 It would be possible to cite many statements to illustrate the Methodist uneasiness about the social habits of Catholics and their unabashed Anglo-Protestant arrogance, but there is more to it. The nub of the Roman Catholic issue had to do with free institutions, education, and assimilation into the American ethos. A few sentences from the Episcopal address at the General Conference of 1872 will suggest the nature of Methodist concern:

> The combined and persistent efforts made by the Bishops and priests of the Romish Church to destroy our system of common schools, attract much public attention. The general diffusion of virtue and intelligence among the people furnish the only sure basis on which civil and religious liberty can rest. 102

The bishops called on the Methodist clergymen and the whole denomination to "cherish the free institutions, " noting that they were bequeathed by Protestant forefathers, and to give an "intelligent, firm and earnest support to the civil authorities" in the maintenance and extension of the schools. Methodists gave enthusiastic support to the common schools because education meant moral and religious elevation. More than that, primary education, especially, meant Americanization and civilization. Methodists saw the parochial schools of Catholicism as an effort to delay the inevitable drift of history. And the "persistent efforts of the priests to keep their people together in towns and cities" was to one Methodist a preventative measure, "lest they should become Protestantized by being Americanized...."103

The challenge of Catholicism came to shape the missionary response of Methodism. The challenge and the peril was in the "un-American character and tendencies" of an alien element whose power was already being felt in the social and political affairs of the nation. Curry put it this way:

> Like a river of pure water, into which some turbid
> affluent pours its muddy current, and the two flow
> on together without uniting; so our native and our
> alien population are only partially fused. And, as
> in the onward course of that stream, the purer
> steadily gains upon turbid, so it may be hoped that
> our traditional American manners, practices, and
> religion shall, at length, fashion all others to our
> own original type. This is the work to which our
> genuine American race is now called. 104

For Curry as for most Protestants, the process of Americanization would develop along Protestant lines. This was the
original model to which he referred. But noteworthy about
the above statement is the use of the term "race." In the
context of all his writings, and recalling that he was, next
to Haven, one of the most vigorous proponents of social and
political equality for American blacks, it may be concluded
that Curry thought blacks were of the "American race."
His racial prejudice was reserved for others. The foreign
elements that threatened to poison the pure stream of nativism
were the Irish and European Catholic immigrants and the so-
called uncivilized Asians.

In the face of increasing tides of immigrants rolling
onto the shores of America, Methodists became convinced
that an important aspect of their ministry had to do with
"Americanizing" the foreign population. Building schools,
colleges and seminaries became one of the chief means of
accomplishing this task. When the Methodist Episcopal
Church planted "the flag of the Gospel on its farthest, its
ocean frontier"--California--Abel Stevens noted that along
the way Methodism had helped to lay the "moral foundations
of the magnificent series of States which now crown there
the continent. "105 Moreover, he thought one of the main
contributions his Church made in safeguarding the nation
from the Asian population flooding the west coast was in the
establishment of schools and colleges. 106 Reviewing this
great benefit he could assert:

> Thus this great commonwealth, chief representative
> of the American Union on the Pacific Coast, stands
> confronting the hoary Asiatic world with all the
> liberties and lights of our civilization. There is
> destiny in its attitude. 107

Bishop Jesse T. Peck, who labored eight years in the States, wrote, "To Methodism belongs the honor of saving the State of California to freedom."[108]

The battle against Romanism in Boston, New York and Chicago was basically the same battle waged by Methodists against foreign Asian elements. The battle was enjoined with an exuberant sense of destiny related to a deep concern for the welfare of the Republic, chosen of God for grand purposes.

One more word needs to be said about the anti-Catholic attitude of Methodists in order to support the contention that much more was involved than Protestant bigotry. It was well known that many of the New York Irish Catholics were participants in the draft riots in the summer of 1863 and that many were pro-South and anti-negro in sentiment and behavior. The opprobrium of such unpatriotism and treasonous guilt left a deep residue of suspicion and anger at the heart of northern Methodism. No less disturbing to New York Methodists was the crime in the city and corruption in its politics, to which Irish Catholic blame was laid. A Methodist editor's indictment, following upon Congressional attempts to conciliate the Fenians after their abortive invasion of Canada, is representative:

> And do these politicians really believe that the vast Protestant majority of American citizens will look with indifference on this chicanery--this favoritism toward a foreign people who fill our prisons and pauper houses--who corrupt our elections, lead our mobs, who made the terrible days of July 1863 in New York one of the saddest seasons of our national struggle, and who, it is now well known, furnished the patriotic army the least proportion of troops of all American religious denominations? The Protestant loyalty of this nation protests against a revival of the old political trucking of the Irish Papists; and the politicians will find this protest a practical power, if they again attempt to compromise the national honor with this generally disloyal people.[109]

The writer, of course, was right in his allegations. The situation did effect "public morals" and did relate to "Christian ethics" as stated by him in the article.[110] As Martin Marty put it, "... nineteenth-century Catholicism was making noises which gave political anti-Catholicism a certain plausibility."[111]

The militant attack of Methodism against the twin perils, infidelity and Romanism, involved a deep-rooted concern for social, cultural and political issues. This concern must be seen as part of the broader mission to the nation. And the evils against which Methodists fought were more numerous than mentioned above. J. T. Crane, a distinguished clergyman from New Jersey and frequent contributor to the Methodist Quarterly Review, declared that "Methodism, at the very beginning, joined battle with the sins that threatened national ruin. "[112] What were the sins that posed a threat to the Republic? He lists: slavery, intemperance, social inequality, rebellion, ignorance, and all of those forces which endangered free institutions and civil liberty. [113] Believing that Methodist theology had infused "a silent yet powerful element into our political life, inculcating a broad humanity ... and asserting everywhere fraternity and the rights of all races and all men, " Crane explained:

> The generous theology of Methodism favors civil liberty. Personal freedom, the ballot, popular education, equality before the law for all citizens, are the natural corollaries of the doctrines of a general atonement and universal grace. [114]

Methodists believed enough in original sin to know that the war they waged was no neighborhood fight. The devil was real and the evils of the age perilous. But they also believed in the saving and renewing activity of God. This faith, coupled with the conviction that the Methodist Episcopal Church was by Providence sent on a mighty mission, was the fount of their energy, aims and hopes. The amalgamation of their Protestant faith and mission with American ideology and destiny had not yet taken place in the first years after the war, though the seeds of this eventuality may be seen in the data presented. A closer look at this problem and a more thorough treatment of the social philosophy implicit in Methodist thought and life is yet to come. It will suffice to say that whatever else may be said about the northern Methodist approach to the solution of social problems, they were not complacent about social sin in the years immediately following the Civil War.

Notes

1. Richard M. Cameron. Methodism and Society in Historical Perspective, I. New York: Abingdon Press,

1961, p. 217. See also, A. Dudly Ward. <u>The Social Creed of the Methodist Church.</u> 2d. ed. rev. New York: Abingdon Press, 1965, pp. 21-25, and Georgie Harkness. <u>The Methodist Church in Social Thought and Action.</u> New York: Abingdon Press, 1964, p. 11. 51f.

2. Gerald Kennedy, "Introduction," <u>History of American Methodism,</u> ed. Emory S. Bucke. New York: Abingdon Press, 1964, III, Part vi, p. 255.

3. Cameron, <u>Methodism and Society...,</u> "Introduction," p. 6.

4. Cameron, <u>Methodism and Society...,</u> p. 187. "Whatever may be said about the "upsurge of social concern," Methodists have scarcely distinguished themselves by the profundity of their social analysis. The fact that they can still be proud of the Social Creed (which includes the following affirmation) ought to be documentation enough for a demurral: "The Methodist Episcopal Church stands--For the recognition of the Golden Rule and the mind of Christ as the supreme law of society and the sure remedy for all social ills." See, Harkness, <u>The Methodist Church,</u> p. 47.

5. "2 Methodists Bid Missions Change," <u>New York Times,</u> (January 11, 1969), p. 19.

6. Jaroslav J. Pelikan, "Methodism's Contribution to America," <u>History of American Methodism,</u> III, p. 607.

7. This is one of the major points of emphasis made by Timothy L. Smith in his book, <u>Revivalism and Social Reform.</u> New York: Harper & Row, 1965. See especially Chapters V, X, and XI See also, Will Herberg, <u>Protestant Catholic Jew,</u> pp. 104-10.

8. Pelikan, "Methodism's Contribution to America," p. 603.

9. "1867-8," (Editorial), <u>Northwestern Christian Advocate,</u> XVI, (January 1, 1868), p. 4. It is probably editor Eddy who remarked that that preceding century had been formative; now Methodism would move into a

period of consolidation. But he was emphatic in declaring that "The old itinerant spirit of aggression lives. "

10. Wade Barclay. History of Methodist Missions, Vol. I. Missionary Motivation and Expansion. New York: Board of Missions of The Methodist Church, 1957, p. vii.

11. Colin Williams. Where in the World? New York: Office of Publication and Distribution National Council of the Churches of Christ, 1963, p. 44.

12. For a typical treatment of this theme see, Jesse T. Peck, "Methodism: Its Method and Mission," Methodist Quarterly Review, XLXI, (April 1869), pp. 242-69.

13. Daniel Dorchester. The Why of Methodism. New York: Phillips and Hunt, 1888, pp. 29, 35.

14. Ibid., pp. 38-40.

15. Ibid., p. 40.

16. W. G. E. Cunnyngham. Thoughts on Missions: Or, An Essay Setting Forth the Principles, Facts and Obligations of Christian Missions. Nashville: Southern Methodist Publishing House, 1874, p. 15.

17. Ibid.

18. John Wesley Johnston. The Home Missions of the Methodist Episcopal Church. Syracuse: Gaylord Brothers, 1908, pp. 3-4.

19. Harkness, The Methodist Church..., p. 11.

20. Ibid., p. 17.

21. Peck, "Methodism...," Methodist Quarterly Review, XLXI, p. 253.

22. New York East Annual Conference Minutes, 1871, p. 253.

23. "The Freedmen and the Methodist Episcopal Church," Zion's Herald, XXXIV, (November 4, 1863), p. 174.

24. Ibid.

25. Church Extension Annual of The Methodist Episcopal Church, 1874, "Address of Rev. Jacob Todd." p. 87.

26. Ibid., p. 85.

27. "Pamphlets-Report of the New England Annual Conference for 1865 on Church Reconstruction," Methodist Quarterly Review, XLVII, (July 1865), p. 483.

28. Ibid.

29. Ibid.

30. Handy, The Protestant Quest..., p. 12.

31. Supra, Chapter 4.

32. B. F. Tefft. Methodism Successful and the Internal Causes of Its Success. New York: Derby & Jackson, 1860, pp. 328, 329.

33. Dorchester, The Why of Methodism, p. 2.

34. Nathan Bangs. An Original Church of Christ: or A Scriptural Vindication of the Orders and Powers of the Ministry of the Methodist Episcopal Church. New York: T. Mason and G. Lane, 1840.

35. Ibid., p. 364.

36. Randolph S. Foster. Centenary Thoughts for the Pew and Pulpit of Methodism. New York: Phillips & Hunt, 1884, p. 36.

37. William Ford, "A Centenary Hymn," Christian Advocate (New York), XLI, (November 15, 1866), p. 362.

38. Stevens, A Compendious History of American Methodism, p. 584.

39. Peck, "Methodism," Methodist Quarterly Review, XLXI, p. 246.

40. Ibid., p. 244. See also, John A. Wright. People and Preachers in the Methodist Episcopal Church. Philadelphia: Lippincott Co., 1866, pp. 21, 22.

41. Tefft, Methodism Successful..., p. 365.

42. Ibid., p. 385.

43. E. S. Janes, "Tests of a Valid Ministry and a True Church," Methodist Quarterly Review, XLXI, (July 1869), p. 329.

44. Ibid.

45. Dorchester, The Why of Methodism, p. 38.

46. Curry, Platform Papers, p. 149.

47. John McClintock, "Distinctive Feature of Methodism," Northwestern Christian Advocate, XV, (December 4, 1867), p. 385.

48. "Methodism and Its Critics," Christian Advocate (New York), XLI, (November 22, 1866), p. 372.

49. Haven, Sermons..., pp. 272-73.

50. Ibid.

51. S. D. Hillman, "The United States and Methodism," Methodist Quarterly Review, XLIX, p. 47.

52. Ibid.

53. Ibid.

54. Curry, Platform Papers, pp. 156-74. The entire chapter represents one of the best treatments of this subject to be found in the literature of the time.

55. See Chapter 4, supra.

56. William Reed Huntington. The Church Idea. New York: Charles Scribner's Sons, 1899. See chapter on "Puritanism: The Idea Diminished," pp. 57-72.

57. "The Puritans," The Methodist, IV, (January 24, 1863), p. 20.

58. Ibid.

59. Ibid.

60. Ibid.

61. Ibid.

62. "Methodist Church Life," The Methodist, VI, (December 30, 1865), p. 412.

63. "Puritanism in Politics," Zion's Herald, XXXV, (September 14, 1864), p. 146.

64. Ibid.

65. Haven, Sermons..., p. v.

66. Ibid., p. ix.

67. Ibid.

68. Ibid.

69. Daniel Boorstin. The Americans, The Colonial Experience. New York: Vintage Books by Alfred Knopf and Random House, 1958, pp. 10-15.

70. Cited by Winthrop Hudson. American Protestantism. Chicago: The University of Chicago Press, 1961, p. 72.

71. Ibid., p. 71. See Hudson for general discussion, pp. 71-74.

72. Haven, Sermons..., pp. v-xxiv.

73. Gilbert Haven, "The Apotheosis of the Camp-Meeting," The Independent, XV, (August 26, 1869), p. 2.

74. "The Puritans," The Methodist, IV, (January 24, 1863), p. 20.

75. George Peck, Our Country..., p. 14.

76. Ibid.

77. "American Methodism, Its Position in American Civilization," The Methodist, V, (July 9, 1864), p. 212.

78. Ibid.

79. Ibid.

80. Ibid.

81. Curry, Platform Papers, pp. 144-45.

82. Ibid.

83. Ibid.

84. "Address of Bishop Baker," Daily Christian Advocate,
     Philadelphia, (May 7, 1864), n. p.

85. Ibid.

86. Paul Hanly Furfey, "The Churches and Social Problems,"
     The Annals of The American Academy of Political
     and Social Science, Vol. 256 (March 1948), p. 109.

87. This judgment would also apply to the National Council
     of Churches and the World Council of Churches.
     When the nineteenth century Methodists embraced
     the Puritan vision of society, they were drawing on
     resources of greater religious and social signifi-
     cance than the "truncated Barthianism" underlying
     most pronouncements coming out of the World and
     National Council of Churches.   The reason for the
     truncation, as Barth said of Amsterdam and as Ram-
     sey said of Geneva, was that the conferences began
     with "man's disorder" (or man's revolutionary pros-
     pects) rather than with "God's design. " See the
     strictures of Paul Ramsey in his Who Speaks for the
     Church.   Nashville and New York: Abingdon Press,
     1967, pp. 73-77.

88. Jesse T. Peck, "Methodism, " Methodist Quarterly Re-
     view, XLXI, p. 252.

89. Church Extension Annual, 1874, p. 89.

90. Abel Stevens.   Supplementary History of American
     Methodism.   New York: Eaton and Mains, 1899,
     p. 40.

91. Matthew Simpson, "The Church of God as an Army: A
     Missionary Sermon, " The Methodist, III, (December
     13, 1862), p. 386.

92. Ibid.

93. Church Extension Society Annual Report, 1871, "Address of Rev. Ira G. Bidwell," p. 64.

94. Church Extension Annual, 1876, "Address of Rev. J. O. Peck," pp. 114, 115.

95. Ibid.

96. Rev. T. H. Pearne. God in the Constitution: A Review of Col. Robert G. Ingersol. Cincinnati: Press of Geo. P. Houston, 1890, p. 21.

97. Ibid., p. 9.

98. Ibid., p. 10.

99. John P. Newman. Christianity Triumphant. New York: Funk and Wagnalls, 1884, p. 59. See Chapter IV, "Great Christians vs. Great Infidels," pp. 43-59.

100. Cited in S. Bucke, ed. The History of American Methodism, Vol. II, "The Methodist Episcopal Church in the Postwar Era," pp. 334-35.

101. Cited by Hiram Mattison, "Romanism in the United States," Methodist Quarterly Review, XLX, (October 1868), pp. 508-09.

102. General Conference Journal..., 1872, p. 456.

103. "Romanism in America and Her School," Northwestern Christian Advocate, XVI, (September 16, 1868), p. 300.

104. Curry, Platform Papers, p. 127.

105. Stevens, Supplementary History of American Methodism, p. 29.

106. Ibid., pp. 32, 33. Among many educational enterprises, Stevens noted the "extensive system of educational institutions under the title, The University of Southern California," p. 33.

107. Ibid., p. 32.

144 / The Sectional Crisis

108.   Cited by Stevens, ibid.

109.   "The Fenians and the Politicians, " Christian Advocate
       (New York), XLI, (July 12, 1866), p. 220.

110.   Ibid.

111.   Marty, Righteous Empire, p. 128.

112.   Jesse T. Peck. History of the Great Republic.   New
       York: Broughton and Wyman, 1868, p. 540.

113.   Ibid. , pp. 540-44.

114.   Ibid. , p. 541.

CHAPTER 6

CIVIL RELIGION AND NATIONAL DESTINY

Most Protestants in mid-nineteenth century had two
religions. One was the religion of the nation; the other, the
religion of evangelical Christianity. These two religions in
near indistinguishable blend formed the substance of conviction and provided a powerful worldview for self-understanding
in northern Methodism during the sectional crisis.

The notion of two religions in American history--the
general religion of Americanism and the particular religion
of Christianity--has been acknowledged and discussed by a
wide range of scholars from Alexis de Tocqueville to Ralph
Gabriel, Will Herberg, Sidney Mead and Martin Marty. And
while they do not all agree on the precise meaning of the
terms and the historical interrelationships, their discussion
and debate has illustrated the usefulness of the "two-religion"
thesis by advancing considerably the understanding of the
American experience.

There is, however, a weakness in much of the discussion and that is the lack of attention to narrow case studies
of particular religious movements in mix and tension with religious nationalism in particular periods. Moreover, much of
the recent reflection on the subject has centered on the twentieth century and what some have called a "post-Protestant
America." In so doing the religion of Protestant Christianity
has been viewed in contrast to the general religion of Ameri-
cans--variously called "culture religion," "the American way
of life," or, "religion in general." This nomenclature suggests a kind of folk religion that is the source of an erosion
of traditional faith and a bland common denominator substi-
tute. Sometimes it has meant that a religion has been made
out of politics. This is emphatically not the case in the mid-
nineteenth century. For most Roman Catholic and Protestant
believers, their civil religion was a fervent nationalism
rooted in a very traditional faith. Cushing Strout, in a very

145

sophisticated study of political religion in America, argues compellingly that Americans have always been prone to making a "politics out of religion" which is not the same thing as making a "religion out of politics."[1] It is in this sense that the term civil religion can be aptly applied to northern Methodists during the Civil War and Reconstruction.

The vital center of this religious mix was a fiercely held conviction that the nation had a vocation uniquely in concert with the mission of the church. The ethical content of this curious blend of traditional Christianity, denominational chauvinism and nationalistic faith was the democratic credo expressed in terms of equal rights and civil liberties.

More than anything else it was the Civil War that had kindled this passionate religious nationalism. "In the hour of bitterest agony," wrote a New England cleric, "we felt the throb of our national vitality as we never had before."[2] The war had brought the nation a "new birth," and with it a new confidence in the vision of America as a chosen people with a special mission. Methodists partook of this widespread summit of nationalist enthusiasm in a special way, for they, perhaps more than any other denomination, had fitted the struggle of the nation into their vocational aims. Fired by a sense of new prestige and power manifested in their political relations with the government, and by a strong conviction that they had to play a crucial role in the nationalizing process, they had unbounded faith in the destiny of the nation. The key to understanding the commingling of religious impulses and nationalistic consciousness that brought together the mission of the Church and national destiny is found in the Methodist belief in Providence. Why was it that in the eighteenth century a new nation and a new form of Christianity were called into being? Because God's providential designs for the redemption of the world could not finally be thwarted by the monarchies, tyranny and barbarism of Europe. The new Republic and American Methodism were thought to have been the chief agents for the fulfillment of Divine purposes. These purposes and the means of achieving them had, for Methodists, become manifest in the struggle and the agonizing climax of the Civil War.

An understanding of this "religious nationalism," deeply felt, clearly articulated and aggressively acted upon, is of major importance for interpreting the social thought and action of northern Methodists in the aftermath of the war. Indeed, it may be the basic interpretive theme for explaining how a revivalistic-oriented denomination came to assume a social mission to the nation. A study of this theme may also help in understanding how northern Methodism could acquiesce, along with the nation, to the compromise of 1877 and gradually lose its concern for civil justice in both the North and the South. That is to say, caught up in the spirit of national destiny when its meaning was religious, Methodists were carried along with the gradual secularization of "manifest destiny" which began in the 1870s and reached its peak in the 1890s and later. [3] Lincoln's vision of the nation as a model Republic accorded well with the mission of the Church in behalf of civil rights and liberties, but when national purposes were expressed in terms of Anglo-Saxon superiority, imperialistic motives and a secular national interest, the cords that bound Church to nation were the cords that pulled Methodism along the stream of an onrushing secularism.

The phrase "religious nationalism," as applied to northern Methodism after the war, contains within it a variety of meanings that can be summed up under three major heads. First, it connotes a sense of common history and an identity with the character and vocation of the nation. Second, it means a strong affirmation of the nation as Christian and as an organic unit. In this sense the nation was defined not so much as a geographic region, but as an ideal incarnated. Third, it is used to describe a faith in the special destiny of the nation to which the mission of the Church closely corresponded.

The United States and Methodism: A Common History

Whenever the doctrine of Providence was invoked, whether in celebrating the first hundred years of Methodism or interpreting the Civil War, there was an almost automatic tendency to articulate a correspondence between the birth, growth and destiny of the Republic and the birth, growth and mission of the Methodist Episcopal Church. Methodists did not think it accidental that they were newly on hand to participate in the struggle for Independence in 1776. Nor did they think it blind fate that accounted for the fact that northern Methodists represented the predominant ecclesiastical power in supporting the Union cause. The idea that the United States had been called to be the chief means of worldwide redemption and that the Methodist Church was the chief agent for helping in the fulfillment of that task was a dominant motif in Methodist interpretations of their own history, the history of the Republic and of the Civil War. [4]

The centennial anniversary of the Declaration of American Independence gave occasion for expressing this understanding. The official action of the General Conference of the Methodist Episcopal Church, at its session of 1872 in preparation for the celebration four years hence, typified the commonly held belief in the unique relationship existing between Methodism and the nation.

> Whereas, the fourth of July, 1876, will be the centennial anniversary of the Declaration of American Independence; and
>
> Whereas, a loyal and patriotic sentiment must prompt every citizen to join in some appropriate commemoration of the event; and,
>
> Whereas, the Methodist Church was the first, through a deputation of her chief ministers, to give a pledge of support to the Government in the days of Washington; and ever maintaining an unswerving loyalty, was second to none in the struggle for the perpetuation of that government in the days of Lincoln.
>
> Therefore, it is meet that we, ... formally express our gratification. ... [5]

In linking the destiny of the nation with the destiny of the Methodist Church there were constant recitals of the long history of loyalty paid to the government. Members of the General Conference in 1864, urging a more vigorous support for the war effort, were reminded that:

> Our church, which was the first to give to the Government under Washington the assurances of allegiance and the promise of support, has ever been loyal and devoted to the best interests of the country. [6]

Commenting on Lincoln's special recognition of Methodist support and loyalty during the war, one preacher employed an unmethodist metaphor in exclaiming that Methodism was the "new wine for the new bottle"--the bottle being the new Republic. He said,

> Asbury and Coke were intimate with Washington--
> they had been guests at Mt. Vernon and Bishop
> Simpson was one of Mr. Lincoln's most trusted
> confidential advisers during the war.   The new
> wine has never ceased to act upon the new bottle,
> and preserve it. [7]

In claiming a very close relationship between their Church
and the nation, Methodists found in the person of Francis Asbury a counterpart to the father of the country.   As the
father of Methodism in America, Asbury "was the only English preacher who adopted the American country, " said Ezra
Wood, and he "was determined to stand or fall with the
cause of independence. "[8]   Thus, a reading of the history of
the American Revolution showed nineteenth-century Methodists
that their own heroic age was coterminous with that of the
founders of the Republic.   "The same convulsion which made
us a nation, " said Bishop Foster, "made us a Church. "[9]
Alluding to the fact that American Methodists organized
nearly at the same time with the organization of the Federal
Republic, another writer informed that Methodism

> has since then kept pace with it almost step by
> step in its wonderful growth in numbers, wealth,
> culture, influence, energy, and prospective useful-
> ness, and this too without loss of spiritual life:
> such a Church may naturally be supposed to have
> characteristics in strong sympathy with the nation,
> and the above census-like similarities holding be-
> tween them may be regarded as the outward signs
> of the inner kinship of common principles. [10]

Among the common principles linking together Methodism and the nation was the "communal idea. "   Other denominations such as the Lutherans, Episcopalians, and Calvinist communions emphasized the sacramental and ceremonial
aspects of the faith, while Methodists stressed "Church fellowship" and "individualism. "   This they believed paralleled more
exactly the doctrine of social equality and individual liberty
in the Federal Republic. [11] Methodists also found a kinship
with the civil government in their common interest in education for the elevation of the masses.   Indeed, it was affirmed
that "the course of our manifest destiny" would lie "in this
popular education, popular refinement and enrichment, " shared
by both Church and state. [12]

The cords of kinship between the Republic and Methodism were found in a common universality. Just as the nation encompassed the whole of the continent, so Methodism through its itinerant system of ministerial labor and connectional system of Church policy spanned the country and adapted itself to the wants of a new and growing nation. [13] Admitting that "the older churches had local strength, " J. T. Crane declared that they had not been as influential in "forming the character and determining the place of this nation in history" as had the Methodist Churches. [14] Why? Because unlike the Methodists, "they lacked the instrumentalities whereby the gospel could be made to keep pace with the advancing lines of settlement and the spread of the population. "[15]

Methodists did not forget that their denomination and the United States both shared a common birth across the seas. Born of mother England and nurtured mutually in the cradle of independence, they were united in origin and destiny. It was acknowledged that the Episcopal Church came from England, but that was different. Episcopalians didn't seem like good Americans. A Methodist expressed it thus: "More than any other, that Church 'hath a foreign air. '"[16] In contrast, he said, "More nearly than any other, the Methodist Church is representative of nineteenth-century American religion. "[17] Unlike the Episcopalians who were thought of as simply transplants, Methodists saw themselves as scions from English stock "grafted into the native tree of our own American society. "[18] "American Methodism, like the American nation," wrote Curry, "was from a foreign source, " but like the nation "it developed an individuality of its own; and as such it grew up and spread itself abroad over the land. "[19] Affectionate as American Methodism was toward its English heritage, prouder still were they of the uniquely American character marking their life and style.

By virtue of this close sense of historical destiny between the new nation and the new Church, Methodists became self-appointed chaplains to the country. As such, "What could be more befitting, " remarked one Methodist, "than the erection of [a] ... living memorial in the capital of our country. "[20] This large cathedral of Methodism was to be a monument representing the great work accomplished by the Methodist Church, and signifying its special contribution to the nation. The writer did not fail to mention that Chief Justice Chase and General Grant were among the trustees and that they greatly favored the project. [21] The Metropolitan Methodist Church of Washington, D. C. stands today as an outward sign of the nineteenth-century consciousness of at-one-ness with the nation.

Patriotism and loyalty were the characteristic expressions of this belief in common origins and purposes with the nation. During the war clergymen besieged the "Throne of God" in behalf of the government and the cause of liberty; American flags were draped over pulpits; ministers took an active part in encouraging enlistments and sometimes, according to Sweet, the minister and recruiting officer stood behind the altar,

> while the preacher urged the young men to come forward and place their names upon the roll; and in not a few cases the first name on the list was the minister's. [22]

A writer for the Western Christian Advocate, commenting on the character of the Central Ohio Conference which was then in session, said:

> In this body of a hundred and twenty ministers of the Gospel, there is not one who is not an earnest, outspoken Union man. Love of country is part of our religion, and manifests itself in every sermon, in every prayer, and even in our business. [23]

Methodists came out of the war years believing that their denomination had played a sublime part in crushing rebellion and destroying slavery. Thus, they felt it to be an essential part of their calling "to maintain heavy and loving loyalty to the United States."[24] Believing that such patriotism and loyalty was rooted in the historical precedent set by Asbury, Coke and company, they saw a providential continuity in the events of the Civil War years. Two quotes will suffice to sum up what lay behind the feeling that love of country was part of their religion. The Christian Advocate of New York was pleased to reprint this statement about the centenary of Methodism found in the New York Tribune:

> It was the first religious body to pledge its unswerving loyalty to the government after the attack on Fort Sumter. It was first to telegraph congratulations to the government on the surrender of Lee. In the cause of the nation it gave a hundred thousand men to war for the Union. The national flag has waved from its spires, and draped its pulpits, and the national struggle has kindled to the highest fervor the characteristic enthusiasm of the sect. [25]

The unrelieved encomium of Methodist patriotism and loyalty is illustrated again by this quotation from Abel Stevens:

> The national flag has waved from its spires and draped its pulpits, and its characteristic enthusiasm has been kindled to the highest fervor by the national struggle. Many of its preachers have followed the army as chaplains, others as officers, and others as privates. Thousands of Methodist martyrs for the Union sleep under the sod of southern battlefields. [26]

Stevens got to the heart of the matter when he expressed directly and succinctly the conclusion of his centenary volume on the history of American Methodism.

> In fine, Methodism, as the chief religious embodiment of the common people, has felt that its destiny is identical with that of the country.... [27]

The Methodist historian was by no means expressing a mere private opinion.

The notion of loyalty and pride in groups or countries was not new to the nineteenth-century Church. John Wesley was eminently loyal to the King; northern Lutherans in Europe were proud of their Swedish, Norwegian or Danish heritage; Medieval loyalties to a manor, a lord or province abounded. What is significant, however, about the kind of loyalty and patriotism expressed by Methodists in the 1860s in America is the shift to a concept of nationalism radically new in the history of the West. Methodists in particular and Americans in general were exhibiting a nationalistic fervor that was sweeping the Western world. It was part of a modern nationalism having origins in the rise of powerful national states occurring between the seventeenth and nineteenth centuries. This new concept comprised a

> fusion of intellectual, emotional and psychological components into that web of common culture, language, sentiments, aims, manners, and ideals called nationalism.... [28]

While American nationalism in the nineteenth century had much in common with the European experience, it cannot be understood in the same terms. The significance of an historical case study of The Methodist Episcopal Church around

the theme of "religious nationalism" is that such a study pro-
vides a focus for looking at what was uniquely American.
And that uniqueness may be construed in terms of the American religious heritage. To understand the inner dynamic of
this new consciousness of nationality, there is no better place
to look than here. The religious impulses toward a uniquely
American nationality were vividly illustrated by the many sug-
gestions and efforts to place explicit Christian symbols and
ceremonies into the national life. Some American Protestants wished to see the national flag modified so as to include
religious symbolism to be used on special national holidays
and in churches. The following is a case in point:

> The country needs, in fine, a religious form of the
> national flag for use on specially religious occa-
> sions or in specially religious places.... Of
> course the complete identity and nationality of the
> banner should be maintained--the colors, stripes
> and stars. But this could be, and yet a religious
> symbolism be its prominent signification. The stars
> are capable of an arrangement in the form of a cross
> or a Bible; the former seems the most befitting as
> the generally recognized emblem of Christianity. 29

The sense of a common history and an identity with
the character and destiny of the nation, of which patriotism
and loyalty were the chief expressions, gave Methodists a
powerful impetus to extend their brand of Christianity into the
whole of society. Without denying legal separation of Church
and State, they could, nevertheless, seek to give the nation
a religious form. The blending of loyalty to the denomination
and to the nation, and of religious and nationalistic impulses
represented another transformed version of the Puritan theocratic tradition. While the union of Church and State remained
invisible, the bond between Methodism and the nation appeared
to Methodists quite visible. With such a consciousness, the
rationale for the Church's right to influence politics became
possible.

The Nation as a Human Writ Large

The previous discussion of nationalism begs the question as to the meaning given to the idea of the nation. A
subsequent consideration of how Methodists viewed the mission
of the nation depends on the answer to that question. Methodists were constantly talking about "the sins of the nation,"

Daniel Denison Whedon (1808-1885), Editor of The Methodist Quarterly Review for twenty-eight years beginning in 1856. He wrote with erudition and ethical sensitivity on issues centering around slavery, war, reconstruction and racial justice.

"the nation under God," "the regeneration of the nation,"
"the character of the nation," and "the mission of the nation."
How was the concept of nation perceived as employed in such
phrases? Put simply, the nation was envisioned as a large
human being. The human metaphor literally abounded in the
colorful rhetoric of nineteenth-century divines. Perhaps the
best exposition of this understanding in the Methodist literature of the times is in an essay by Daniel Whedon, editor
of the Methodist Quarterly Review (1856-1884). The title of
the essay, "The Man-Republic," reveals the line of his
thought. Drawing on one of what he called the "very truth-
like hallucinations of that most splendid of all mono-maniacs,
Immanuel Swedenborg," Whedon expressed appreciation for
his image of the universe existing in "the human shape."[30]
Narrowing the figure to an analogy between the individual and
the nation, Whedon could propound the concept that "a nation
is a great organic personality." Therefore,

> ... the national person, like the individual person,
> has its character, its responsibility and its retri-
> bution. ...[31]

He regarded a nation as an organism with a life of its own,
a national character, a national spirit, a national mind, a
national will and a national destiny. Worth stressing here is
the Romantic emphasis on particularity, individuality, and
difference, as opposed to the Enlightenment's respect for
universalism, cosmopolitanism, and likeness.[32] Also worth
noting is the idea of "character" as the true meaning of
nationality. In the first and most important sense of the
term, nation meant a "way of life," not a region. Only in
a secondary sense would the term nation refer to a place.
When Whedon described the new "man-collective" or "man-
continent" he did not mention geographic boundaries, nor was
it assumed that every citizen of the country was an American. Rather, he drew a verbal portrait of a national
character comprising a national "INTELLECT," a national
"HEART," a national "WILL," and a national "SOUL."[33]
An American was not simply a person who gave allegiance
to the United States government and lived on the continent.
He was a particular kind of citizen whose manner and morals
corresponded with the American way represented by pictures
of the model Republic.

From the beginning the United States has been the
embodiment of our ideal. As Richard Hofstadter has aptly
put it, "It has been our fate as a nation, not to have ideolo-

gies but to be one. "[34]   Illustrating this assertion, a Methodist writer for the Zion's Herald discussed national purposes
with reference to the "American Idea. "[35]   What was the
American Way?   It was faithfulness to the "true American
Idea, which is the Christian Idea embodied in government. ... "[36]
Thus, the national character, as representative of the American Idea, embraced all the elements of national destiny. [37]

        Unless we understand the meaning attributed to the
idea of the nation as an organic human entity embodying the
Christian idea, we fail to appreciate how a Methodist Bishop
such as Matthew Simpson could extend the evangelical witness
of the gospel from a narrow individualistic concern to include
the character and destiny of the nation.   James Kirby quite
rightly rejected Robert Clark's conclusion that Simpson had
turned from the evangelical message to "worshiping and
praising the things of mammon and state. "[38]   When Methodist Bishops and Elders spoke of the nation and its destiny
they did not think they had departed from the evangelical
message of the Church.   Because nations, as individuals, are
called into being by divine providence, nations, as organic
collectivities, are objects of divine judgment and regeneration.
Methodists were out to save souls, but nations too had souls.
The logical implication of such a view resulted in an aggressive mission to form the soul of America and to save and fit
it for immortal destiny. [39]   Further, as the minds of men
had to be formed by Christian ideas, so the public mind and
its formation became part of the Church's responsibility.
Whedon noted sarcastically that politicians talked of "manu-
facturing public opinion. "[40]   That was small business compared to the momentous business of the Church, which was
the "creation of a public mind. "[41]   It was this concern that
sent Methodism out over the country establishing schools and
colleges, and motivated the Methodist press to presume to
instruct the "powers that be" on national goals and policy.

        Again, as the human heart was an object of God's
cleansing activity, so the national heart, that "organic bundle
of sensibilities and appetites, natural and moral ... within
which destiny is enveloped, "[42] had to be cleansed of barbarism, crime, intemperance and all forms of injustice. [43]
With this doctrine of the nation, Methodists could define the
evangelical task in concrete social and political terms.   It
was this theoretical ground that lay back of appeals for political equality.   "... [T]he true American Idea, which is
the Christian Idea embodied in government, " wrote an editor,
"is annihilation of all caste before the law. "[44]

As of the individual, the nation has a will. Whedon stated that the executor and controller of the corporate mind and heart is the national will embodied in "governmental power." The sensibility and the sense of the nation is represented and executed by the power of the "SWORD" ordained of God. And beyond the power of the magistracy "to wield the sword of self-preservation and justice," he stated that,

> a nation and a government are bound, as an individual, by the laws of God. [45]

Whedon's own conclusion can serve as a summary of this discussion:

> In our model MAN-REPUBLIC, finally, we have seen, that the INTELLECT should be stored with all the treasures of knowledge, trained to the liveliest activity of thought, and quickened to the highest point of self-consciousness; of the HEART, the natural sensibilities should be exorcised from their great organic evils, and the moral animated by a holy religion; while the governmental WILL, firm and energetic, the true representative and executive of the entire soul, its destiny in the pathway of holy right and noble enterprise. Condense and enshrine this soul in the individual, within a manly and majestic form, and where in human history will you find the embodiment of the picture I have drawn, save in him--our nation's model, as well as our nation's founder--WASHINGTON?

The foregoing articulation of the nation as an organic unit with a life, character and destiny dependent upon God, in addition to the conviction that America was a Christian Idea incarnate, represented the common mind of northern Methodism around the time of the sectional conflict. Whedon's position may be taken as typical. This being true, then the relevance of Christianity to social and political life was believed by Methodists to be clear and direct. Christianity, they believed, had a duty to pervade every department of life, private or public. Politics became the business of the Church. The Methodist pulpit asserted over and over again its right to instruct the civil authorities as well as the gathered believers. The Church that proclaimed America a Christian nation assumed direct responsibility for its welfare and destiny. Sometimes the social task was expressed in terms of indirect influence; sometimes it meant

direct action, but always and uniformly Methodists held that
the Church was to the nation what the conscience was to the
man--"its moral monitor and guide. "[46] This could mean
that the true mission of the Church was to "overrule even
the 'politics' of the country with ... the laws of eternal truth
and justice. "[47] Or, it could mean constantly reminding the
politicians and statesmen that there was a higher majesty
over the nation to whom they were responsible. Whedon said
that the man who would say religion has nothing to do with
politics or advise the pulpit not to meddle in politics would
in effect be saying to the omniscient eye, "Be shut. "[48] The
presence of the corporate body of northern Methodists was
a visible sign to the government that the omniscient eye was
not closed.

By proclaiming the nation to be Christian, Abel Stevens
could dismiss the question, "Whether or not the Republic is
organically a Christian government?"[49] The nation, not the
government, was Christian. With such a view, Stevens ob-
jected to efforts to adopt an amendment to the Constitution
formally recognizing Christianity. That course of action
would mean an abrogation of the 'voluntary principle' which
was vitally important to Methodists, and, at the same time,
erode reliance on the unwritten law that Christianity was indeed the undergirding, dominant fact of the Republic. [50] Why
have a Constitutional amendment when the Churches bore constant witness to American Christianity? Legal separation and
the voluntary principle had been affirmed, but the theme of
the Christian nation had not been surrendered. Methodist
views on the mission of America can be understood only if
seen in the context of this intense religious nationalism--
and theoretical conception of nationhood.

The Mission of America

It had been the Civil War that engendered a dynamic
nationalistic fervor among northern Methodists as well as the
renewed belief that the nation, cleansed from the blight of
slavery, was truly a Christian country. The fusion of nationalism with Christianity that occurred resulted in the persuasion that the United States had been called to be the chief
agency of world-wide redemption and that Methodism, along
with the other Protestant Churches, would play a crucial role
in accomplishing this goal. The theological and ideological
frame out of which this civil religion was expressed sets the
Methodist belief in national destiny, during the reconstruction
period, apart from usual meanings of Manifest Destiny.

The Puritan vision of a "city upon a hill" as a light
to all the nations had been described in religio-nationalistic
terms, but it was not the secularized version of the Puritan
dream associated with Protestants in a later period. It
would be a mistake to think that Haven, Curry, Stevens,
Whedon, Eddy, Simpson, the Peck brothers, including other
northern Methodists in leadership positions after the war, had
imperialistic interests in mind when they spoke of the mission of America. [51]   Kenneth Mackenzie has documented very
ably how Methodists came to incorporate American imperialism into their belief in America as a chosen people, but important to note is that this thesis described the period following 1876, with special emphasis on the late 1880s and
the 1890s when major changes occurred in the nation as a
whole. While there were traces of the doctrine of Anglo-
Saxon superiority in the preachments of northern Methodists
after the war, the gospel of America as a redeemer nation
is not to be identified with the gospel of Josiah Strong two
decades later.

When the potent phrase Manifest Destiny was first
coined by John L. Sullivan in 1844, it had obvious and direct
reference to expansionism. But Frederick Merk has convincingly shown that the program of Manifest Destiny was
never consummated. With the acquisition of California, con-
tinentalist enthusiasm died off in the nation and the enterprise
to expand the bounds from the frozen north to the torrid south
remained uncompleted. [52] According to Merk, the public evidenced little interest in expansion and acquisition of provinces
outside the continental limits from 1848 to the 1880s. Certainly this was true of the period after the Civil War. Seward, for instance, persistently sought insular positions or
outposts of American defense in the years 1865-68 while he
faced massive public indifference to his campaigns. The annexation of Alaska could be taken as proof of Seward's liking
for territory, but the phrase "Seward's Folly" hardly indicates a public enthusiasm for Manifest Destiny. Speaking of
the Seward era, Merk wrote:

> Certainly the era was a continuous demonstration
> of a temper in the American public the opposite of
> expansionism. [53]

The point is worthy of emphasis in order to make distinctions between the national destiny theme as formulated in the
1860s and the way it was expressed in an earlier and later
period. Apart from this distinction, the Methodist notions

of the national vocation cannot be rightly understood. This recognition is especially important with regard to race.

Ralph Gabriel has pointed out that attending the belief in America's grand mission was an emphasis "upon the God-given superiority of the American Anglo-Saxon. "[54] Merk underscores this fact but adds precision to its meaning when he writes that in the 1890s with the revival of agitation for expansion came a "revival of racism in the United States. "[55] "As in the 1840s, " he declares, "expansionism synchronized with racism. "[56] This is not to suggest that a conviction of ethnic and racial superiority was absent from the cultural ethos in the transition period. It is to suggest that Protestant clergymen in the North, coming out of the anti-slavery struggle and the Civil War to face the task of Reconstruction, are found to have been more immune from the form of racism inherent in the more virulent doctrines of Manifest Destiny. [57] Particularly was this true for northern Methodists. Moreover, when ethnocentrism was injected into their rhetoric, more often than not it had reference to the Irish Catholics, the southern Europeans and the Asians than to Afro-Americans. What then was the Methodist belief in the destiny and mission of America after Appomatox? The inquiry may now turn to this question.

Having argued that Methodist belief in Manifest Destiny during the Johnson and Grant era is not to be equated with the more obviously secularistic phases of American nationalistic fervor, it is the contention of this study that belief in the redemptive mission of America on the part of Methodists in the northern states was fundamentally religious. To put it negatively, the notion that Manifest Destiny was a "nationalistic theology" serving as a religious justification for imperialistic and racist designs and practices flies in the face of overwhelming evidence to the contrary. [58] Also rejected is the idea that Methodist enthusiasm for the mission of America represents a simple identification of revivalistic Protestantism with American culture. [59] What has been neglected in many studies of this subject is the central place of the doctrine of the Providence of God; the inner directed sense of the Church as Mission-sent, and the element of millennial mission--a basically religious vision of divine purpose for both Church and Nation. On the latter point, it should be acknowledged that it is a commonplace to suggest that the notions of a grandiose American destiny resemble Hebraic images of God's chosen people and appear like those of apocalyptic prophecy. What has not been fully realized is that they are literally apocalyptic. [60]

Admittedly, the doctrine of Providence was bereft of some of the mystery and transcendence of Biblical faith, and the apocalypticism was expressed as a realized eschatology. But the assertion pertaining to the fundamental religious orientation of the millennial belief still stands. The secular dimension of this belief can be accounted for in a variety of ways. Ideologically understood, the pervasive nineteenth-century dogma of inevitable historical progress and the new historical thinking accounts not a little for a this-worldly view of the Kingdom of God. But the belief that the redemptive purposes of God would be manifested in a visible historical community has unique religious sources in seventeenth-century Puritanism. The combination of the secular and religious comprising Methodist views of America's role in history is illustrated here in a quotation from an article appearing in the Zion's Herald:

> The underlying philosophy of our government is millennial in its character: it is what shall be hereafter, it is that for which good men have prayed, of which philanthropists have dreamed, and in behalf of which the martyrs of many ages have toiled and died. Whatever may have been the practice of the nation, it still remains true, that constantly in our governmental institutions, the absolute brotherhood of man has been recognized.
> ....
> A nation thus constituted may properly be considered as chosen of Heaven to bear the ark of God in the grand procession of humanity toward the ultimate bounds of human progress. [61]

The scope of the task was nothing less than humanity itself. The nation was on a "millennial march"--to use one of Whedon's phrases. [62]

Results of the Civil War indicated to Methodists the divine mandate and the nature of the marching orders. In an 1876 Centennial sermon delivered before the New York East Conference, a Methodist cleric expressed a common view when he asserted that the American Republic not only established liberty for itself one hundred years ago, "but for all the world ten years ago, by the power of God." The work that remained,

> was that of making the kingdoms of this world the kingdom of our Lord and of his Christ. [63]

A nation tried by fire and triumphant in the establishment of liberty now faced a this-worldly, millennial destiny by which all nations would benefit. 64

      This view was perhaps no more imaginatively expressed than in an obscure little book, The American Republic and Human Liberty Foreshadowed in Scripture, by George S. Phillips. 65 The author was a Methodist preacher from Ohio and served as chaplain of the 49th Regiment of the Ohio Volunteer Infantry. It was during the pressing duties of camp life that he began to trace in his Bible prophetic indications of God's plan to raise up the American republic as a means of redeeming the world. His central thesis was that America was the restored nation of prophecy, a new Israel. After detailing exact parallels between the "Hebrew Commonwealth" and the "American Commonwealth" he asked:

> Who will question, in the light of all these facts,
> that the United States of Israel was a type of the
> United States of America? 66

An example of his biblical exposition may be seen in his treatment of Isaiah xxxiii, 21. "But there the glorious Lord will be unto us a place of broad rivers and streams...." "This, " he said, "cannot apply to Palestine with its single river and two or three small brooks. " The reader should have no trouble filling in the rest.

> The Mississippi River has fifty navigable tribu-
> taries, saying nothing of the other great rivers in
> the land, This is literally a country of 'broad
> rivers and streams. '67

Such theological vulgarity ought not be cause to dismiss the book as an aberrant stream of thought in the 1860s. While it lacks the sophistication of essays by Daniel Curry and Daniel Whedon, the central theme of America as a redeemer nation is the same. Countless tracts, pamphlets and sermons treated the subject in much the same way. William Clebsch, who discussed Phillips' book at some length, could say,

> The patent unoriginality of Phillips' book signifies
> its representing a major body of religious and
> nationalistic sentiment in the north. Neither the
> threads of argument nor the cloth of conception
> belonged uniquely to the author. 68

Noteworthy about the book is that he could adduce argument upon argument from long quotations borrowed from a long list of statesmen and clergymen, from Jefferson and Adams to Bushnell and Lincoln, in order to establish his conclusion that:

> Surely a high destiny awaits the United States of America. That will be a glorious day for mankind, when free government shall prevail throughout the world ... when the 'earth shall be full of the glory of the Lord,' and the universal shout ascend the skies, 'Halleluia, the Lord God omnipotent reigneth!'[69]

It should be remembered that Methodist allusions to the biblical imagery of a chosen people were not new in the American tradition. Of the many places one could go to find this idea, there is no better place than to Philadelphia in the summer of 1776. On July 4th of that year the Continental Congress recognized the need of a seal for the new nation by commissioning Benjamin Franklin, John Adams and Thomas Jefferson "to bring in a device for a seal for the United States of America."[70] Franklin's design pictured Moses with hand held high, the Red Sea dividing, while Pharaoh in his chariot was being engulfed by the waters. Jefferson's design depicted the children of Israel in the wilderness, led by a cloud by day and a pillar of fire by night.[71] The final form of the seal adopted on June 20, 1782, which may be seen on a dollar bill, shows an unfinished pyramid on the reverse side of the seal over which is the eye of God. Arching over the eye is the motto, "Annuit Coeptis" and beneath the pyramid, "Novus Ordo Seclorum." It may be translated, "he has prospered our beginnings, a new order of the ages."[72]

It is not necessary to trace the theocratic tradition in American Protestantism to make the point that Methodist millennial ideas were not new.[73] What is important is that in the decade following the Civil War it was the revivalist churches with a conservative biblical theology which were sustaining and even reviving the theocratic ideal in very literal eschatological terms. This may be taken as one of the key reasons for the sense of social urgency that marked Methodists in contrast to the Congregationalists, who were forsaking the theocratic traditions of Emmons and Lyman Beecher. Gilbert Haven in New England--not Henry Ward Beecher--preserved the Puritan heritage of relating political

and social analysis to the judging and redeeming dimensions
of God. It was he more than the Princeton theologians who
placed political preaching, decision and action firmly in the
context of eschatology.

Haven's views on the right of ministers to dwell on
social and civil sins were constantly related to the immanent
millennial reign. [74] He denounced ministers who yielded to
the pressure of those who urged them to shun politics, saying that they were yielding to the antichrist who seeks to
thwart God's redemptive purposes. His robust denunciations
of color-caste were not infrequently proclaimed in the setting
of millennial hope. [75] The God of nations had called on
America to be the great light that

> The nations that have so long sat in darkness, and
> have now seen the great light, will come to that
> light, and kings to the brightness of its rising.
> Thus and then will wars cease to the end of the
> earth, the millennial glory rest upon the world-
> republic, and universal liberty, equality, and
> brotherhood bring universal peace. [76]

For Haven the "Millennium is a world of men, equal, brotherly, united, and holy. "[77] Though this millennial hope is suf-
fused with democratic ideology and requires courageous human
efforts, it is by no means a humanistic version of inevitable
progress. It was God's millennium. "He is pushing us forward to His, not our, Millennium, " he said. He was, to
Haven and similarly conservative Methodists, still the transcendent God who proposes and disposes as He will. He could
cause "our wrath or righteousness alike to praise and prosper
Him. " He could work "gradually ... by the operation of
laws ... or suddenly, and by the breaking up of the present
order and institutions. "[78] The call was to respond in repentance and active love.

This was not the concept of Manifest Destiny that
carried with it the necessity of extending America's physical
and political authority over the world. It was not the notion
of a Kingdom of God that could be readily and easily built
by good republicans and American Christians. And in spite
of grandiose dreams of world-wide redemption, the direct
application of the eschatological demand and hope was made
to the domestic scene. Exporting democratic principles became the luxury of a later generation. The belief in national
destiny with universal implications was of course strong, but
it was a manifest millennial destiny.

The nineteenth century has been thought of as the period of secularistic positivism and the triumph of natural science, "but," wrote Tuveson,

> it was also the last time in history when many responsible thinkers thought of human life and history as dominated or at least strongly affected by angels and demons. [79]

The secularism was mostly in the academies, and these were not the colleges that shaped the thought of Methodist clergymen who, in their frank supernaturalism, reflected quite accurately the mode of thought and belief of the vast majority of Americans.

If the millennial idea can be easily detected as the paramount dogma behind the American sense of mission as conceived by Methodist leaders of the northern states, the actual definition they gave to the national vocation is a more difficult task. A complex of ideas and a variety of beliefs may be comprehended in official and unofficial statements on the subject. Recognizing obvious overlapping of categories and differing emphasis placed on the definition of national purposes, it is possible to see three major definitions given to the mission of the United States. First, the United States was described as a laboratory for working out democratic principles, experimenting in human rights and proving that man could govern himself with freedom without violating order and justice. Second, the United States would be not only a laboratory but a model Republic actively beguiling other nations to follow its lead. The characteristics of the model were democratic and Christian. Witnessing for democratic principles and aiming for the moral renovation and Christian evangelization of the world comprised its chief purposes. Third, the United States was defined as a human-saving and human-making order. It would serve as an asylum for the weary and a melting pot for heterogeneous masses having the primary goal of creating the new man.

Each definition of mission is interrelated and interdependent. The first is exemplary, the second evangelical, the third priestly. All presupposed America as a Christian nation. [80]

The first part of the American mission, to be a laboratory in which the great experiment of democracy could be tested, had been a perpetual theme during the first century of the Republic. Lincoln, it will be recalled, noted that, "Our popular government has often been called an experiment. "[81] This nation, "conceived in liberty and dedicated to the proposition that all men are created equal, " was being tested on the battlefields of the war. The depth of the struggle for Lincoln was focused in the question, "whether that nation, or any nation so conceived and so dedicated, can long endure. "[82] It should be remembered that when Lincoln set forth the themes and meanings of the Civil War, he was not originating new ideas. It would be difficult to assess just how much he influenced the thinking of the churches, the chief bearers of the American dream, and how much the churches influenced him. Certainly, Lincoln had heard the ideas before. The notion that America was divinely called to be a peculiar experiment in human liberty and equality was part of the warp and woof of Northern Methodist thinking and action during and after the war.

Up to the fateful years of the early 1860s the success of the experiment was great enough to indicate a "noble destiny, " and make of America "the light of the world. "[83] The image of America as a light to the nation makes it clear that it was no private experiment. "When she shall have triumphed in the holy cause of freedom ... when she shall again come out of the struggle for independence ... then, " said one Methodist,

> will her light shine forth with such dazzling splendor, that tyranny shall be blinded and fall to rise no more, and her example be followed by all the nations of the earth. [84]

But while the final aim of America's mission was to lead other nations along the path to political, social and religious regeneration, some Methodists were cautionary in their appeals. The ideal had not been fully realized. The time, even after the war, was a time of testing. The problems had not been worked out. Thus, in the first instance, the mission of America was to test experimentally the unrealized ideals of the nation. The northern Methodist penetration into the South during the reconstruction period, and their efforts to "institute a new civilization" and "renovate" the southern social order, must be estimated in the broader context of their belief in the grand mission of America. The triumph of the North at Appomattox insured the preservation of the union but did not insure the viability of democratic principles. The noble experiment was at the heart of the

second phase of the war--Reconstruction--in the minds of
Methodists.   This experiment was at the center of efforts
to plant churches and schools across the nation in the interest of assimilating and elevating the masses.   Behind
every domestic missionary endeavor was the belief that,

> ... this continent was reserved, as it was, ...
> that the Almighty had here provided a new field
> upon which in the fullness of time there might be
> wrought out some of the grandest problems of hu-
> man life. [85]

In a discourse on "The American Nation" during the
national Centenary celebration of 1876, Daniel Curry spoke
of the mission of America in the tentative terms of risk and
experiment.

> Our position is a very simple one, and very grand;
> it may also be a very perilous one.   The experi-
> ment of a really free government is worthy of
> some risk in seeking for its realization. [86]

By 1876 Curry was sufficiently chastened.   It was the Christian Advocate of New York under the editorship of Curry that
promised vehemently an aggressive reconstruction policy for
the Methodist Episcopal Church.   And it was Curry, as much
as any northern Methodist, who came under bitter attack by
southern Churchmen.   In light of the continuing division between the sections of the nation and the failure of reconstruction policies, keenly felt by this robust New Yorker, he could
not be completely sanguine about the future.   Curry spoke
as though America was still working out her deep problems
and still had crucial decisions to make.   The legend, e
pluribus unum, had been set forth and the political unity of
the nation had been assured, "But, " asked Curry, "who were
'the people of the United States' in whose behalf this constitution had been formed?"[87]   Noting that there were "three
widely diverse races of men--Caucasians, or White man;
Africans, or Negroes; and native Indians, " he correctly
pointed out that "only the first of these were contemplated
by the framers of that instrument. "[88]   Curry could not talk
about American destiny without agonizing over this problem.
He said:

> We are now just past the threshold of the second
> century of our independent national career, and the
> unsolved problem of the right disposition of these

Daniel Curry (1809-1887), Editor of the New York Christian Advocate from 1864 to 1876. He was a vigorous proponent of radical Reconstruction.

alien, though native-born, races, still stares us
in the face. ... Till recently the Indian question
seemed likely to solve itself by their complete
extermination; but by reason of the civilization and
Christianization of large bodies of that people, even
that terrible mode of relief seems no longer prob-
able. Like Japhet, dwelling in the tents of Shem,
these 'dark Americans,' who antedate all others
in the land, seem destined to continue; and any adjustment of the 'American Nation' of the future must
consider them among its factors. [89]

The Negro question was much more urgent and an-
guishing for Curry. Recalling the time of his address--
1876--the following passage is remarkable in many ways.
From the vantage point of 1969, in the aftermath of the
second reconstruction, [90] this statement seems extraordinarily
perspicacious, realistic, and prophetic.

The negro race presents a still more difficult study
for our statesmen and social philosophers than the
Indians. They have been among us from a very
early date, not as semi-independent tribes, living
apart from us, but in our midst, and making a
part of our social and domestic life; and now they
are, numerically, a very considerable factor in
our population. ... From extreme barbarism of
their original estate they have advanced to a not
contemptible stage of culture; and in whatever the
Africo-American excels the wild savages of his
father-land, he is an American. This race, now
numbering about five million souls--nearly an eighth
part of the nation--all native-born, and with no
foreign memories or associations, are with us, to
stay, for they can not be either deported, or ex-
terminated; and since they seem to flourish in
spite of hard treatment, they are evidently destined to rise in the social scale. [91]

Seeing the Negro as an American with capacities for upward
movement in spite of hardships, and assessing the demo-
graphic facts of their presence, Curry saw the folly of "colonization" efforts and correctly anticipated the upward mobility of this minority group. The continuing presence of
Negroes and their gradual movement up the social scale,
made race the major unsolved social problem, in Curry's
estimate. He noted that many were asking the question,

"What shall we do with him?"--referring to the Negro. In complete candor Curry said it was a question "to which no satisfactory answer can be rendered. "[92] Curry then remarked, with uncommon prescience:

> But while we are asking and wondering and proposing impracticable schemes the colored man is laboring and praying and learning. By and by he will assert his rights. [93]

The destiny of the nation was problematic, though not without hope. The options facing America were fateful.

> A Republic that shall eclipse the dreams of Plato and more than realize the Utopia of Sir Thomas More, or a destructive social disorganization and anarchy are our alternatives. And we are not without hope for the issue. [94]

In a similar vein, Gilbert Haven wrote on "God's Purpose for America, " during the Centenary year of American Independence. [95] He set forth three qualifications in answering the question, "What is God's purpose for America?" First, he declared it was such as He intended for every nation and that it was foolish conceit to suppose "God has especial love for this bit of earth. "[96] The biblical truth still stands: "God is no respecter of persons. No more is he of lands or nations. "[97] Second, he thought it was folly to indulge in self-exaltation and claim special favor because of rich natural resources and a picturesque land. The soil, the broad rivers and majestic mountains were not to be despised, but Haven did remind his readers that in this regard other continents could make the same-- even greater--claims. [98] Third, he admonished his readers that God's purpose for America was not especially illustrated by the stock of people planted in America. He noted that much had been made of the superior quality of Pilgrim blood. Rejecting this feeble assertion, he said:

> It is not unworthy blood; but it has had the most trifling effect on New England itself. The Puritans were a much more powerful stock. ... They have driven their influence through all the land. [99]

But even this was not cause for exultation. "Our stock is simply and solely human, " wrote Haven. [100]

The great resource was not blood, nor was it race;

rather the fount of destinal possibilities was "Christ and Christianity."[101] In keeping with the theme of America as a new experiment in history, Haven said God's purpose in respect to America was "To give the human race a new territory to work out its destiny."[102] The final goal would be the achievement of a new and "perfect humanity in Christ."[103] In another context he specified the twofold requirement for accomplishing the national purpose:

> First. Universal toleration of religion, with the acknowledged supremacy of Christianity.
> Second. The universal equality and fraternity of man. [104]

The mission of America was to set an example for the nations of the world, that with Christ as the principle of unity, a common brotherhood could be achieved. With this as his definition of national vocation, it is not surprising that he directed almost exclusive attention to the question of caste in the social order, which he said, "now rules us with its rod and iron as tyrannically as it does the Brahmins of India...."[105]

Bishop Jesse T. Peck, in his giant book The Great Republic, propounded the thesis that here was

> a model nation, with the opportunity of working out, as an example to the nations, the problem of government by the people. [106]

But his nationalistic fervor was tempered by the facts. As with Curry and Haven, he admitted that liberty had been slow of growth, and that at the time of writing the question of suffrage in both the North and the South provided a critical testing ground for the grand experiment. [107]

The consequence of nationalistic fervor and a revived theocratic ideal beginning with the Civil War years and reaching a climax during the celebration of the national Centennial was a vital awareness of national vices. Proclamations of America as a country with a providential mission forced northern clergymen to give close attention to the public school question, the temperance question, corruption in city politics, among many other public issues that had a bearing on the destiny of the nation. More important than any issue, however, were the questions of social caste, civil rights and liberties. In spite of the failure to include the economic questions in their catalogue of national problems, northern Methodist leaders exhibited a high degree of social awareness. Indeed, when many northern abolitionists had turned their eyes from the race question after the Emancipation Proclamation, Methodist leaders were in their initial phase of concern for this perplexing question. In accounting for this social liberalism in the context of a conservative Christianity, many complex factors are involved, not the least of which, is the manifest destiny theme. The vision of America as a model Republic enabled them to break through the narrow confines of an individualist conservatism.

Methodists conceived of their nation as exemplary, or, as Bishop Simpson expressed it,

> ... by presenting to the world an illustration of the happiness of a free people with a free people, with a free church, in a free state, under laws of their own enactment, and under rulers of their own selection ... may the mission of America, under divine inspiration be one of affection, brotherhood and love for all our race. And may the coming centuries be filled with the glory of our Christian civilization. [108]

The concept of national destiny was taken to the altar and baptized. Democratic principles and evangelical faith merged in the belief that the mission of America was a great experiment in human rights and a model Christian Republic. If the experiment proved out, the United States would eventually allure the world to freedom and Christianity by the beauty of illustration.

The second aspect of national destiny, to witness for democratic principles and actively aim for the moral renovation and evangelization of the world, is inextricably related to the first, and as such has already been discussed. But distinctions can be made. In the first instance, the churchmen turned inward with emphasis on the nation as experimental, on the road to being a new model. The second portion was an emphasis on the evangelical task, the experiment being made for the sake of the world. The direction was outward.

Haven expressed what he believed as a "peculiarity of American feeling" when in the early period of the Civil War he said America was "fighting the battle for the world. "[109]

Another Methodist clergyman boldly declared that America was an "evangelist." His thesis was this:

> The August Ruler of all the nations designed the United States of America as the grand depository and evangelist of civil liberty and of a pure religious faith. And these two are one. [110]

It was for him and for many, "the grandest mission ever committed to any nation."[111] Bishop Simpson agreed that the mission of America was to "reconstruct society, and bring the world to the foot of the cross."[112] Another time Simpson said,

> God has given us a peculiar position before the nations of the earth.... Ours is almost a theological school for the world. [113]

Some northern Methodists, far less restrained than Curry and Haven about the destiny of the nation, anticipated a religiously motivated imperialistic role for the United States. After glorying in the natural richness, the acquired wealth and power, and superior social qualities of the nation, one writer said this:

> But we have seen that the American nation does in a most wonderful manner possess each and all of these qualifications, and hence it must be conceded that the benevolent plans of God look to the further enlargement of this nation in numbers, wealth, power and influence, in order that it may become the channel through which the infinite mercies of God shall flow to all the nations of the earth. [114]

Worthy of mention is the position of George Philips. Although his notions of an aggressive national mission are extreme, they do represent a minority opinion among northern Methodists. Philips, in a chapter titled, "The American Republic Destined to Become Universal," said the task of the United States was to destroy the monarchies of the world.[115] The destiny of the republic was "to rule all nations."[116]

> Here, then, it is declared that the Republic of the United States is to fill the earth; that is, it is so to occupy the place of government in the world, as to leave room for no other government. Under its

mild sway all nations shall be brought, and the nation's prophetic insignia of 'E Pluribus Unum' be fully realized. This view is not only in harmony with the Word of God, but with the desires and expectations of mankind. [117]

Simpson, while not as politically oriented as Philips, was no less modest about America's role when he said,

> ... how could the world do without us? The people of all nations look to us. If our country goes down, one-half of the world would raise a wail of woe, and sink lower. God ... cannot afford to lose the United States. [118]

The Bishop's confidence in the greatness of America was not shared by his colleague of the Episcopacy, Gilbert Haven, who looked out over the continent and saw impiety, insolent scorn of God, infidelity, worldliness and crime. [119] Nevertheless, he believed that God's plan could not be thwarted, "He will redeem us," said Haven, "the world's future shall not be blotted out with our destruction. "[120] He believed that America was a divinely appointed illustration and defender of democracy, but, with characteristic caution, he also suggested a more aggressive role; "we may be its divinely armed and appointed propagandists. "[121]

Methodists sensed that the United States was soon to take the lead in world affairs. Hence, it was not enough simply to set an example by building a model republic. America, placed strategically in history, endowed with wealth and population, "seems," said Bishop Thompson, "intended to be the great missionary nation. "[122] Professor Hillman said,

> ... our confident hope is, that as westward the course of civilization has taken its way around the world, so the seat of American civilization westward it shall again follow the sun, blessing all lands with its light of truth and its privileges of freedom. [123]

With such a projection of America's destiny it became extremely important that the American nation be thoroughly Christian, thoroughly democratic, and thoroughly civilized. Not only the destiny of the nation, but the future of the world depended on it. This was what was at stake in the question of slavery and the freedmen. When Methodists talked about Christianizing and civilizing the nation, not infrequently they had in mind concrete political change. The following passage appearing in the Western Christian Advocate is illustrative:

> It is God's will that every yoke shall be broken, and that the oppressed shall go free; and he who lifts his puny arm against the inexorable decree of Jehovah will be ground to powder, while the great work of civilization and christianization shall go on till the whole earth shall be full of the knowledge of the Lord.

> Let us thankfully recognize the good hand of our God upon us, humble ourselves in his sight, and be willing to fulfill the mission he has committed to us as a nation. Then shall we be a free, a united, a happy people. We believe the Lord has ordained it and will bring it to pass. [124]

The third part of Methodist belief in the mission of America, to be a human-saving and human-making order, was presupposed in the above two portions of the theme. To be a missionary nation for the cause of freedom, the United States certainly had to be a haven of rest for the weary and oppressed, and had to make over those schooled in European tyranny to conform to a nation of the free. It is a common and perennial theme in American history that this nation is an asylum from poverty and oppression. Inscribed on the Statue of Liberty is Emma Lazarus' poem:

> Give me your tired, your poor,
> Your huddled masses yearning to be free,
> The wretched refuse of your teeming shore.
> Send these, the homeless, tempest-tost, to me.

The destiny of America was tied up with its boundless wealth and resources to feed and clothe the poor. One writer said America not only could care for her own, but she could feed and clothe the world. [125] Bishop Simpson said,

> Here is a reform society, a society to care for the poor, for the drunkards and lunatics, for the disabled, for the aged. [126]

The humane services of the Sanitary and Christian Commis-

sions during the war indicated to George Peck that a Christian nation such as the United States was capable of acting
the part of the "Good Samaritan. "127

More than a refuge and an asylum, America was the
land of opportunity. Its Methodist missionary agents could
say to the foreign millions that would flood the shores,

> Here you may plant, and there not; here you may
> live, and here you may die, here you may be
> buried, and there not. 128

The role of the United States was contrasted with that of
England by this writer. "One hundred and fifteen men own
half of England, " he instructed, "and only one out of a
thousand of the population have any stake in the soil. "129
He continued:

> No wonder that to the poverty-stricken millions
> of Europe there has been the thrill of millennial
> music in the offer of a farm to any man who would
> till it. 130

Beyond this the destiny of the nation was to take the
heterogeneous populations and fuse them into a new humanity. 131   Haven put it directly:

> This, then, is God's Purpose for America, --to
> make this great continent the mother of a new
> race in Christ. We may fight it down, by en-
> slavement, by ostracism, by refusal to admit them
> to our shores. Nothing will avail. Who art thou
> to fight against God?132

The use of the term "American race" by so many Methodists actually pointed to what they believed was a new man
under the sun. The nation was a composite people made up
of "all the peoples, molded into one under the guidance of
the Puritan spirit. "133 The task of the Church and nation
was not merely assimilation. It was molding and making.

Methodists were emphatic in their belief that to reform humanity from every nation into one, two things were
of utmost importance, education and religion. One Methodist used this figure to express his conviction:

> We have in this country a great mill; the lower

stone of it is our common school system, the up-
per stone the Bible; we pour into the hopper the
heterogeneous immigrant from all lands and it
comes out an enlightened and Christianized Protestantism. [134]

Daniel Whedon wrote that in order to make manifest the destiny of the nation two things were required, a regeneration
of the heart and an enlightenment of the mind. For the first,
the Bible was required, for the second, education. [135]
George Peck said that the success of the nation would depend
on the "intellectual and moral elevation of the masses. "[136]
To redeem the nation and be a redeemer nation for the world,
the Church and the schoolhouse, religion and education, must
go hand-in-hand in forming the manner, morals and spirit of
the common people. In this great enterprise of creating a
new humanity, Methodists in the North viewed the vocation
of their denomination as identical with the national vocation.
The nation, conceived as a Christian Commonwealth, was
literally an order of redemption in the minds of most Protestants during the post Civil War period. In this sense, as
Gordon Harland has put it,

> The destiny of the nation and the mission of the
> Church had become one--to spread across the
> world the fruits of a Christian civilization shaped
> by evangelical Protestantism. [137]

As an experiment in democracy, the national purpose
was defined as exemplary; as a model republic raised up for
the redemption of the world, the national purpose was defined as evangelistic; as a haven, a school, an order of redemption where salvation of body, mind and spirit became
available, the purpose of the nation was defined as priestly.
These were the primary ingredients in the northern Methodist
conception of the Mission of America. These were the animating images of a Protestant piety that may aptly be called
civil religion. [138]

Historically, the post-Civil War years of dynamic religious nationalism may be seen as transition years. Protestantism as expressed and lived by northern Methodists was
evangelical, militant, and conservative Christianity. National
destiny was cast in apocalyptic terms and the message of
the Church still had a transcendent source and a prophetic
function. [139] In fact, it was because the mission of America
was taken with religious seriousness that Methodists could

and did bring judgment to bear on the nation and its ways.
It is a gross injustice to the facts to equate this period of
Manifest Destiny thinking with a later period when there was
an almost complete capitulation of the Church to imperialistic
interests and American culture. It is, however, consistent
with the facts to say the decades of the 1860s and 1870s
mark a telling and crucial phase in the accommodation of
the Church to the American way of life. This period is
more accurately identified as a prelude to imperialism and
a prelude to ideological and cultural amalgamation of Protestantism with Americanism.

There is a significant difference between the unity of
Church and nation and the commonality of their respective
mission in 1865, and the identity of Church and nation a century later. At the close of the Civil War an aggressive
Protestantism held sway in the syncretistic mingling of the
democratic faith and the Christian faith. The nation had a
grand mission, but basically her vocation was an agent of
God and a helpful instrument of the Church for the promotion
of Protestant Christianity. A century later, as Will Herberg
has so convincingly demonstrated, things were turned around.
In the twentieth century the fusion of religion with national
purpose meant an exploitation of religion. Where once the
nation was regarded as functional to the Church, now the
Church becomes a public utility. 140

Notes

1. Cushing Strout. The New Heavens and New Earth:
Political Religion in America. New York: Harper
and Row, 1975, p. x. See also Sidney E. Mead.
The Nation With the Soul of a Church. New York:
Harper and Row, 1975, chapter 2, for an interest-
ing assessment of the current discussion.

2. "Freedman and Freeman," Zion's Herald, XXXVII (January 3, 1866), p. 1.

3. A very good study in which distinctions between Manifest
Destiny themes as they were understood in the 1840s,
the 1890s and the period in between is contained in
Frederick Merk, Manifest Destiny and Mission in
American History. New York: Vintage Books, A
Division of Random House, 1966. See especially
chapters X, XI, and XII. Another very excellent

discussion is contained in Ralph Gabriel, The Course of American Democratic Thought. New York: The Ronald Press Co., 1956, chapter 26.

4. Abel Stevens. History of the Methodist Episcopal Church in the United States of America, Vol. L New York: Carlton & Porter, 1865, p. 28. Here Stevens noted that it had been said that, "Methodism thus seems to have been providentially designed more for the new world than for the old. The coincidence of its history with that of the United States does indeed seem providential; and, if such an assumption might have appeared presumptuous in its beginning, its historical results, as impressed on all the civil geography of the country and attested by the national statistics, now amply justify the opinion."

5. Journal of the General Conference, 1872, p. 388.

6. Journal of the General Conference, 1864, p. 240.

7. Moore, The Republic to Methodism, Dr., p. 90.

8. Ezra M. Wood. Methodism and the Centennial of American Independence. New York: Nelson & Phillips, 1876, p. 40.

9. Foster, Centenary Thoughts, p. 11. See also Curry, Platform Papers, p. 182.

10. S. D. Hillman, "The United States and Methodism," Methodist Quarterly Review, XLIX, (January 1867), p. 31.

11. Ibid., pp. 40-42.

12. Ibid., p. 43.

13. Jesse T. Peck. History of the Great Republic, p. 537. Peck quoted from a paper written by Rev. J. T. Crane.

14. Ibid.

15. Ibid.

16. Moore, The Republic to Methodism, Dr., p. 9.

17. Ibid.

18. Curry, Platform Papers, p. 183.

19. Ibid.

20. F. S. DeHass, "Metropolitan M. E. Church, Washington," Christian Advocate, XLI, (September 20, 1866), p. 298.

21. Ibid.

22. Sweet, Methodism in American History, pp. 284-85.

23. "Central Ohio Conference," Western Christian Advocate, XXXI, (October 3, 1864), p. 313.

24. "The Sham Baltimore Conference," The Methodist, VII, (February 10, 1866), p. 44. See also "The Bishops Address," General Conference Journal, --1864, p. 274.

25. "The N. Y. Tribune and the M. E. Church," Christian Advocate (New York), XLI, (January 4, 1866), p. 4. (n. d., n. p. on the New York Tribune article).

26. Stevens, Centenary of American Methodism, p. 210.

27. Ibid.

28. Russel B. Nye. This Almost Chosen People. Michigan State University Press, 1966, p. 44. This is a good collection of essays in the History of American Ideas with special relevance to this subject.

29. "Methodism--A Church," The Methodist, VI, (December 9, 1865), p. 338.

30. Whedon, Public Addresses, p. 65.

31. Ibid.

32. Nye, Almost Chosen People, p. 52. See his discussion of this subject.

33. Whedon, Public Addresses, p. 66.

34. Quoted in Hans Kohn, American Nationalism. New

York: Macmillan Co., 1957, p. 13. This remark
was picked up by Gordon Harland in his essay,
"American Protestantism: Its Genius and Its Problem," Drew Gateway, (Winter, 1964), p. 76. This
essay presents a lucid and insightful discussion of
what Harland calls the dominant theme of American
Protestantism, "the need to shape a Christian civilization."

35. "Freedman and the Freeman," Zion's Herald, XXXVII,
      p. 1.

36. Ibid.

37. Ibid.

38. Kirby, "The Ecclesiastical and Social Thought of
      Matthew Simpson," pp. 279-80; Clark, The Life of
      Matthew Simpson, p. 433.

39. Whedon, Public Addresses, pp. 66, 67.

40. Ibid., p. 65.

41. Ibid.

42. Ibid., p. 74.

43. Ibid., pp. 74-82.

44. "Freedman and the Freeman," Zion's Herald, XXXVII,
      p. 1.

45. Whedon, Public Addresses, pp. 82, 83, 84.

46. "The New York East Conference and the Southern Gen-
      eral Conference," Methodist Quarterly Review,
      XLVIII, (July 1866), p. 456.

47. Ibid.

48. Whedon, Public Addresses, p. 80.

49. Abel Stevens, "The National Christianity," Western
      Christian Advocate, XXXVII, (July 6, 1870), from
      "Clippings" by Abel Stevens, Drew University Li-
      brary.

50. Ibid. In this connection, it should be mentioned that Methodists frequently made reference to the fact that higher law was recognized as an important aspect of jurisprudence and that Christianity was a part of common law. For an example see, "Our Land and Its Religion, " Northwestern Christian Advocate, XV, (December 11, 1867), p. 396.

51. Of course there was a strong conviction that the United States would eventually lead the nations of the world and that democracy and Christianity would finally win out over aristocracy and paganism. In this sense it could be said there were imperialistic visions, yet Simpson's vision of a day when "every land shall be Christian" and Haven's belief that "to save this land to universal liberty and universal brotherhood, supported by universal law and sanctified by universal piety, is to save all lands, "--both are more pietistic and millennial than imperialistic. The completion of Simpson's quote will further illustrate. "Some of you will live until there shall be missionary centers in every land; some of you may live till the brightness of millennial glory shall sweep over this earth and make it but the threshold to the greater glory on high. " See "Bishop Simpson's Address, " Northwestern Christian Advocate, II, (November 6, 1861), p. 356; Haven, Sermons..., pp. 358-59.

52. Merk, Manifest Destiny, pp. 215-27.

53. Ibid., p. 230. See also, Scrapbook, Matthew Simpson Papers, Library of Congress, p. 13. Simpson was representative of a large majority of Americans when he said, "I am not anxious for annexation. It will come soon enough; it will come, not because we are anxious to gather other people in, but because they will be anxious to come to us. "

54. Gabriel, The Course of American Democratic Thought, p. 371.

55. Merk, Manifest Destiny, p. 237.

56. Ibid.

57. Russell Nye argues that "American nationalism was never

deeply rooted in race or place, " compared to European nationalism. While the statement has a degree
of validity it does ignore the importance of the
Anglo-Saxon model in shaping the cultural ethos and
does not account for the period between 1890 and
1920 which was a time of intense racial thinking.
Nye, The Almost Chosen People, p. 47.

58.　Albert K. Weinberg. Manifest Destiny. Chicago: Quad-
rangle Books, 1963, p. 17. See discussion of Weinberg's position in Earnest Lee Tuveson. Redeemer
Nation. Chicago: University of Chicago Press,
1968, pp. 91-92 and all of Chapter IV.

59.　Kirby, "The Ecclesiastical and Social Thought of Matthew Simpson, " p. 280.

60.　Tuveson, Redeemer Nation, p. 91.

61.　"The Plans of God in Regard to the American People, "
Zion's Herald, XXXVII (May 2, 1866), p. 69.

62.　Whedon, Public Addresses, p. 84.

63.　Henry Warren. Past Successes--Future Possibilities:
A Centennial Sermon. New York: Nelson & Phillips, 1876, p. 23.

64.　The following quote is given to show the close blending
of nationalism and religion in the context of the millennial idea: "Christianity and Republicanism--faith
and freedom--still go hand in hand, yielding each
other a mutual support--yet each the more firm for
standing by their own strength upon the moveless
platform of reason, truth and human good. Still on
and onward shall be their associate march. Advancing time shall deepen the intensity of their lustre,
establish the centralism of their power, and spread
the area of their triumph and dominion. Their
struggle is the moral battle of the world; and the
millennium of their reign shall be the joy of the
earth, and the salvation of the race. " In Whedon,
Public Addresses, pp. 58-9.

65.　Phillips, The American Republic in Prophecy. Cincinnati: Poe & Hitchcock, 1864.

66.　Ibid. , p. 52.

67. Ibid., p. 63.

68. William A. Clebsch. From Sacred to Profane America. New York: Harper & Row, 1968, pp. 191-92.

69. Phillips, American Republic..., p. 236.

70. Bernard J. Cigrand, "The Great Seal of the United States," Encyclopedia Americana, 1967, XIII, p. 362.

71. Ibid.

72. Ibid.

73. For good treatments of this theme see Gordon Harland, "American Protestantism: Its Genius and Its Problem," Drew Gateway, Winter, 1964, pp. 71-82, and James Fulton Maclear, "The True American Union of Church and State: The Reconstruction of the Theocratic Tradition," Church History, Vol. 29, 1959, pp. 41-62.

74. Haven, Sermons..., pp. 330-40.

75. Ibid., pp. 340-41, 361-71.

76. Ibid., p. 472.

77. Ibid., p. 384.

78. Ibid.

79. Tuveson, Redeemer Nation, p. 205.

80. This categorization is similar to the one Russell B. Nye employs to represent American national purpose as defined over three hundred years. With some variation in emphasis, especially with respect to evangelical Christianity, his threefold scheme holds true for the brief slice of history represented in this study.

81. Richard Hofstadter, ed. Great Issues in American History: A Documentary Record. Vol. I, 1765-1865. New York: Vintage Books, Random House, 1958, p. 405.

82. Ibid.

83. "True Americanism: or, Our Duties to Our Government," Zion's Herald, XXXV, (May 11, 1864), p. 73.

84. Ibid.

85. "The Plan of God in Regard to the American People," Zion's Herald, XXXVII, p. 69.

86. Curry, Platform Papers, p. 128.

87. Ibid., p. 124.

88. Ibid.

89. Ibid., pp. 125-26.

90. C. Vann Woodward has used the terms "second Reconstruction" with reference to the civil rights movement in the 1950s and early 1960s. See, "Seeds of Failure in Radical Race Policy," Proceedings of the American Philosophical Society, Vol. 110, No. 1, (February 18, 1966), p. 9.

91. Curry, Platform Papers, p. 126.

92. Ibid.

93. Ibid.

94. Ibid., p. 129.

95. Gilbert Haven, "God's Purpose for America," Ladies Home Repository (December, 1876), pp. 522-33.

96. Ibid., p. 522.

97. Ibid.

98. Ibid., pp. 523-24.

99. Ibid., p. 524.

100. Ibid., p. 525. Similarly, Bishop Peck said that in America men cease to be "Anglo-Saxon, Teutonic,

Slavonic, or Celt ... and ... become ... simply and only Americans. " Jesse T. Peck, The Great Republic, p. 342.

101. Haven, "God's Purpose for America, " p. 525.

102. Ibid.

103. Ibid.

104. Haven, Sermons..., p. 321.

105. Ibid. , p. 349.

106. Jesse T. Peck, The Great Republic, p. 354.

107. Ibid. , pp. 687-90.

108. Scrapbook (Newspaper Clipping), 1875. Matthew Simpson Papers, Library of Congress, pb. Cited by Kirby, "The Ecclesiastical and Social Thought of Matthew Simpson, " p. 298.

109. Haven, Sermons..., p. 303.

110. Cyrus D. Foss, "The Mission of Our Country, " Christian Advocate (New York), LI, (July 6, 1876), p. 210.

111. Ibid.

112. Matthew Simpson, "Speech at Boston Centenary Festival, Zion's Herald, XXXVII, (June 20, 1866), p. 97.

113. "Indiana Conference, " The Methodist, II, (October 12, 1861), p. 313. Cited by Kirby, p. 296.

114. "The Plan of God in Regard to the American People, " Zion's Herald, XXXVII, p. 69.

115. George S. Philips, The American Republic in Prophecy, p. 231.

116. Ibid.

117. Ibid. , p. 232.

118. "Indiana Conference, " The Methodist, II, p. 313.

119. Haven, Sermons..., p. 438.

120. Ibid.

121. Ibid., p. 471.

122. Kenneth M. MacKenzie, The Robe and the Sword, p. 13.

123. Prof. S. D. Hillman, "The United States and Methodism," Methodist Quarterly Review, XLIX, (January 1867), p. 49.

124. "The Situation Yet Again," Western Christian Advocate, XXXI, (March 22, 1864), p. 92.

125. "Position and Prospects of the American Union," Methodist Quarterly Review, LVI, (1874), p. 49, 59.

126. George R. Crooks, ed. Sermons by Bishop Matthew Simpson. New York: Harper & Brothers, 1885, p. 8.

127. George Peck, Our Country Its Trial and Triumph, pp. 256-300.

128. Cyrus D. Foss, "The Mission of Our Country," Christian Advocate (New York), LI, (July 6, 1876), p. 210.

129. Ibid.

130. Ibid.

131. Hillman, "The United States and Methodism," Methodist Quarterly Review, XLIX, p. 29.

132. Haven, "God's Purpose for America," Ladies Home Repository, XXXVI, (December 1876), p. 529.

133. Cyrus D. Foss, "The Mission of Our Country," Christian Advocate (New York), LI, p. 210. The belief that a new man was being created was reiterated often in Methodist literature. Another good example of the way this was expressed is seen in the following statement. "Thus forming, moulding, assimilating all to itself, the Great Republic of America goes on with the process of constructing a race of

its own, strangely and even miraculously adjusted to its providential purposes, and the accomplishment of its grand mission among the governments of the earth. " See the section, "The American Race, " in Jesse T. Peck, The Great Republic, pp. 342-46.

134. Cyrus D. Foss, "The Mission of Our Country, " Christian Advocate (New York), LI, p. 210.

135. Whedon, Public Addresses, p. 77.

136. George Peck, Our Country: Its Trial and Its Triumph, p. 38.

137. Gordon Harland, "American Protestantism: Its Genius and Its Problem, " Drew Gateway, Winter 1964, p. 76.

138. Russell Richey and Donald Jones, American Civil Religion, p. 17.

139. This has not always been seen by interpreters of religion in America. For instance, Sidney Mead suggests that an ideological amalgamation had taken place between the religion of democracy and the religion of Christianity resulting in Protestantism's acceptance of the church-state status quo. See Sydney Mead. The Lively Experiment. New York: Harper & Row, 1963, chapter VIII (see pp. 134-35).

140. Herberg, Protestant Catholic Jew, p. 264f.

PART III

CHRISTIANITY AND SOCIETY

CHAPTER 7

NORTHERN METHODISM AND THE SOCIAL ORDER

Social Responsibility

Throughout the Civil War and the decade following, Methodist spokesmen of the North had not been aloof to the vexatious and urgent social questions that faced the nation and the Church. The preceding chapters have been devoted to an assessment of external and internal factors that could provide a basis for making intelligible both the social action and the social teaching of the Methodist Episcopal Church during this period. This large and influential denomination found itself intimately woven into the social fabric of the nation and with considerable influence in public affairs. This fact alone made it difficult for Methodists to divorce themselves from social and political matters. Thus, they were not innocent bystanders during the sectional struggle. On the contrary, Methodist leaders exercised their right to speak to the two fundamental issues involved in the war--the meaning of the nation and the question of slavery--as well as to other related social issues.

Heady with denominational success and public prominence, they were further energized to assume social responsibility by firm acceptance of a philosophy of history rooted in the doctrine of Providence. Where the doctrine of Providence led to a social quietism in the first half of the nineteenth century, it became a source of social activism in the post-bellum period. Protestant Christianity and American democracy, they believed, were the providentially chosen agents for evangelizing and civilizing the world. To sum it up briefly, a sense of social responsibility was prompted by a strong conviction of being mission-sent into the world; a logical outgrowth of a fervent religious nationalism; and a felt requirement of a providential Lord who was judging, renewing and calling them to obedience. This, then, represented the broad but basic rationale for an aggressive social mission.

The problem of presenting and interpreting the social philosophy operative here is at once simple and complex. For instance, it is a simple but true fact that Methodists loved their country. To know this is to understand that patriotism, and sometimes frenzied chauvinism, was a powerful motivation for accepting responsibility for the whole of national life as they saw it. But penetrating what appears on the surface to be patriotic fervor, it may be seen that at the deeper level is a millennial hope containing a religious imperative. It becomes a complex task to assess the causal nexus of nationalistic consciousness and a religious eschatological expectation. In the same vein, the observation that the Methodist Episcopal Church was a large, self-aggrandizing denomination is a simple truism that becomes an important factor in understanding Methodist involvement in politics and aggressive policies in the South during Reconstruction. But to see the interrelationships between denominational self-interest, evangelical zeal, humanitarian impulses and democratic principles would be to preclude all oversimplified judgments concerning the motives of Northern Methodists in attempting to explain their political and social activity.

Again, it is a simple commonplace that Protestants were on quest for a Christian America. This obviously accounts for the energetic and programmatic activism so characteristic of the evangelical churches. But when Methodists talked about permeating society with Christianity, it becomes a complex matter to discern when the moral and religious categories shift to social and political considerations. The opposite is equally problematic because there are times when the rhetoric seems to point in the direction of social and political approaches, when in fact the meaning is moral and religious. An added problem in ferreting out the social thought of Northern Methodists is that they had no formal, systematic understanding of what the proper role of Christianity was to society. However, while the existence of an explicit social philosophy may not be assumed, it can, nevertheless, be surmised that these churchmen at this particular time were being forced to clarify the relation between faith and the social order.

Because they had been rebuked for meddling in politics by their own laymen, the southern Methodists, and politicians--primarily in the Democratic party--northern Methodist clergy were being impelled to justify their ways. There is also available for study a vast literature on the relationship of Church and state as focused on the common school-Roman-

ist debate and the question of southern loyalty to the government. In a word, within the ranks of northern Methodism
there was a lively religious and political debate going on as
to the relevance of Christianity to social life. It is possible,
therefore, to glimpse an emerging social ethic.

How Methodists came to assume a sense of social responsibility and how they justified it are questions already
answered in part. But more needs to be said. On the practical level they had been imbued with a great sense of confidence as a result of venturing out into the political arena,
starting with the debates over the Fugitive Slave Bill and
through anti-slavery agitation to the end of the war. They
did not hesitate to assert that the Protestant Churches had
been "the strongholds of freedom, and the sources of power"
that not only turned back "the floods of treason" but "asserted
the inviolability of our nationality."[1] One Methodist unblush-
ingly surmised

> that the Protestant pulpit and press have been under
> God, the agency of the nation's deliverance. . . . [2]

On the theoretical level they had become convinced
that Christianity embraced the whole of life. In an essay on
politics and Christianity, Bostwick Hawley, a New York
clergyman, argued the right of Christianity to "enter and supervise the relations of social and civil life" on the grounds
that Christianity was

> . . . the genius of the world, which intermeddles
> with all knowledge, all truth, all facts, and which
> aims to bring all things into harmony with the best
> interests of mankind. [3]

Because politics was the business of establishing principles
of justice that Christianity proclaimed, Hawley thought it
necessary for the Church to go beyond "spiritual renovation"
and enter the political arena to make sure their principles
were properly established. He said,

> And though Christianity has no organic connection
> with civil government, it has a real and vital one,
> such as exists between religion and education, re-
> ligion and social life. And only when it shall have
> attained its greatest triumphs, not only in the
> spiritual renovation of the people, but in the es-
> tablishing of righteousness, truth, and freedom in
> all the earth, will its mission be complete. [4]

The unshakable conviction that Christianity comprehended the whole of life came to be the foundational affirmation that at once gave impetus to a broader social ministry and at the same time provided a convincing theoretical justification for social pioneering. [5] Essential to this notion that Christianity was the "genius of the world, " that it touched all of life, was the doctrine of divine law. It was variously called "higher law, " "the law of God, " "the moral laws of God. " The editor for the Western Christian Advocate reminded his readers that when they entered the region of politics they did "not pass beyond the domain of the law of God. "[6] Refusing to make radical distinctions between the sacred and the profane, he enjoined Methodists to heed the teaching of the Apostle.

> Whether we eat or drink, or whatsoever we do, we are bound to do all for the glory of our Divine Lord. Christian obligation binds us, not only on the Sabbath and in the sanctuary, but on the secular days of the week, and in the marts of trade, in society, and at the caucus and the ballot-box. We must not only pray religiously, we must buy, and sell and vote religiously. [7]

Similarly, Daniel Whedon contended that Almighty God was present to the civil order in terms of "divine law. " Consequently, it became the task of the Church to be the conscience of politicians who, he thought, would no doubt "be very glad to know that over their domains the divine law is suspended. "[8] Whedon, like most clergymen, was not at all sanguine about the capacity or the willingness of the political profession to relate the divine law to temporal affairs. Hence, it became the duty of the pulpit to firmly apply "the divine law to all crime, high and low, individual and governmental. "[9] In speaking to public questions the pulpit performed its proper teaching function and "served to complete the formation of the public conscience. "[10] He firmly believed that

> Christianity has a right to pervade every department of the life of responsible beings, private or public. [11]

Presupposed in such declarations was the belief that this was a Christian nation. For this reason Jesse T. Peck could say:

> Americans reason. As they pass from the house of God to the civil assembly of the citizens, they

> cannot in either place wholly forget what they hear
> in the other.... He who listened to the arguments
> of the Methodist ministry, and was convinced that
> God is no respecter of persons, and went thence
> to the popular meeting, and heard the great truths
> of the Declaration of Independence, felt that his re-
> ligious belief, and the American theory of civil
> government, rest on the same foundation of eternal
> truth. Thus Methodism has re-enforced the funda-
> mental principles of our Republic, and strengthened
> their hold upon the popular mind. [12]

What is operative here is a revised version of the
Christian Commonwealth idea fitted to the American experience. To be sure, the functions of Church and state were
discrete; the task of statesmen and clergymen were not held
to be identical. The overarching theological postulate that
precluded a sharp dualism between the temporal and spiritual
spheres was this belief in divine law above human law. "It
is the duty of the Church to enforce obedience to the civil
law," wrote a Methodist editor, "so it is to urge upon the
government obedience to the divine law."[13] This line of
thought was used many times over as a rational justification
for proclaiming the right of the Church to assume its proper
mission in the political and social order.

At the New York State Methodist Convention in 1871
several speakers called for a new understanding of the relations between Christianity and society. A Rev. W. H. Goodwin of the East Genesee Conference clamored against those
who would separate religion from the political sphere. Such
a one-sided view of Christianity, he thought, would lead to
a form of Christianity "with only an eye for the petty field
of ecclesiastical ambition," while at the same time "a sickly
asceticism grows eloquent in its denunciation of politics in
the Church."[14] He decried the dualistic view that implied
special purity for the Church that stayed out of political
matters. "The necessities of the times demand ... a clearer
definition of Christian duty."[15] Many speakers met Goodwin's challenge by invoking arguments based on divine law in
human life. But there were other warrants for social responsibility offered. The Rev. George Lansing asserted that
inasmuch as God's rule was over all of life and that man's
piety toward God was inherently tied up with duty to his fellow man, the relevance of Christianity to political life was
inescapable. He even took a biblical passage that could well
be used to defend a conservative quietism. Here is a brief
example of his exposition:

The man whose piety toward God cannot stand the
test of his duty toward man had better get a ro-
buster piety right away.   It [is] as much a divine
command that we 'render to Caesar the things that
are Caesar's' as 'to God the things that are God's. '
Nor does this duty to Caesar consist merely in
tame obedience.   It demands action as well as sub-
mission, intelligent, independent, manful action. 16

Another argument produced was based on a biblical
text frequently used for missionary sermons.   The editor
saw in the "great commission" a divine mandate for the pulpit to relate the Gospel to questions of the State.   In the
lines, "Go ye therefore and teach all nations, " and "teaching them to observe all things ... " he lifted up the word,
"all. "17   The command to "teach all nations" meant that the
scope of teaching encompassed the institutions and offices
that made up a nation.   In the second instance, he said ministers had no discretion as to the message, for the duty "is
prescribed and required, and embraces all that is taught in
the Word of God. "18   Against those who thought the aim of
preaching Christ was exclusively for personal salvation, he
had this to say:

> We have no right to limit ourselves merely to what
> is technically called the Cross.   We may so inter-
> pret Paul's determination to know only 'Jesus
> Christ and him crucified, ' as to make it the vilest
> heresy.   Christ is only preached when he is
> preached in all his relations and offices.   Christ
> is a Prophet and King as well as a Priest and
> Savior, and that would be a defective ministry
> which omitted his teachings and laws, however
> sweetly and constantly it presented the bare atone-
> ment. 19

The readers who had taken the vows of ordination no
doubt recalled the solemn injunction in their Discipline.
Paragraph 185 in the section under the title, "The Matter
and Manner of Preaching, " contains this advice:

> The most effectual way of preaching Christ is, to
> preach him in all his offices; and to declare his
> law, as well as his Gospel, both to believers and
> unbelievers. 20

Gilbert Haven's answer to the reiterated declaration

that the clergyman should stick to the business of preaching
"Christ and Him crucified" was put this way:

> What matters it [sic] that you gather round the flag
> if you desert the outposts? Wellington was de-
> fending London when campaigning in the Peninsula.
> So is it with the Gospel of the Cross. Christ
> crucified is the grand banner of the Church in its
> conflict with the world. It must be always and
> every-where defended. But to come and hug that
> flag-staff with apparent fondness, while the enemy
> is plowing the outer lines with diabolic artillery,
> is not affection--it is cowardice; and the officer
> who thus comports himself receives contempt, not
> commendation, from his Master. Take your flag
> with you, and rush thither. Smite down the foe in
> this remotest assault, and you preserve your army
> from more central peril. 21

In another instance, the dauntless New England moralist said
that if the pulpit did not preach against usury, "the besetting
sin of business communities"; did not denounce the "insane
passion for fiction"; did not talk against the "opera or
theater"; did not condemn the politician who "goes on establishing the State on injustice"; then, "Christ and Him Crucified" would not be preached. Instead the preacher would be
setting before the world, "the savorless salt of an exhausted
and tasteless Gospel. "22

> Even Matthew Simpson, who said many times, "I have
but one work to do: I must preach Christ and him crucified,"
could lecture the theological students at Yale on the duty of
the minister who

> should ever announce great principles which lie at
> the foundation of society--principles affecting the
> rights of man and the duties of government. 23

Simpson did not think that preachers should veer too far or
often from the great themes of salvation but he did allow
that there were public events that called for preaching on
social issues. The test was whether such issues touched
Christian morality. His advice to young ministers was to
spend most of their time reading the Bible and studying sound
theological works. The rest of the study time could be spent
in mastering subsidiary disciplines and keeping abreast of
the times. 24 In the interest of keeping up on current events,

he noted the importance of reading the daily press. He did, however, caution the students with this interesting bit of counsel:

> In keeping abreast of the day it is not best to spend
> too much time on the daily press or the lighter
> class of magazines. It is one of the triumphs of
> Christian civilization that we can have news at our
> breakfast table from all parts of the globe; but the
> daily press is not of itself an unmixed benefit--it
> tempts the student to dissipation of thought. ...
> Like a bee, he should know how in a few moments
> to extract the honey from the flower, and then fly
> on. ...   He should be like the business man who
> rapidly glances over the most important items, and
> then confines himself to the duties of his counting-
> room or office. 25

Though Simpson was utterly convinced that Christianity related to all of life, including institutions, his language was usually couched in moral-religious categories.   His justification for addressing social issues was based on belief in the universal- ity of divine law and a "high and pure morality, " of which the church was custodian. 26

Of all the arguments presented by Northern Methodists to sustain their case that the Church had a right to invade the social and political orders, the one most commonly given had to do with the moral dimension of practical questions. Ministers of the New York Annual Conference received a resolution which stated that they would allow none of their pulpits ever to become subservient to a political party, yet when wrong appeared they reserved the right to speak out.

> ... whether in the State or the Church, whether it
> be the immorality of violated civil rights, or of
> Divine moral rights, we would close no lips, re-
> strain no animadversions. ... 27

It is not at all surprising that churchmen, who thought of their denomination as the modern revival of Apostolic purity and morality, should speak out courageously on public issues where moral questions were involved.   The formula for de- ciding when to speak out on public issues was stated this way by Abel Stevens:

> it should make its voice heard on public questions

which are legitimate to its moral relations to the
commonwealth. 28

What were those public questions? The most obvious
and pressing questions in New York State in the 1870s, according to the Methodist clergymen, had to do with the com-
mon-school system and the Catholic question; the temperance
question; and political corruption in the cities. The moderate
Abel Stevens, always cautious about involvement in extra-
ecclesiastical matters, saw the dilemma. Each of these issues contained moral and political ingredients. Public morality was inescapably bound up with politics. Intensifying the
dilemma was the fact that Church involvement could "hardly
escape complications with political parties."29 Stevens urged
that such considerations should not deter his denomination
from entering the battle. In fact, he thought the possible
complications with partisan politics was all the more reason
to act quickly, "before it gets too deeply immersed in the
mire of party politics."30 At the heart of his position was
the common belief that the Church was the guardian of public
morals. But his plea was buttressed by citing historical
precedent.

> Methodism, and, at last, nearly the whole evan-
> gelical Christianity of the land, established a de-
> terminate precedent for such cases in the slavery
> contest and the consequent war. Lincoln applauded
> Methodism for its powerful intervention then, and
> its record, for that part of its history, will ever
> be one of the most luminous and exemplary chap-
> ters of its annals. 31

This is a point worth emphasis. It has already been
stated that the early debates of slavery, starting with the
Fugitive Slave issue in 1850 and Methodist involvement in
the Civil War, wrought a major shift in how northern Methodist leaders viewed moral questions. They did not fail to
see that public morality involved institutional and, therefore,
political considerations. The Methodist pulpit was released
for a wider social ministry. The historian Stevens, in a
review of Gilbert Haven's National Sermons, put it well:

> ... this volume is an illustration, and equally a
> model, of that freedom of the pulpit which arose
> with the antislavery struggle, and culminated with
> the war. That struggle not only emancipated our
> slaves, it emancipated our clergy. 32

Referring to the Colonial period, he averred that "The original American pulpit was free enough; it molded the social and even the political life of the colonies."[33] Then, after the Revolution the Church subsided into a "merely theologic attitude," which to Stevens represented a capitulation to a public opinion that would not admit to political preachments. But at last the spell broke and the pulpit spoke out, recalled Stevens, "and not till it thus bravely spoke did the national conscience act effectively against slavery."[34] The following lengthy quote is included as an example of how a moderate spokesman for northern Methodism agonized and reasoned about the Church's relations to the social order. It becomes all the more instructive when it is known that Abel Stevens frequently rebuked Gilbert Haven, Daniel Curry and others who he thought were too radical on certain issues.[35] Speaking of the role of the pulpit, he said:

> We admit the difficulty of defining precisely its function in such cases. We would not have it become a political organ; it should stand sacredly independent of party, yet a terror to partisan evil doers; and no public question involving Christian ethics should be allowed to evade its scrutiny and its verdict. That such freedom may be abused-- that it demands the greatest prudence and conscientiousness--we admit; but such remarks are commonplace truisms, as relevent to other positions as to that of the clergy. They are, or ought to be, our most considerate and cultivated men. Their office presupposes that they shall have the capacity and discretion to know their duty and how to do it, as well as the moral courage to do it. With the restraints of public opinion, not to say public prejudice, and their pecuniary dependence upon public support, they are far more liable to error on the side of reticence than on that of truculence. Having been emancipated, we hope they will now retain their liberty, and retain it by both their prudence and their courage.[36]

The ministers of Methodism in the North could no longer enjoy the luxury of simply relating the gospel to the need for personal conversion, upright living and denominational expansion. A lively dispute was taking place concerning the relations of the Christian to social life. Not only the opprobrium of social evil demanded a new understanding of Christian duty, but their own theology and faith commitment seemed to require it.

In sum, many different views on the social mission of the Church existed during the post-Civil War period. It would be hopeless to attempt a systematic analysis of all the different attitudes. The assumption that Christianity related to all of life; that God was ruler of all domains; that Christian piety meant duty to men as well as God; that Christ in all of his offices implied teaching "all things"; that the divine moral law was the basis of human law and life--all of this and more went into the stew of a developing social teaching. This tentative and ill-defined mix of views could in no way be described as a social theology or ethic. It was, rather, a confident and aggressive approach to applied Christianity. In seeking to apply Christianity, confrontation with the political order became unavoidable. It will further an understanding of northern Methodist social thought to view the response of ecclesiastics to the problem posed in such a confrontation.

Religion and Politics

Two questions will help to focus the discussion: 1) What was the immediate cause of the "religion-politics" dispute? 2) What was the definition of politics that required intervention into the political domain? At the close of this section some generalizations will be offered as to the significance of this subject for an understanding of the over-all social thought of northern Methodist clergymen.

Practical-minded Methodists, more concerned with the moral renovation of society and less with the fine points of theology or moral philosophy, had no theoretical rationale for a social mission in society as they faced absorbing and increasingly complex social issues. A line of demarcation between personal and social Christianity had seldom been made by Methodists. They knew they were out to save souls and permeate society with Christianity. Their emphasis on the latter and on the fruits of faith as expressed by the morally-upright life, by works of charity, and by good citizenship prepared them for a more self-conscious delineation of the two spheres and a more sharply defined social ministry.

Many different reasons have been offered in an attempt

to explain how these northern preachers, editors and bishops came to make distinctions between the personal and social spheres. But the most immediate, though by no means the most important, cause was the sharp attack on the Methodist Episcopal Church from several quarters. Methodist clerics were stung by charges that their denomination was a "political Church." Accusations to this effect came from politicians, the laity, southern Methodists, and sometimes from fellow clergy.

Politicians in the Democratic party were particularly hostile to the Methodist Episcopal Church for several reasons. "Our Church has been stigmatized as a political organization," exclaimed a contributor to the Northwestern Christian Advocate. [37] Why? The writer noted that the source of agitation could be traced to the fact that "our preachers and members have almost unanimously supported the Republican party," and also the fear among Germans that Methodists would take away the "beer-mug and meerschaum." [38] Commenting on the same issue at a later date, another writer for this journal justified the action of the Wisconsin Conference in pledging support for Republican candidates on grounds that the Democratic party opposed the moral platform of Methodists in their stand on "the absorbing political issues of the day." [39] The issues were Sunday laws, temperance and disloyalty.

New York Methodists bristled at charges by Roman Catholic politicians that they were meddling in politics. Far from denying it, speaker after speaker in the New York convention of Methodists in 1871 arose to defend the right of the Church to speak and act politically. The accusations had the affect of impelling the ministers to frame platforms on political involvement. Typical of the responses was a paper presented by the Rev. Alonzo Flack, President of Claverack College, who stated his purpose as a consideration of "the relations of Temperance to the Church, to society, and to politics." [40] He cited statistics and impressive documentation to show that there was a direct correlation between the "dram shop" and social problems, chief among which were political corruption, pauperism, and crime. The solution proposed was not just changing men's hearts. He declared the minister guilty if he "did not use every legal means to suppress that which corrupts men." [41] He did not shrink from the political implications of this.

Temperance has a political as well as a moral

aspect, and in a republic like ours we are under
religious obligations to advocate it politically as
well as morally. [42]

He fearlessly asserted that the Church in supporting temperance reform was dealing with the same kind of question
it faced in the anti-slavery struggle. His statement in this
regard is worth looking at:

It is the height of folly to talk of keeping this subject out of politics. It is already in politics. The
first and last questions every politician asks is,
'How will this move be looked upon by lager and
rum?' Pro-slavery men always cried out against
bringing the slavery question into politics, when it
was really the only political question. Politics is
the stronghold of rum. We must fight the enemy
in his intrenchment and drive him out. Politics
sustains the dramshop. Nothing but political action
will ever destroy it. Be not deceived. This political war is inevitable, and 'let it come. We repeat
it, sir, let it come. '[43]

The Zion's Herald adroitly turned the issue around on
the politicians who criticized the Church for meddling. When
politicians presume to prevent the Church from speaking on
questions of evil and attempt "to frame iniquity into a law
of the land, " they themselves are "pushing party creeds over
the bounds of their rightful empire, into the preacher's realm
of moral questions. "[44] The writer then gave fair warning
that the more the Methodist moral hero is embraced with the
title of "political preacher ... the more rabid he becomes
in politics. "[45]

Responding to supporters of the peace platform and
draft resisters who railed against the pulpit for enthusiastic
support of the war, and charging them with "political preaching, " George Peck argued that

To enforce obedience to the civil authorities is part
of the duty of the pulpit, whatever party politicians
may say. [46]

He admitted the governance of a line of propriety on the matter of clergymen entering politics, "yet, " he said, "there are
multitudes of so-called peace men who do not discern where
this line is. "[47] Illustrating how ludicrous his opponent's position was, he told this story:

A certain preacher not long since in a sermon
quoted the words of St. Paul, in the 13th of Romans,
'Let every soul be subject to the higher powers, '
etc. , when, before he had made a remark, one of
our sensitive souls took himself away with evident
indignation at hearing politics introduced into the
pulpit. With him the language of St. Paul was
downright abolitionism. [48]

If Western and Northern politicians incited northern
Methodists to develop a justification for political preaching
and acting, the Methodists of the South were equally successful in this regard. Among the charges laid against the
Methodist Episcopal Church by southern Methodists, the principal one was that the northern branch had become a "political body. "[49] Reacting to the oft-reiterated condemnation, a
northerner insisted on the legitimacy of the Church holding a
political position and engaging in political activity by adducing
three good reasons. The first was historical precedent. He
noted that "from the beginning our Church has occupied a
well defined political position. "[50] Referring to the article
on loyalty to the government, he said this "strictly political
article" is the most sacredly preserved of all. And on the
question of slavery, he averred that Methodists who did not
regard it as an evil were running against Methodist foundations. [51]

The second argument was an appeal to logic tinged
with some irony. Asserting that because most of the important points of morality were involved in political issues,
he judged it "impossible that Churches should not have some
political position. "[52] Alluding to their own tacit support of
slavery, loyalty to southern politicians and support of the
war, the writer made this point:

> Probably no religious body in the land has been
> more decidedly and intensely political, in the po-
> sitions and influence of its members and ministers,
> than the Southern Methodist Church, but, unhappily,
> all on the wrong side of a question of high moral-
> ity. [53]

Aside from the merits of the debate on slavery and the war,
the position of northern Methodists was commendable for the
lucidity with which they saw the inextricable relation of the
moral question to the political realities. To this writer it
was obvious that the Sabbath question was a political one; the

temperance question was a political one; and certainly the
slavery question was a political one. But, as political questions, they all, especially slavery, "have moral relations. "
For that reason, he concludes "the Church is bound by her
fidelity to speak out respecting it. "[54] Expanding this contention, the article turned to a third argument having to do
with faithfulness to the Bible. Nearly all of the duties enjoined in the decalogue and the injunction to follow the golden
rule, he thought, could involve the Church in politics if it
were to be true to scripture. [55] In another context a northern editor spoke of this matter by declaring that the Church
would find it impossible to enforce the golden rule "without
evolving Magna Chartas, and declarations of rights, and de-
crees of emancipation. "[56]

It is a fair inference from the foregoing discussion,
representing a mere sample of the many articles and statements produced by Methodist ecclesiastics in the North that
they did not retreat in the face of rebukes for their political
activity. Far from falling back on simple moral and religious
categories in making their case, they candidly admitted the
political ramifications of their moral battle and proceeded to
develop a rather convincing vindication of their policy.

To bring their underlying social philosophy into clearer
focus, it would be well to look briefly into certain northern
Methodist views of political science and ethics and inquire
into their operative definition of politics.

From the editorial chair of the New York Christian
Advocate came this classical understanding:

> Political science is a department of ethics, and all
> questions within its domain must be discussed and
> determined accordingly. [57]

As an aspect of ethics, politics was considered by the writer
as the science of "relating right and wrong" in the administration "of public affairs. " Thus, statecraft would involve
discerning "fundamental principles" and relating them to
"practical expedients, " being careful that "the latter should
always be made to accord with the former. " In a word, the
task of politics was the creation of justice.

Assuming that ethics was a department of religion,
the writer presumed to address the suffrage question as it
related to blacks. Of special interest in this judicious and

incisive article is the way the editor related moral principles
to practical considerations.

He started by making a distinction between natural and
conventional rights.

> Natural rights, (among which are usually enumer-
> ated 'life, liberty, and the pursuit of happiness, ')
> as they are not acquired, but God-given, so they
> are inalienable. ... But the right to govern, as
> expressed in the existing form of government, to
> which the governed assent, is conventional. ...
> We grant that in forming governmental institutions
> de novo, the common rules of political ethics are
> applicable; but it very seldom happens that political
> societies are found without an existing order of
> government. [58]

From here he argued that while equality was a universal
ethical principle, he was not therefore prepared to say that
"in the distribution of political authority the law of universal
equality must always prevail. " He did not insist that it was
an absolute moral right for every man to have the franchise,
but did declare that in the American situation it was wrong
both morally and politically to discriminate between races.
The article bitterly denounced President Johnson's reconstruction policy which in effect excluded the loyal freedmen
from political power, and at the same time the writer opted
for impartial suffrage as a compromise required by practical
political considerations. In rebuking Johnson, he declared
his policy wrong because it was "impolitic" and a practical
"blunder, " because he could see that until the government
gave political equality to the Negro the agitation and the
strife that would be inevitable would tear apart the social
fabric of the nation. Stating his case from a strictly realistic premise he said:

> Sambo, like the frogs in Egypt, will find his way
> into all our affairs, a plague and an offense. [59]

But do him justice and he will subside. Concluding the article he asked, "Will the American people permit him to subside. "[60] The debate that went on between universal and impartial suffrage will be treated in the next chapter. It is
sufficient to say that the foregoing approach to a burning
social question, which has remained as one of the most urgent issues in American domestic life to this day, belies

all caricatures of nineteenth-century Methodists as simple
moralists flying high above the realm of politics.

The biblical affirmation that civil government was ordained of God provided some Methodists with a starting point
for their understanding of politics. In an earlier editorial
appearing in the New York Christian Advocate it was put this
way:

> As God has established civil government and sub-
> jected it to his laws, political science is intimately
> related both to theology and ethics. [61]

The touchstone between theology and politics was ethics. Insofar as theology was the science dealing with deity and politics the science dealing with laws and government, ethics
was the discipline embracing the two. With this formulation
the writer endorsed the right of the pulpit to deal with "political principles" and to enforce obedience to "Civil government." [62]

Abel Stevens, reacting to an accusation printed in
Scribners Monthly, to the effect that the Protestant pulpit
had lacked "moral courage" and "intellectual independence, "
admitted a partial truth to this charge, but indicated that
since the advent of the anti-slavery cause, "The American
pulpit has generally improved in boldness and directness."[63]
In urging the pulpit to do better, he declared that politics
had to do with all relevant questions of morality. "Was not
slavery a matter of 'politics'? ... Is not the temperance
question one of law?" he asked. [64] Believing that these
questions "involving Christian ethics are legitimate to the
pulpit, " he queried,

> Would you have the pulpit dumb or compromising,
> on these subjects? Would it not become contempt-
> ible should it be so, and deserve contempt?[65]

Stevens' plea depended on his understanding of politics as a
means of institutionalizing morality. Hence, he believed
the Church should use its "public" and "moral" power to
"address the conscience of the nation" in order to influence
political decisions. [66]

If politics was viewed at best as a means of ordering
public life and civil affairs according to moral right, it was
also a means of sin and crime. Methodists never tired of

inveighing against powerful statesmen or political demagogues who "attempt great public crimes and sap the foundations of public morals. "[67] In a centenary address given three years earlier than the above article, Abel Stevens warned what could happen if the pulpit evaded the responsibility of "political preaching. " To drive his point home he cited some extreme possibilities for his fellow Methodists to consider.

> If a legislature should reduce again to slavery our long suffering people of color, or open the African slave-trade, or abolish the sacredness of marriage or the Sabbath, or restore judicial torture, or ... abrogate religious freedom ... must the pulpits of the land stand in helpless silence? And if not in such cases the fallacy fails, and the neutrality of pulpit becomes a mere question of prudence. [68]

Working, no doubt, from the same notes as before, he concluded his remarks with this:

> There is no question whatever, which involves Christian ethics, that is not a legitimate question for his public instruction, and none that he should not be competent prudently to discuss. [69]

The Western Christian Advocate came out with an editorial endorsing the legitimacy of mixing politics with religion. It was noted that some people had the idea that religion was a "matter of the heart, " having only to do "with the spirit, and the motives of men's lives. ... "[70] The rest of the statement gives added insight into congregational life in 1867 and would seem to indicate that Methodism at the grass roots has not changed much in a hundred years. The writer perceived that many in the Church thought of religion as a

> regulator and a sweetener of men's tempers, a determiner of their faith, a comforter of those that mourn. Such views still prevail. If, in congregations that we know, the minister to-day should speak of the equal rights of the race, there are auditors whose facial muscles would contract, and whose inclinations would prompt them to take their hats and hunt the Church door. [71]

Against such a view of religion, the editorial quoted Richard Watson who said the Gospel came "sometimes as a goad and a reproof. " Citing the common argument, "But has not politics to do with the State and with legislation. . . ?" the editor answered,

> Yes, but wise legislation and good morals are in-
> separably married. . . . The harmlessness of the
> dove is to be conjoined with the wisdom of the ser-
> pent. Let the minister . . . ever bear in mind
> that he is an ambassador from the Highest Court
> in the Universe, and that it is his duty with a
> loving heart, but with a true one also, to 're-
> prove, ' and 'rebuke'. . . . [72]

Most northern Methodists who were actively engaged in the great social struggles of the times were convinced that the strange repugnance to such activity on the part of laity and some members of the clergy was due to ignorance of what constituted politics and their relations to Christian-ity. Consequently, the pulpit and the press were at great pains to clarify characteristics of politics that invited and even necessitated a religious-political interaction. The Rev. Bostwick Hawley attempted to correct defective understand-ings of politics in an article in the Methodist Quarterly Re-view. "What the word religion expresses in the relations of man to God, " he said, "the word politics expresses in the civil relations of man to man. "[73] He approvingly quoted Ruskin, who said,

> Politics are the essential laws of social and civil
> life, out of which grow the great principles that
> healthfully agitate and firmly bind society together. [74]

Hawley then gave a succinct and representative statement of what was involved in politics.

> Politics are, then, nothing less than the relations
> and duties of men to each other, in which are in-
> volved the fact and influence of truth and righteous-
> ness, and the power and danger of vice. [75]

In the first instance, the task of the Church was to help the statesmen in determining truth, righteousness and "those great principles of equity" by which men and nations govern "relations to each other. "[76] Simply put, it was thought that the Church could function responsibly by advising on ethical principles, while the task of politicians was to establish and adjust them in society. To make sure the advice was followed, Hawley thought that Christianity should "enter and supervise the relations of social and civil life."[77] In the second instance, because politics was also the opportunity for "the power and danger of vice," and because wrong may "be found in social and civil matters," the Church should admonish and correct. Christianity and its distinctive truths, its ideas and forces "are the only and sure purifying elements and powers," he asserted.[78]

Underlying all such formulations of the relations between Christianity and politics was the belief that politics was a moral science, a part of ethics. This persuasion gave the basic sanction to Church involvement in the political realm. Politics was not just a matter of adjusting clashes of interest and balancing powers. It was, rather, an expression of the human spirit, of the deepest interests of man, of eternal truths and moral laws.[79] It was a moral science more than an art of the possible. Consequently Methodist divines were moved to action by moral appeals.

This does not mean, however, that they eschewed all pragmatic considerations and reasoning when they uttered social criticisms or attempted to achieve a higher morality in public life. On the temperance question Methodists based their contention that drinking posed a serious moral issue on very practical grounds. Intoxicating drink was not referred to as inherently evil; rather, as the source of social evils.[80] In achieving the desired goal of prohibition, some Methodist moralists insisted that there ought not be any compromise, that they should declare themselves in favor of total prohibition. But the majority at the 1871 Conference in New York decided that this was unrealistic. The Rev. Dr. Goodwin said,

> In itself prohibition is practicable, and the thing
> which we need, and in the end must have; but if
> we cannot have it now, our next best thing is to
> make such approaches to it as we can main-
> tain. ... [81]

The approach that he and the more practical-minded men favored was a law which would authorize and empower a majority of voters in counties, towns, villages and cities to prohibit the sale of intoxicating liquors as a beverage or at least to regulate the sale of liquors by license on the local level. A compromise resolution was then offered and adopted by the convention. The resolution was as follows:

> Resolved, 'That while we declare total prohibition
> to be our right and aim, ' we respectfully ask the
> passage of a law which will make it necessary to
> obtain the consent of a majority of legal voters,
> 'at an election held for that purpose, ' in a ward,
> town, or county, before one may sell 'therein' in-
> toxicating liquors as a beverage. [82]

Most clergymen rejected appeals to form a prohibition
party in the 1860s and '70s, desiring instead to maintain a
strong, loud witness as a Church to the necessity for social
change and political reform. They were willing to work with
and on partisan politicians and even offer tentative support
to the Republican party when their goals accorded with Methodist goals, but for the most part they were loath to identify
Christian principles with any secular political position or
group. What they did see was the importance of political
power as a means of achieving moral aims. And they did
not hesitate to use their vast numbers and their tightly organized denomination to coerce politicians and legislatures in
the interest of social reform. Nor did they fail to see that
the moral question of temperance was intimately related to
political and legal matters. Bostwick Hawley, for instance,
saw that the Church ought to speak to the issue of Federal
revenue laws inasmuch as they related directly to "the manu-
facture, rectification, and sale of alcoholic liquors. "[83]

All of which is to say that Methodists, in grappling
with the temperance question, could not dismiss political
issues. They evidenced a willingness to compromise; saw
the necessity of power; were able to relate final goals to
provisional possibility; and could come to terms with legal
aspects of morality. Of course, the moral element was the
vital ingredient controlling their approach to social matters.
They thought of themselves as moral reformers. Nevertheless, in taking the temperance question as a case in point,
it is patently clear that these moral prophets were not without social wisdom and a certain expertise as they endeavored
to come to terms with the practical side of the matter. The
least that can be said, after a study of the social and ecclesiastical history of this period, is that northern Methodists
were seriously engaged in a struggle to reconcile Christian
morality with practical politics. The fact that this has not
always been recognized makes this assessment worthy of
special note.

Church and State

Methodists discovered early that in order to clarify the Church's position on slavery and related issues disclosed in the sectional conflict, it was necessary for them to determine those things which were due Caesar and those that belonged to God. In the period after the war, the principal issues which occupied the thought and energies of Methodist clergymen were temperance, public schools, religious liberty, national destiny, political reconstruction and the freedman question. Each of these problems involved the perennial issue of church-state relations.

Stow Persons has written that one of the most important contributions of denominationalism to American culture was the way Church bodies defined the relationship between church and state. [84] If the Congregationalists, after disestablishment, made the chief contribution, the Methodist Episcopal Church, no less than any other protestant body, contributed to the distinction between church and state in post-Appomattox America. There may have been confusion and disagreement concerning the Church's relations to politics and society in general, but northern Methodists were totally clear about the church-state relationship. Each sphere was regarded as distinct and separate, with unique functions and authority, and yet, they were convinced of a profound interdependence of the two orders harmonized by an invisible union which was rooted in the belief that America was a Christian nation, having a common destiny with the Church. This dualism, comprehended in terms of a Christian commonwealth, was neither the theocracy of Boniface VIII nor the Erastian view of a temporal dominance. It was new and uniquely American.

The normative theory of church-state relations was enunciated at the 1868 General Conference of the Methodist Episcopal Church in the "Report of the Committee of the State of the Country. "

> The Church and the civil Government have their separate spheres; but in this they agree, that they are both delegations of power from the same sovereign Lord, and co-ordinate agencies of Providence in the accomplishment of the highest elevation and well-being of our race. They are the two grand public institutions of God for the purity and conservation of society; and they become helps to each

> other, not by political union nor by interference
> with each other's powers, but by performing each
> of its own functions in its own legitimate sphere. [85]

Methodists could applaud and support legal separation because
of their own successes as a voluntary Church. They also believed that by being released from its unchaste alliance with
the civil power, the Church in America had "with that release
wrought the more powerfully on public opinion" and thereby
exerted a greater influence on the "legislation and judicial
processes of the country. "[86] It was explained that the power
of the Church as a voluntary institution far transcended the
power of an established Church. And Methodists could not
be dislodged from the conviction that it was the voluntary
Church

> that saved for the American people their liberties
> and their civilization during the perilous times of
> colonization, revolution, and rebellion. [87]

New York Methodist preachers were furious about the
political tendencies and increasing power of Catholicism in
the state. An excerpt from a resolution passed in their annual Conference of 1871 will indicate their grievance and how
they viewed the separation of powers.

> And whenever we consider the prosperity of the
> Church as intimately related to the civil condition
> of the State, and that each is best subserved by
> moving in distinct lines, never blending, but in
> close proximity--not allowing one to usurp the rights
> of the other or imperiously dictate the policy of the
> other. And that all such assumptions of preroga-
> tive by any branch of the Christian Church meet
> with our earnest and unqualified remonstrance. [88]

The Syllabus of Errors, enunciated by Pius the IX,
greatly distressed Methodists. The statement above was in
reference to just this. The ultramontanism of the Papal
Encyclical prompted a torrent of articles, sermons, scholarly
papers and official resolutions--all defending the traditional
doctrine of civil and ecclesiastical separation. George L.
Crooks made an historical survey of Catholic thought on the
relations of Church and state, citing key documents all the
way from the forged Isidorian Decretals and the theories of
Gregory VII to the views of Leo X and Pio Nono. His conclusion was that the conflict with Rome over the school ques-

tion was a "conflict of fundamental principles. "[89] The crux
of the matter for Methodists was this:

> ... we claim that the Church shall not encroach
> upon the State, nor presume to override it, as by
> a divine authority; Rome claims to be supreme
> over the State, and that in any conflict between the
> civil and spiritual powers the civil must submit;
> we maintain the right of the State to education, for
> its own protection and in the interest of civiliza-
> tion; Rome denies all such right to the State, and
> maintains that she alone is the divinely appointed
> educator of mankind. [90]

Crooks mentioned with chagrin that men such as Brownson
and Hecker, who were friendly to the American type of religious and civil liberty, were flatly contradicted by Rome.
This meant to him that Americans now had to deal with "Ultramontanism of the most pronounced type, " and that the
question of Bible reading was a trivial matter compared with
the real issue, which was to him, "schools or no schools."[91]

It may seem a contradiction that Methodists could on
the one hand vigorously defend the separation principle and
on the other hand, simply assume the Protestant orientation
of public education which Roman Catholics, with equal vigor,
resisted. To Methodists it was no contradiction at all, for
this did not represent a confusion of the two spheres. It
was, rather, a proper blending of Christianity with American
social institutions. They concluded that "Catholics do not
want their children to be Americanized. "[92] Some Methodists
boldly stated that the government was Christian. [93] Most
settled for the assertion that it was not the government that
was Christian; rather, the nation was Christian and Protestant. [94]

Daniel Curry represented a more circumspect position
when he declared that though the country was still largely
Protestant, "yet even Protestantism and Americanism are
not the same thing. "[95] He did not hesitate to affirm the importance of religion in public life, but insisted that the American idea excluded notions of a state religion. "The state, "
he said, "is neither religious nor irreligious, since it is
not ... among the legitimate functions of government to inter-
meddle with these things. "[96] Expressing a traditional view
of religion's function in society, he wrote this:

> It is not denied that the stability of society requires

> the salutary influence of religion to fashion the
> character of the people; but it is believed that all
> these advantages are best secured through uncon-
> strained personal and social action. But if, in
> any case, under the name of religion, the peace
> and safety of society shall be invaded, or personal
> rights violated, it is clearly the duty of the state
> to restrain such an abuse of religious freedom. [97]

Methodists saw the American system of church-state
relations as a compromise between the high theocratic notions of Romanism and the scandalous secularism of France.
Against the Catholics they contended for religious freedom.
In the face of the French experience they argued for the inclusion of religion in public life and as the only stable basis
for legitimate government. Reviewing a book on the French
Revolution, a Rev. J. A. McCauley traced the failure of the
French experiment to notions of the secular state. [98] To ally
freedom with irreligion was the height of folly, according to
this cleric. As an example of how most Protestants in America viewed the Revolution, the following excerpt from his review is included:

> The sorest perplexities and saddest failures of the
> Revolution were largely the result of the ill-con-
> sidered attitude it early took, and the policy it
> afterward pursued, regarding questions of religion.
> Its treatment of the Church as a creature of the
> State, and its mad endeavor to bind conscience with
> the shackles of human law, awakened that resistance
> which, in turn, provoked those storms of infidel
> rage whose final fury wrecked so many of its
> hopes. [99]

Against both the Romanists and the "atheistical" French,
Methodists could and did sharpen their understanding of the
spiritual and civil orders. They were clearly for separation
and yet equally sure that the basis for legitimate government
had to be religion if not Christianity of the Protestant kind.

What, then, was the function of the state? The answer of northern Methodists was clear: the preservation of
the social order. It was a conservative theory of the state
based on the Pauline doctrine found in Romans 13. George
Peck stated categorically that,

> Government is a coercive power. It holds 'the

sword. ' It is a 'revenger to execute wrath upon
him that doeth evil. '100

Daniel Whedon said with equal bluntness, "the magistrate is
armed with the 'sword' to execute even capital penalty upon
the domestic foe, or, " his comment went on, "prosecute war
upon a foreign aggressor. "101 A writer for the Zion's Herald
defined government as "exercise of authority, restraint, control. ... "102

The ground upon which this negative view of civil
authority was based is to be found in the Pauline proposition
that the "powers that be are ordained of God. " The magistrate was regarded in classical Protestant terms as "the
minister of God. "103 In this respect the Rev. Joseph Horner asserted that governmental authority was "somewhat
analogous to that of a parent, who ... is also representative
of God. "104 This line of reasoning was not uncommon. The
Rev. John P. Newman, in a sermon to his congregation in
the Metropolitan Memorial Church, Washington, D. C. , declared,

> By divine appointment the father is the legislator,
> the judge and the executive; and the first family of
> our race foreshadowed the civil order of society. ...
> Hence, out of the family came the state, which de-
> fined the duties of the individual. 105

Another clergyman said that just as it was the duty of ministers to enforce "obedience of wives to their husbands, of
children to their parents, " so he should enforce obedience to
the requirements of civil government. 106

Because civil authority had the sanction of divine
claim and because the magistrate was "the minister of God, "
it was hard for Methodists to conceive of a case when civil
disobedience or rebellion against the government would be
allowed. Ministers were charged with the responsibility of
enforcing and teaching obedience. Laymen were enjoined to
obey civil authority "for conscience sake. " And the minister
of justice was appointed to require obedience at all costs and
should "pursue the track of the disloyal and disturber of public peace. " Then, at the hands of the magistrate, "engines
of divine power will be set in motion ... and will break upon
their heads. "107

Behind such forceful language was not only the Pauline

doctrine of the state, but also the odium of certain groups in American society which were regarded by Methodists as disloyal and disturbers of the public peace. It would be wrong to conclude that the firmness on the part of northern Methodists with reference to the absolute authority of the state over secular matters was a convenient but passing justification for condemning their enemies. But the potent language and energy with which they presented their case cannot be understood apart from their aggravation with groups such as the Mormons with their infamous polygamy, the Whisky Ring of New York, the draft rioters, anti-American Romanists, the insurgent Fenians, and, most contemptible of all, the treasonous southerners. The alleged criminality and sinfulness of these groups was understood in terms that went beyond civil disobedience, to be sure. But any estimate of northern Methodist social criticism regarding social sins will be defective if the Methodist teaching on temporal authority is not taken seriously. Certainly, the notion that civil magistrates function as executors of divine wrath was a central feature in the attitude of Methodists of the North as they inaugurated their plan for southern reconstruction and as they advised federal authorities of their duties on the question of reconstruction.

The Methodist teaching on temporal authority was plain and unequivocal. John Newman said, "the State in all secular matters is absolute, and must be obeyed."[108] But when does loyalty to God come into conflict with the temporal powers? Newman said, "there is but one exception ... where the civil law is in contravention of the plain precepts of religion."[109] The one exception was the earthly ruler who arrogates to himself that which belongs only to God.

> 'Render unto Caesar the things which are Caesar's, and unto God the things which are God's.' Whatever bears his 'image and superscription,' give it to Caesar, and God says, Caesar shall have it. But if Caesar demands that whereon are not his 'image and superscription'; if he asks your homage to his idol; if he claims the right to control your conscience; then in the language of St. Peter, 'We ought to obey God, rather than men.' (Acts, V: 29)[110]

The teaching here is in line with essential Christianity traditionally understood. All Methodists agreed the Christian must not submit to earthly rulers when they required ultimate devotion or attempted to control conscience. There were, however, a variety of views expressed concerning other possible exceptions to the rule of obedience. Whedon stated that if a government required him as a military officer to fight an unjust war, he would have to send in at once his moral protest and resignation. Or, he said,

> If a government require me, beyond its right of securing self-preservation and justice, to violate eternal right, or the law of God, such a requirement is null, and I must disregard it. If I have ever taken any oath to support the Constitution, regardless of God's law, my conscience has been entrapped, and that oath is so far null. If called to repeat that oath, to support an unrighteous constitution, audibly and firmly must I utter the reserve. 'Except it reverse the law of God'; and the government which would make that reserve a ban of ostracism upon me, is a government of blasphemy. [111]

There were limits beyond which the state could not go. But if the state did exceed its rightful limits and require obedience, Whedon would not allow revolution as a Christian response. "I must neither obey nor resist, but suffer." [112]

Haven saw reasons for civil disobedience when the "human law is opposed to the evident decisions of divine law." [113] The Fugitive Slave Law passed in 1850 posed such an occasion. The proper Christian response to a government which endorses slavery by ordering the recovery of those who have escaped was twofold. First, Haven said there should be "one general outburst of execration, one united prayer and effort for the repeal" of such a law. Second, if the government calls upon Christians to assist in the execution of this law, "we must refuse," he declared

> Ready as we should be to aid the executors of laws which we have no sound reasons to consider morally wrong, we should refuse any assistance in the execution of those clearly criminal. [114]

As radical as Haven was on matters of social justice, he was no anarchist. With Whedon, he said,

> We must suffer, if need be, the penalty of disobedience, rejoicing that we are counted worthy to

> endure such contradiction of sinners, and that
> Christ gives us strength sufficient for the high re-
> solve. [115]

A minister from Philadelphia advised that Christians
should resist the state when it attempted to

> monopolize the pulpit; to gag the press; to assume
> the paternity of the household; to run inquisitorial
> commissions to every fireside; and always, and
> everywhere, to inaugurate a system of black and
> damning espionage upon the territory of private
> thought. ... [116]

The purpose of government, for him, was "to secure the
rights of individuals"; when it has done this, its mission is
fulfilled and beyond this governments "become arrogant and
despotic; beyond this they have no rights, and they cease to
be governments. "[117] This Methodist minister went beyond
most when he declared the necessity of remedial action when
a government becomes unjust and oppressive. He proposed
a moderate form of revolution. In suggesting the remedy, he
cautioned that it was not the business "of the rabble and the
mob" nor was it the right of a party "maddened with rage
for dreamy abstractions. ... "[118] "Revolution, " he believed,
"is the business of the people, under the restrictions of
sound judgment and general right. "[119] The following quotation indicates both caution and resolution:

> If the government be a monarchy, the redress may
> be, to dethrone the king; but if a republic, to alter
> the constitution. There is usually a mode of doing
> either, without violence to person or property.
> Sometimes, it is true, when the throne is occupied
> by a Nimrod or a Nero; when a Charles the First,
> or a George the Fourth, sways the sceptre, armed
> resistance becomes necessary. There can be, as
> doubtless there have been, occasions on which the
> opinions should be made into cartridges, and prin-
> ciples should be primed with gun-powder; some-
> times the most pointed arguments are sword-points,
> and the most effective speeches are made from
> howitzers and long nines; but these are the reme-
> dies of desperate times, and the weapons of des-
> perate men. [120]

Theologically conservative Methodists in the nineteenth

century believed in original sin and had a healthy respect for the social consequences of sin unchecked. This was part of the logic that undergirded their insistence on civil obedience. It was also what lay back of their teaching on limits of earthly powers. In an extremely sophisticated article appearing in the Methodist Quarterly Review, a Methodist author articulated the view that governments should always function under well-defined principles and laws. "It is an axiom in constitutional government, " he said, "that no man can be trusted with undefined power."[121] Thus he saw the importance of checks and limitations of authority which were found in constitutions, as well as the division of governmental functions into the legislative, the executive, and judicial branches. These necessary checks and balances were necessary by reason of man's propensity for self-aggrandizement. "All history, " he said, "is illustrative of man's love of power."[122] It is clearly the political realism of a James Madison or Reinhold Niebuhr.

The prevailing view of the state was that it was an order of preservation, having clearly circumscribed limits, with internal arrangements to check possible excesses in wielding power. As an order of preservation, the state's actions were appropriate to its own purposes not only when it maintained law and order and punished the evil doer, but when it acted to achieve justice; contributed to the "wealth, the happiness and the glory of the body-politic";[123] and when it provided a system and monies "for common school instruction."[124] It must be understood that even these more constructive tasks of state were understood by Methodists as conserving courses of action. The state was not charged with the duty of forming the characters and directing the lives of its subjects. It did not exist as an ideal moral power. And Methodists were most emphatic that government was not a reforming agent.[125] That was the prerogative of the Church. The state was not to be indifferent to reforming society, but it could make its appropriate contribution by protecting the Churches and offering benefits and incentives that would assure the free course of the gospel and the moral power of Christianity.

Having discussed Methodist theories on the separation of powers and the authority, function and limits of temporal authority, the inquiry now turns to the role of the Church in relation to the state and to the broader society. Because the teaching on the duties of the Church in society have already been treated extensively under a variety of heads in

previous chapters, this section will serve to give only a
brief summary and synopsis.

Church and Society

A sense of loyalty to government had always been
deeply engrained in the ethos of the Church of Wesley.   It
was probably this fact as much as any other that exasperated
the northerners in the face of disloyalty in the South.   And
when their southern colleagues in the ministry went along with
Jeff Davis and Confederate politicians to the very last, a
sensitive nerve was struck.   Hence, with great assiduity the
Northern Methodist press, pulpit and official conferences denounced the sin of treason. [126]

For themselves and their congregations in the North,
Methodist clergymen thought the peace of the state was to a
large extent the peace of the Church.   This practical reason,
added to theological cannons already discussed, provided the
basis for strong declarations of duty to the state.   Three
things were required of the Church.   First, it was the duty
of the Church to be loyal; second, to teach reverence for the
magistracy; and third, to offer supplications and prayers for
all that are in authority. [127]   Beyond this official teaching
were many other views as to what the Church ought to do to
help the state and society in general.

What were some of the aims of the Methodist Episcopal Church and how were they stated?   Out of the maze of
words used to state broad goals for the Church, three phrases
emerge as dominant: the salvation of souls; the education of
the masses; and Christianization of the country.   A preacher
from the Southwest called upon the Church to send them a
bishop, more clergymen, a better religious press and some
money.   Why?   To give Methodism more power to "convert,
educate, and Christianize...."[128]   These expressed goals,
used over and over and put in a number of ways, became
determinative for the northern Methodist reconstruction policies just as they provided impetus for Church extension,
home and foreign missions and efforts to found schools and
colleges.   On the face of it, these directions would appear
to be highly moralistic in tone and substance.   Certain
scholars have used terms such as "conversionist ethic,"
"revivalistic ethic," and "evangelical moralism" to describe
the underlying social thought operative here.   Milton Powell,
for instance, stated that mid-nineteenth-century Methodists

were not aiming for the reconstruction of society; rather the aims were of "a purely spiritual nature, " and, he went on, "the purpose of Christianity was not therefore to reconstruct society but to redeem mankind by evangelical means. "[129] James Kirby, in his study on Matthew Simpson, concluded that the operative concept in the Bishop's social thought was

> a revival or conversionist ethic which depends upon the conversion of the individual for the reformation of society. [130]

Richard Cameron, in the same vein, asserted that political considerations entered very little into northern Methodist protests against evil in society. Instead, they "summoned the sanctions of religion and morality, " he said. [131] These and similar judgments, however, do not contain the whole truth of the matter. To get beneath the surface into the meaning of phrases that sound moralistic, and to look at the action of men who uttered the words, is to come out with a different picture.

Daniel Curry said the Church was a "civilizing force" and "Christianizing the nation" was its main task. [132] Concretely, that meant the Church had the duty of seeing to it that civil law came more into conformity with the divine law. To Christianize the nation meant to abolish unChristian institutions such as slavery and repeal unChristian laws that made it legal to sell alcoholic beverages. [133] To educate meant, for Methodists, the necessity of putting the right laws on the books to assure the free course of public instruction. It frequently meant the education of the public conscience concerning moral issues in public matters.

A phrase commonly used to state the aim of the Church was, the "moral renovation of society. " The phrase encompasses the meaning of the three broad goals stated above. This, of course, meant inculcating morality into the lives of individuals. But it also meant elevating institutions of society to a greater conformity to democratic and Christian principles. Sometimes Methodists talked about permeating the nation with religion as a "cement and sustainer of society. " This included a religious influence on the consciousness of individuals as well as incorporating religion in the very "structure of society. "[134] Bishop Simpson was for the elevation of morality in individuals, but he did not hesitate to speak on the wider issues of morality in government. Nor did he fail to relate and even compromise moral principles to political necessity, as was evidenced in his role in saving Maryland for the Union cause. [135]

Most Methodist leaders, as they engaged in the task of moral renovation, were not blind to the social implications of such a task. A writer for the Christian Advocate advised his readers that while temperance was a moral issue, it was also a social issue and "in all cases involving social issues, politics, of course, must enter."[136] "When the object is simply the suppression of vice, and the promotion of virtue in society," he exclaimed, "we have no dread of mingling politics and religion."[137]

The quest was for a Christian society. The meaning of that quest included religious, moral, social and political elements. Having said this, the question is still begged as to the means of achieving the aims. Put more precisely, how did northern Methodists approach their social mission and how did they contribute to the solution of social problems? A review of their writing and activities reveals four related approaches that may be classified as follows: prophetic ministry, social action, pastoral responsibility, and social pioneering. The prophetic ministry includes church judgments on social conditions and church teachings about moral principles and social ideals. Social action refers to individual and corporate means of bringing about institutional change and directly or indirectly influencing the course of public affairs. Pastoral responsibility means the organized effort of the Church to help society by works of charity aimed at helping those who have fallen out of the orders of society. Social pioneering is the Church out ahead of society in practicing equality, in achieving reconciliation and in representing model morality for the sake of society.

The Prophetic Ministry. Methodists employed their powers and their wits in the task of bringing the nation to an "understanding and recognition of God, of justice, and of principles as related to the national life."[138] The aim was to accent the moral component of public issues and to arouse and form the conscience of political leaders and citizens. During the Civil War, it was the northern Methodist Church, as much as any religious body, that proclaimed the moral issue at the heart of the struggle.[139] During the debates on Reconstruction between Congress and the President, Methodists played the part of the prophetic watchman. When President Andrew Johnson turned back the reconstruction bill,

an editorial in the Christian Advocate came right to the point
in stating that while many people did not see the significance
of the event, beneath the surface lurked an old issue. "It
is simply the negro question of the past in another shape ..."
he said, "the spirit of slavery is very much alive. "[140]

Methodists thought of their Church as the guardian of
the heritage of God's law and moral truth and assumed the
responsibility of being on constant watch to see that such was
not ignored by policy makers. They did not presume to
make policy, but they did want to point up the moral dimension in statecraft. As much as most Methodists liked Lincoln, there was some uneasiness about his political pragmatism. The following quotation stands as an illustration of
this concern:

> Our good president--honest man that he is--con-
> fesses in a recent letter, that he has not sought to
> make national events conform to the moral standard
> of God's unutterable law, but he has been controlled
> by events, and has shaped the executive policy of
> the government by the demands of the war rather
> than by the question of moral right. We admire
> his honesty, but all of us cannot in all things ap-
> prove of his principles of action. [141]

George Prentice, professor at Wesleyan University
and good friend of Gilbert Haven, stated the prophetic task
of the religious journalist this way:

> The religious journalist must be ready to utter the
> judgment of the Christian conscience upon such
> events, to interpret their bearing on public morals
> and religious interests, and to turn public opinion
> in favor of Christian ideas. [142]

In the same fashion, a reviewer for the Methodist Quarterly
Review wrote that the Church had "a direct, authoritative,
divine mission in the state...." He went on,

> When great ethical questions, deep interests of ab-
> solute right or of vital religion, are made to under-
> lie a political platform, the divine reprobation is
> upon her if she shrink from uttering the eternal
> truths committed to her trust. [143]

A New York preacher claimed that the role of the Church in

society was as a keeper of the public welfare. Thus, it was
the duty of Methodists to apply ethical truths "as fearlessly
in politics as in any other science or practice."[144]

It can be said that as these Methodist seers stood
upon their walls of Zion, they did see the deeper issue in
many public questions; they did exhibit great moral courage
in denouncing social evil; and they did portray a measure of
social wisdom. And insofar as politics does involve determining moral priorities, perhaps they played a more significant role in the public life of the nation than might appear
at first glance. It should also be noted that whatever strengths
there might have been in the northern Methodist approach to
prophetic Christianity there was a failure to comprehend the
fact that in most social problems there is the dilemma of
competing moral principles. Methodist social critics showed
little capacity to harmonize multiple moral norms which
regularly are in conflict.

Social Action. The activity of the Methodist Episcopal Church
directed toward changing laws, policy and institutions, and
influencing elections was an important part of its social
ministry. In 1850 many northern Methodists took a decided
stand on the question of slavery. It was the first time the
Church had attempted to directly influence public opinion in
the interest of changing a law and an institution. With the
slavery issue, northern Methodists began to see that the
most promising method of securing such goals as freedom
and equality would be through political action. In a laissez
faire society and in a period of rough and tumble competition,
Methodists proved themselves men of their times. With a
sense of moral urgency and a virile toughmindedness, the
Methodist Church entered into competition with other power
groups for the attention of temporal authority. Counseling
officials, passing resolutions, publicity campaigns, legislative lobbying, and electioneering for the right candidates
were all allowed as means of achieving their goals.[145]

Methodists in New York thought it a matter of Christian stewardship to exercise their power in direct political
action.[146] Speaking of the "dram shop," the Rev. Flack
exclaimed, "Nothing but political power will destroy it."[147]
And he had boundless faith that "the Christian Church has
the power ... as soon as it wakes up."[148] The Methodists
in New York had 1,457 traveling and 817 local preachers
with 200,000 members. It was the largest single Protestant

body in the state. Flack believed that if Methodists could combine with the other 400,000 Protestants in New York, "rum making" and "rum drinking" would be "speedily swept out of existence."[149] An avalanche of petitions went out all over the country in the interest of influencing legislators on the temperance question. But some thought that petitions could have more effect by a corporate presence. "We should not be so afraid of being called politicians ...," remarked a spirited Methodist layman. "We should be sending petitions to the Legislature in boots rather than on paper."[150]

The lusty attitude of Methodists toward the affairs of state was expressed not only in condemnation of evil, but in praise and support of the good. In the dispute between Johnson and the legislature, Methodists unanimously praised the thirty-ninth Congress. It wasn't just because the Tennessee President reportedly came to the inauguration drunk. Methodists were ready to forgive or disbelieve that, until he chose not to follow the advice of virtually every northern Methodist journal by vetoing the Civil Rights Bill in 1866. From that moment on northern Methodists sought to influence public sentiment by vitriolic attacks on Johnson, the "Tennessee slaveholder," the "drunkard and tyrant," the "boor and ignoramus."[151] On the other hand the legislative body was referred to as "The magnificent Congress," "The best we ever had," "the most enlightened legislative (assembly) in the world."[152] And Methodists put action behind their words in valiant efforts to help embattled radical Congressmen get re-elected during the elections of the fall of 1866. [153]

Prayer has normally not been thought of as a means of social action, but the doughty piety of some northern Methodist clerics proved an exception to the rule. Resolutions for public prayer at official conferences, not infrequently, were intended to serve as a warning to politicians and instruction for the public. An example may be adduced from the record of the 1868 General Conference proceedings. Meeting in Chicago during the actual impeachment proceedings, Methodists spent four days in deliberations over what they could do to make a witness and help influence the outcome. In the course of it, Gilbert Haven offered the following resolution:

> Whereas, The most solemn act to which the Government of the United States in its judicial capacity has been called in all its history is near its

consummation; and whereas, the failure of the impeachment of the President will subject the greatest
of our Generals and all under his authority to the
power of an infuriated Executive, who has opposed
every law that has been made to heal the nation on
the only true and permanent basis of equal rights
to loyal men; and whereas, his release will also
re-animate the dying embers of the rebellion
throughout all the South, sacrifice the lives of many
of our fellow-citizens, and cast all that region into
terror, distress, and danger; therefore,

Resolved, That the General Conference of the Methodist Episcopal Church ... earnestly invokes upon
the Senate ... the blessing of Almighty God ...
that tyrannical usurpation may be rebuked.... 154

Daniel Curry, in the discussion that followed, demurred,
thinking that "he could pray in his closet."[155] Others suggested the action would be "indecorous and improper"; that
it might convey the impression "of an attempt to interfere"
with the judicial process.[156] In the end a very moderately
worded resolution was adopted rather than the Haven pro-
posal. However, the next day Bishop Simpson, in an extra-
ordinary departure from parliamentary procedure, took the
floor and, completely ignoring the fact that a resolution had
already been adopted by the Conference, set forth a series
of grievances, including the charge that Senators were being
influenced improperly by corrupt influences. Believing that
it was the duty of the Methodist Church to counter that influence, the Bishop beseeched the Conference--in a new reso-
lution--to "appoint an hour of prayer ... to invoke ... the
mercy of God, " and "to save our Senators from error."[157]
The resolution was adopted without debate or dissent. The
Nation wryly suggested that it had been "aimed at Senator
Willey of West Virginia, rather than at the Throne of
Grace."[158]

Prominent Methodist laymen and clergymen took an
active part in the election campaign of 1868. Of the journals,
all, except for the Western Christian Advocate, came out for
Grant. In some quarters the men of northern Methodism
earned the reputation of being "the most desirable and effi-
cient political speakers of the day."[159] Some analysts concluded that because of the electioneering efforts of Methodist preachers and bishops, Grant had "surrounded himself
with a Methodist court."[160] The Rev. J. P. Newman

boastfully exclaimed that no class of citizens were received in Washington "by our public men with more respect than the bishops of our church. "[161]

One cannot help but marvel at the organizing power of northern Methodism, both to serve its own ends and to serve the interests of the country. With Grant, Methodists thought they would receive their just rewards in political patronage and support for ecclesiastical reconstruction. At the same time, the famous General was regarded as a "second and greater Saviour of his country, " who would bring "justice to the South. "[162]

Methodists in the cities, deeply distressed at the political corruption and all attending evil, saw the need for direct action. As in the national elections, "organization" became the key word. Jesse T. Peck referred to their social procedure as "organizing moral power for political action. "[163] Representing the prevailing view, he did not think that a separate reform political party should be formed. What was needed, instead, was for "good men" to band together, to drop all Church preferences; to stay within their parties; and to act in concert "for the high purpose of political regeneration. "[164] The editor of The Methodist had the same idea when he set forth a plan for the

> organization of a competent number of honest voters, of any party, to hold the 'balance of power' at the polls. [165]

The leadership of Methodism may have seen social problems in the cities in simple moralistic terms, but when it came to the means for eradicating evil, they displayed a hearty taste for the battle and a realistic grasp of the necessities of power for the achievement of their goals. Given the history of Methodist involvement in social and political matters during the Civil War and reconstruction periods, Peck believed that his denomination was uniquely equipped to lead other Churches and reform groups in the exercise of moral power.

> We are at home, therefore, when we come to the question of putting together forces which are existent, and which have been hitherto chiefly latent in the Church, upon the great moral interests that are involved in the elective franchise of the State and the nation. [166]

The awareness that the forces of evil were powerfully organized prompted Methodists to look to their own political resources. The following statement says it directly:

> Besides, the enemies of liberty and personal, civil
> and political rights are organized--organized most
> thoroughly--under the power of party discipline, so
> that we are compelled, in order to meet these an-
> tagonistic forces, to come together to find out
> what are the limits of our power, and to bring
> into operation the forces, that God has ordained
> to secure the public against the assaults of per-
> sonal malignity and vaulting ambition. We are
> compelled to organize in order that we may be
> one in spirit and action.... 167

On the whole, the social action of northern Methodism represents a curious mixture of moralism and ethical realism. There was little recognition of the ambiguity involved in exercising power. The tendency to see the enemy as "bad men" and the forces of right as "good men" betrays an uncritical view of objective structural sources of evil and good. On the other hand, there was a lucid realization among Methodist reformers that in order to ameliorate social problems and cure moral evil, organization was necessary; power had to be exerted; and institutions had to be changed. They most emphatically did not believe that to solve social problems all that was required was "changing the heart." And most Methodists would never be caught saying, "you can't legislate morals."

Pastoral Responsibility. Another feature of the social mission of Methodism was its social work. In discharging its responsibilities to God for society, the Methodist Episcopal Church carried out pastoral functions as well as assuming the prophetic task and engaging in social action. Because this aspect of Methodism and society has been emphasized and thoroughly treated in previous studies, it is not necessary to go into a detailed analysis. It will be sufficient to make some general comments and offer a few specific quotations.

Bishop Simpson expressed the broad scope of pastoral responsibility for society in these terms:

> to save the fallen and the outcasts, to guard

against cruelty to little children, and even to dumb
animals, to found orphanages, to provide homes
for the aged who are friendless and destitute, and
to furnish education to the deaf and dumb, the
blind and the imbecile, to aid the poor, and to support hospitals. [168]

He thought it quite proper and necessary for churchmen to
extend their pastoral interest beyond the limits of any one
denomination. But he and other Methodists were very chary
about the state or federal government doing welfare and social work. Save for the field of education, secular institutions and governmental agencies were thought of as incom-
petent to deal with the basic social problems.

The Methodist, with editorial offices in New York
City, made a canvas of the wide variety of charitable societies in the metropolis and noted that those societies "receive and disburse annually $2,000,000."[169] The enormous
sum of money and extensive effort of the various charitable
organizations raised a pertinent question. The editor asked:

How is it that there is so much misery, destitu-
tion, and wickedness in the metropolis? How is
it that the moral atmosphere is so infected?[170]

His answer was typical. He was all for social remedies to
help solve the problems of human misery, but the consequences of those efforts would be nugatory, apart from
attacking the deeper moral and spiritual conditions that lay
at the heart of social illness.

While our charities afford relief, and reform to a
certain extent, they are by no means effective
agencies of reformation. It may be that the material aid they dispense, in many cases, even en-
courages indigence. Our Churches and missions
are the best means of elevating the moral condition of the people, and an improved moral condition will save them from poverty. [171]

The writer concluded that only when social work is combined
with evangelism will it bear the intended fruits. [172] Hence,
The Methodist and other Church periodicals made frequent
appeals for city evangelism, along with the call for creating
immigrant aid societies, for supporting the YMCA movement
and a variety of other instruments under the heading of "city
missions."

In preaching the gospel and shepherding the weak and disinherited in social service, Methodists believed that they were being true to their own Christian heritage and at the same time faithful to their providential role in the destiny of America. In aiding the immigrants, for instance, the motivation was twofold: to save souls and Americanize them. Healing, clothing, feeding, and educating served the purposes of Christianizing and civilizing. Thus, Methodists could think of themselves as "bulwarks of our land, " and true children of Wesley as they assumed a pastoral mission to society. [173]

Social Pioneering. Finally, Methodist responsibility for society took the form of what may be called pioneering responsibility. [174] That is to say, there was a notion that just as Providence called America to be a model nation for the whole world to see, so the Church was called to be a model community for the nation to see. In going out ahead of the broader community in the practice of brotherhood; in illustrating the viability of civilization in the wilderness; in exemplifying patriotism and loyalty to the nation; in acts of public repentance; and in publicly acknowledging the guiding hand of God's providence, Methodists believed that they were the apostolic remnant by which the whole society would eventually be blessed.

The Rev. J. A. McCauley declared that Methodist work and evangelism in the West "pioneered the way" in establishing civilization and by its "example" led to the creation of "agencies of large avail for good. "[175] With "ardent zeal, and with machinery of peculiar adaptation, " he said Methodists went West when "there was no one else to do it. "[176] And in so doing they exhibited "the foundations of civilization not inferior to the best" in the nation. [177] McCauley further stated that,

> by means of pulpit and press and school, diffusing light creating moral sentiment, leading multitudes in every generation to fear God and work righteousness, it has helped to base and build our civil polity. [178]

Simpson thought that the minister and the Church were uniquely called to serve as a "bond of union" between the various classes of society. Where society in general could not bring the rich and poor together, the Church could lead

the way. [179] The clergyman, he thought, was distinctively
equipped to serve as a minister of reconciliation.

> He is a bond of union, and the only bond of union,
> between the various classes of society. Educated
> and refined, he can associate with the wealthiest
> and highest; at the same time, with limited means,
> and visiting among the masses, his heart is drawn
> toward them. If he be truly a man of God, he be-
> comes a nucleus around which all the elements
> gather, attracted by his purity, benevolence and
> love. [180]

Simpson truly believed that the ministry of the Church, if
faithful in reconciling the rich and poor within its own fellowship, could serve to "remedy ... this fearful state in society. " "Without this, " he said, "we may fear the Commu-
nism of Europe. "[181]

During the Civil War the Churches acknowledged the
judgment of God on the nation and in public confession re-
pented on behalf of their own denomination and of all society. [182] Whenever this happened in the religious press,
at public meetings, in the Sunday chapel service or at official conferences, Methodists were quite conscious that they
were engaging in a social as well as a religious act. At
the close of the war some ministers and bishops pleaded
with local Churches to abolish color caste in their communion; to invite black ministers into their pulpits; and called
for abolition of color lines in the annual conference. Among
the reasons given, the most common was that by representing
the "unity, the fraternity of man, " the Church could lead
society by example. [183] One writer said caste should be
abolished in the Church because "political duties demanded
it. "[184] Another said, "the theory of 'color blindness' should
be ... enunciated and at once reduced to practice. " Then
with a clearer conscience northerners could go South on mission to the freedmen. [185] The efforts of those in the northern Church to undertake institutional change within their denomination may be seen as social pioneering. They thought
that if the Methodist Church could practice equality, this
might show the wider community it was possible.

Finally, northern Methodists thought of their social
responsibility in terms of conscience formation and thought
of themselves as primary shapers of the social ethos. In
the ministry of prophetic preaching and social pronouncements

and in the area of social action the effect was direct. But there was also a confident belief that if the Church would be the Church; would "be herself the public conscience ... " by the way she lived her own corporate life, then she could "complete the formation of the public conscience. "[186] Bishop Foster thought that in the history of Methodism in America perhaps the inadvertent influence of the Church in transforming the cultural and political life of the country was greater than the results of direct action. [187]

> If it were possible to adequately separate and estimate these external effects, it might appear that by far the greatest work Methodism has wrought has been in lines wholly outside of its own pale--the indirect greater than the direct results. For myself I have no doubt upon that point. If, as a distinct organization, it should now at once disappear or become absorbed, these influences, which have permanently incorporated themselves into the civil and religious consciousness of the race and structure of society, would make it still, though undiscerned, one of the most tremendous factors in the world's life. [188]

The point that needs underscoring here is that Methodists rarely thought of their institutions and the life of the denomination apart from social consequences. An interesting illustration of this way of thinking is found in a suggestion that the proper place for a seminary was in a city. A writer for the Methodist Quarterly Review in an 1866 issue said:

> For a college, the proper place is a rural town far from a great city; for a theological seminary, the true position is a Metropolis. For the young minister, and especially for the live young Methodist, the great city is not only an outside educator, furnishing models and means for improvement unknown to rural life; but it furnishes a great field for action blended with study, through which he is trained to the highest practical power, and by which

---

Opposite: Mead Hall, Drew Theological Seminary, founded 1867. The former ante-bellum mansion of William Gibbons, later presented as a gift to the M. E. Church, North by Daniel Drew.

the institution makes an impression upon the population. [189]

In rhetoric having a strikingly contemporary ring, the writer speaks of the possible destiny of the yet unborn Drew Theological Seminary.

> Place a great Methodist seminary here, (New York City) and it will be not only such an honor to its founding as it can nowhere else be, but it will be a power in the great metropolis, to be felt by the nation and the world. Place it on the same ground with our Mission Rooms and our Book Rooms and its impression will be world-wide. Let New York herself, for instance, place a seminary sixty miles distant and it would be a monumental mistake. A whole half century would suffer for the error, and 1966 would wonder at the unwisdom that committed it. Let New England place her theological seminary in Boston and it will be the commanding success. New York would show the grounds and buildings; New England would show the students, and Boston would take religious character from their perpetual presence and labors. [190]

The preceding discussion has indicated a profound concern for society among Methodist churchmen. And while this chapter has given more systematic form to their social thought than in fact existed at the time, it can be said that what is here represented is the nascence of the social gospel movement and the prelude to a time of more conscious and ordered reflection on the relations of Christianity to society. That succeeding generations of churchmen have not paused to look back; that they have not sufficiently drawn upon the rich resources of this heritage, has been to their own impoverishment.

Notes

1. "The Late Election--Its Lessons, " Christian Advocate (New York), XLI (November 24, 1864), p. 372.

2. Ibid.

3. Bostwick Hawley, "Relations of Politics and Christianity," Methodist Quarterly Review, LXI (July, 1879), pp. 468-69, 472.

4. Ibid., pp. 471-72.

5. "Religion and Secular Life," Christian Advocate (New York), XLIV (October 7, 1869), p. 318.

6. "How Shall We Vote?" Western Christian Advocate, XXXI (October 12, 1864), p. 324.

7. Ibid.

8. Whedon, Public Addresses, p. 80.

9. Ibid.

10. Ibid. See also "Religion in Secular Life," Christian Advocate (New York), XLIV, p. 318.

11. Ibid.

12. Jesse T. Peck, The Great Republic, p. 542.

13. "Divine Law Above Human," Christian Advocate (New York), XXXVIII (March 12, 1863), p. 84.

14. Second New York State Convention, December 5-8, 1871. New York: Carlton and Lanahan, 1872, p. 122.

15. Ibid.

16. Ibid.

17. "The Pulpit and Politics," Western Christian Advocate, XXXI (November 9, 1864), p. 356.

18. Ibid.

19. Ibid. For a similar treatment of the "great commission" see, "Address of General Albright," Christian Advocate (New York), XLIV (December 9, 1869), p. 386.

20. The Doctrines and Discipline of the Methodist Episcopal Church, 1872. Cincinnati: Hitchcock and Walden, 1872, p. 81.

21. Quoted in Rev. Professor Steele, "Politics and the Pulpit," Methodist Quarterly Review, LII (April 1870),

p. 203. This is a good review of Gilbert Haven's volume of National Sermons.

22. Haven, Sermons..., p. 339.

23. Matthew Simpson. Lectures on Preaching. New York: Phillips & Hunt, 1879, pp. 306-07. The lectures contained in this volume were given under the auspices of the "Lyman-Beecher Lectureship."

24. Ibid., pp. 123-24.

25. Ibid., p. 124.

26. Ibid., pp. 125-27.

27. Minutes of the New York Annual Conference, 1871, p. 40.

28. Abel Stevens, "The State Methodist Convention," February 5, 1870. (Publication not known.) Taken from Clippings in collected form, Drew University Library.

29. Ibid.

30. Ibid.

31. Ibid.

32. Abel Stevens, "G. Haven's Sermons ... Liberty of the Pulpit," Christian Advocate (New York), XLIV (December 30, 1869), p. 410.

33. Ibid.

34. Ibid.

35. Ralph Morrow has noted that Abel Stevens was often "ridiculed by fellow Methodists for his political conservatism...." See Morrow, Northern Methodism and Reconstruction, p. 210.

36. Abel Stevens, "G. Haven's Sermons ... Liberty of the Pulpit," Christian Advocate (New York), XLIV, p. 410.

Northern Methodism / 237

37. George C. Haddock, "Politics and the Church," North-western Christian Advocate, XVI (February 19, 1868), p. 62. See also, "Our Land and Its Religion," Ibid. (December 11, 1867), p. 396.

38. Haddock; also, "The Sabbath in Politics," Western Christian Advocate, XXXIV (October 16, 1867), p. 332.

39. Samuel Fallows, "Politics and Religion," Northwestern Christian Advocate, XVI (March 11, 1868), p. 86.

40. Second New York State Convention, p. 45.

41. Ibid., p. 48.

42. Ibid.

43. Ibid., p. 50.

44. "Religious Not Political," Zion's Herald, XXXV (February 17, 1864), p. 26.

45. Ibid.

46. George Peck, Our Country..., p. 183.

47. Ibid., p. 184.

48. Ibid.

49. "Political Tests," Christian Advocate (New York), XLI (May 17, 1866), p. 156.

50. Ibid.

51. Ibid.

52. Ibid.

53. Ibid. See also, "Religion and Politics," Western Christian Advocate, XXXIII (August 21, 1867), p. 268. The article states: "'Meddling with politics' has always been a relative question. It depends on the minister's views and how closely they are shared by his congregation ... such as: if both minister and congregation were pro-slavery, he might denounce

anti-slavery sentiments by the hour, and not only
not be considered political, but be pronounced eminently gospel and religious in the work."

54. "Political Tests," Christian Advocate (New York), XLI,
    p. 156.

55. Ibid. For a similar statement see, Hawley, "Relations
    of Politics and Christianity," Methodist Quarterly Re-
    view, LXI, pp. 473-74.

56. "Divine Law Above Human," Christian Advocate (New
    York), XXXVIII (March 12, 1863), p. 84.

57. "The Suffrage Question," Christian Advocate (New York),
    XLI (February 1, 1866), p. 36.

58. Ibid.

59. Ibid.

60. Ibid.

61. "Respect for Government," Christian Advocate (New
    York), XXXVIII (March 5, 1863), p. 76.

62. Ibid.

63. Abel Stevens, "Criticism of the American Pulpit," North-
    western Christian Advocate, XVIII (November 23,
    1870), p. 372.

64. Ibid.

65. Ibid.

66. Ibid.

67. Abel Stevens, "Centenary Discourse," Christian Advo-
    cate (New York), XLI (May 24, 1866), p. 162.

68. Ibid.

69. Ibid.

70. "Religion and Politics," Western Christian Advocate,
    XXXIII, p. 268.

71. Ibid.

72. Ibid.

73. Hawley, "Relations of Politics and Christianity," Methodist Quarterly Review, LXI, p. 468.

74. Ibid.

75. Ibid.

76. Ibid., pp. 468, 472.

77. Ibid., pp. 468-69.

78. Ibid., p. 469.

79. Rev. J. Linebarger, "Religion and Politics of Luthardt,"
Northwestern Christian Advocate, XVI (August 12,
1868), p. 262.

80. See the speech by Rev. M. S. Hard on "The Social
Evils of Temperance," New York State Methodist
Convention 1876. New York: Carlton & Lanahan,
1870, pp. 30-35. Also see, "Temperance and Politics," Christian Advocate (New York), XLIV (September 16, 1869), p. 292. It should also be noted
that at this time there was no Disciplinary rule
precluding the use of wine in the Communion ritual.

81. Second New York State Methodist Convention 1871, p.
61.

82. Ibid., p. 64.

83. Hawley, "Relations of Politics and Christianity," Methodist Quarterly Review, LXI, p. 462.

84. Stow Persons, "Religion and Modernity," Religious
Perspectives in American Culture, Vol. II of Re-
ligion in American Life. 2 vols. Princeton:
Princeton University Press, 1961, p. 371.

85. Journal of the General Conference ..., 1868, p. 628.

86. S. D. Hillman, "The United States and Methodism,"
Methodist Quarterly Review, XLIX, p. 29.

87. Ibid.

88. Minutes of the New York Annual Conference, 1871, p. 40.

89. Second New York State Methodist Convention 1871, pp. 25-29.

90. Ibid., p. 29.

91. Ibid.

92. Ibid., p. 32.

93. Ibid., p. 42.

94. Ibid.

95. Curry, Platform Papers, p. 127.

96. Ibid., p. 131.

97. Ibid. See also, Daniel Curry, "New York State Schools," Methodist Quarterly Review, LVI (April 1874), pp. 181-212. In this article Curry exclaimed, "It is not the least of the duties devolved by Providence upon our nation and people to develop into active forms, at once, the complete organic segregation, and the mutual and effective co-operation, of the State and the Church in an enlightened, self-governing Christian society" (pp. 184-85).

98. J. A. McCauley, "Religion and the Reign of Terror," Methodist Quarterly Review, XXI (October 1869), p. 569.

99. Ibid., p. 571.

100. George Peck, Our Country..., p. 22.

101. Whedon, Public Addresses, p. 84.

102. "True Americanism: or, Our Duties to Our Govn't.," Zion's Herald, XXXV (May 11, 1864), p. 73.

103. Joseph Horner, "Christianity and the War Power," Methodist Quarterly Review, XLVII (April 1865), p. 180.

104. Ibid.

105. John P. Newman, "Religious Liberty." Washington,
D. C.   Printed at the Office of the "National Republican," 1875, p. 7.

106. "Respect for Government," Christian Advocate (New
York), XXXVIII (March 5, 1863), p. 76.

107. George Peck, Our Country..., pp. 24, 25.

108. John P. Newman, "Religious Liberty," p. 8.

109. Ibid.

110. Whedon, Public Addresses, p. 85.

111. Ibid., p. 84.

112. Haven, Sermons..., p. 22.

113. Ibid., p. 23.

114. Ibid., pp. 23-24.

115. J. S. Willis.   Temporal Authority.   Philadelphia:
Wm. S. Young, Book and Job Printer, 1860, p. 13.

116. Ibid., p. 14.

117. Ibid.

118. Ibid.

119. Ibid., pp. 14-15.

120. J. Pullman, "Methodism and Heresy," Methodist
Quarterly Review LXI (April 1879), pp. 334-35.

121. Ibid.

122. John Newman, "Religious Liberty," p. 9.

123. For a good argument on the right of the State to provide education as a means of its own self-preservation, see: "A Coming Question," Northwestern
Christian Advocate, XVI (November 4, 1868), p. 356.

124. James Bryce, The American Commonwealth, pp. 574-
76. In contrasting the American system of church-
state relations with the European pattern, Bryce
rightly noted that Americans had a less glamorized
conception of the state. "The State is not to them,
as to Germans or Frenchmen, and even to some
English thinkers, an ideal moral power, charged with
the duty of forming the characters and guiding the
lives of its subjects. It is more like a commercial
company, or perhaps a huge municipality created
for the management of certain business in which all
who reside within its bounds are interested, levying
contributions and expending them on this business
of common interest, but for the most part leaving
the shareholders or burgesses to themselves" (pp.
575-76).

125. For numerous citations see, Sweet, The Methodist
Episcopal Church and the Civil War, chapter VI,
especially pp. 115-17.

126. Journal of the General Conference ..., 1868, p. 629.

127. Robert Allyn, "The Moral and Religious Needs of the
Great Center and Southwest," Western Christian Advocate, XXX (March 30, 1864), p. 98.

128. Milton B. Powell, "The Abolitionist Controversy...,"
p. 7.

129. Ibid.

130. James Kirby, "The Ecclesiastical and Social Thought
of Matthew Simpson," p. 182.

131. Richard Cameron, Methodism and Society in Historical
Perspective, p. 187.

132. Curry, Platform Papers, pp. 150, 182.

133. Ibid. See Chapters VI and IX.

134. Randolf S. Foster, Centenary Thoughts, pp. 14-15.

135. Crooks, The Life of Bishop Simpson, pp. 370-71.

136. "Temperance and Politics," Christian Advocate (New
York), XLIV, p. 292.

137. Ibid.

138. Sweet, The Methodist Episcopal Church and the Civil War, p. 116.

139. Crooks, The Life of Bishop Simpson, pp. 368-69.

140. "Public Affairs," Christian Advocate (New York), XLI (March 1, 1866), p. 68.

141. "Our Freedmen," Zion's Herald, XXXV (June 8, 1864), p. 89.

142. George Prentice. The Life of Gilbert Haven. New York: Phillips & Hunt, 1883, p. 338.

143. "Review of Christianity and Statesmanship," by Wm. Hague, Methodist Quarterly Review, XLVIII (January 1866), p. 160.

144. Second New York State Methodist Convention--1871, p. 129.

145. For good accounts of the political acitivity of northern Methodists, see, Sweet, "Methodist Church Influence in Southern Activities," Mississippi Valley Historical Review, I (March 1915) and Morrow, Northern Methodists and Reconstruction, Chapter VIII.

146. Second New York State Methodist Convention--1871, p. 50.

147. Ibid.

148. Ibid.

149. Ibid.

150. New York State Methodist Convention--1870, p. 39.

151. Morrow, Northern Methodism and Reconstruction, pp. 207-08.

152. Ibid.

153. William A. Russ, Jr., "The Influence of the Methodist Press on Radical Reconstruction," Susquehanna University Studies, I (January 1937), p. 57.

154. The Daily Christian Advocate, (May 14, 1868), p. 47.

155. Ibid.

156. Ibid.

157. Ibid.

158. Noted by Clark, The Life of Matthew Simpson, p. 261.
     For an interesting account of Simpson's role in
     attempting to influence his good friend and Method-
     ist layman, Senator Waitman T. Willey, see pp.
     260-61.

159. Morrow, Northern Methodism and Reconstruction, p.
     213.

160. Ibid., pp. 213-14.

161. John P. Newman, "A Letter From Washington," The
     Methodist, X (December 25, 1869), p. 417.

162. "General Grant Elected President," Zion's Herald,
     XLV (October 22, 1868), p. 505.

163. Second New York State Convention--1871, p. 142.

164. Ibid., p. 43.

165. "Political Reform," The Methodist, XI (October 22,
     1870), p. 340.

166. Second New York State Convention--1871, p. 142.

167. Ibid.

168. Simpson, Lectures on Preaching, p. 283.

169. "Religion and Benevolence in N.Y.C.," The Method-
     ist (January 29, 1870), p. 36.

170. Ibid.

171. Ibid.

172. Ibid.

173. George Peck, Our Country..., p. 16; Daniel

Dorchester, The Why of Methodism, pp. 41-42. Wesley's formula, "Get all you can; save all you can; and give all you can, " became a familiar text for urging pecuniary and philanthropic benevolence.

174. The phrase, "pioneering responsibility, " or "social pioneering, " is taken from H. R. Niebuhr, "The Responsibility of the Church for Society, " The Gospel, The Church and The World, ed. Kenneth S. Latourette. New York: Harper & Bros. , 1946, pp. 132-33.

175. J. A. McCauley. "The Nation and the Churches: A Centennial Sermon. " Baltimore: Methodist Episcopal Book Depository, 1876, p. 21.

176. Ibid.

177. Ibid.

178. Ibid.

179. Simpson, Lectures on Preaching, pp. 331-32.

180. Ibid. , p. 332.

181. Ibid.

182. See Chapter 4, supra.

183. Gilbert Haven, "The Great Election, " Methodist Quarterly Review, XLVII (April 1865), p. 272.

184. "No Caste in the Church of God, " Zion's Herald, XXXVIII (April 10, 1867), p. 57.

185. "The Church and the Freedmen, " Christian Advocate, XLI (November 8, 1866), p. 356.

186. Whedon, Public Addresses, p. 80.

187. Foster, Centenary Thoughts, pp. 14-15.

188. Ibid.

189. Review of Manual of Information Respecting the American Methodist Ladies Centenary Association (author

not listed), <u>Methodist Quarterly Review</u>, XLVIII (April 1866), p. 322.

190. <u>Ibid.</u>, pp. 322-23. The Drew Theological Seminary, incidentally, yet flourishes in the Drew Forest in Madison, New Jersey just twenty miles from New York City. It's record of social, political and theological influence has been second to none among Methodist schools. Certainly, Drew has competed favorably with the Boston Brethren.

CHAPTER 8

THE FREEDMEN AND RECONSTRUCTION

The Prolonged Conflict

The great ethical concerns of the Methodist Episcopal Church during the decade following the Civil War centered around the interests of the freedman and the destiny of the nation. [1] There was, of course, a lively interest in such questions as temperance reform, the common schools, political corruption, crime, and immigration. Nevertheless, the dominant social questions that engaged the life of northern Methodism were the questions raised during the war. This being the case, it would be impossible to understand the social attitudes and actions of Methodist bishops and preachers during Reconstruction apart from the meaning they ascribed to the Civil War. In fact, to them, the meaning of Reconstruction was the meaning of the Civil War and the struggle after Appomattox was simply a new phase of the campaign begun at Fort Sumter. If slavery was the chief cause of the war, like Banquo's ghost the spirit of slavery stalked the stage of Reconstruction. If preservation of the Union was the prime aim of the war, cementing national unity and fulfilling the dreams of national destiny were at the very heart of reconstruction policies.

As has already been discussed, Methodists viewed the war as a grand arbitrament of Providence. Far from being just a sectional conflict of competing economic, political and ideological interests, the tragic altercation was thought to have been a divine drama played out on the stage of God's own history. Thus, there was Providence at Appomattox and not just a local armistice. Methodists, by virtue of close political ties with the federal government and a deep moral commitment to the purposes of the war, had been awakened to a vital sense of responsibility for the whole of society--especially those aspects related to the war effort. All of which is to say that unless northern Methodist involve-

247

ment in the social questions of Reconstruction are seen in the context of the total sectional struggle and unless it is understood that the Civil War served an obstetric function in bringing forth a new birth of social ministry, it would be impossible to give a proper or balanced assessment of the Methodist Episcopal Church's role during Reconstruction.

Historians who have written on this subject have usually suggested that the denomination was dominated by moods of vindictiveness and sentimental expectations as to the future of the freedman. Many writers have suggested that "war psychosis," "self righteousness," and "sectarian interests" lay back of the mission to the South. [2] However, while it has been demonstrated with sufficient evidence that some of the motives and methods were less than noble, most writings leave many aspects of motivation unexplored and fail to do justice to the social realities encompassing the social thought and action of the Church. For instance, those commentators from a later period who have expressed the opinion that the welfare of the nation depended on a more generous and forgiving spirit ignore both the tragic character of the war and the tragic dilemma posed in political and moral decision-making. [3]

The ethical problems facing northern Methodists in 1865 were real and perplexing. The dilemma of harmonizing the need for magnanimity and the requirements of moral righteousness was not academic. Daniel Whedon, the influential editor of the Methodist Quarterly Review, knew this better than most. In seeking to steer a conciliatory course with regard to the southern policy of the Methodist Episcopal Church, he posed the crucial question: "If you harmonize with the Church, South, [do] you forsake the negro?"[4] Whedon answered in the negative. He believed that the northern connection could "assert the rights of the negro, yet gain the hearts of the Church South. ... "[5] Daniel Curry, the hardy editor of the New York Christian Advocate, was less sanguine about the prospects of blending racial justice and harmony with the ex-slaveholders. Indeed, he feared the war had ended

> too soon and too abruptly for the good of the South or the peace of the Country. [6]

Between the placatory views of Whedon and the more truculent position of Curry were a variety of answers to the problem. During the summer of 1865 there was a virtual

battle of the journals over the question of political and ecclesiastical Reconstruction. The Methodist Quarterly Review,
the Northwestern Advocate, and The Methodist urged a charitable policy toward the South while at the same time taking
a firm stand in favor of civil rights and freedmen's aid. On
the other side, the Christian Advocate of New York, the
Western Christian Advocate, and the Zion's Herald depre-
cated all policies for reunion with the Church South which
might compromise their stand on racial justice and inhibit
programs of religious and social work among the freedmen. [7]
A perusal of annual conference resolutions and the avalanche
of articles devoted to this subject, in addition to an acquaintance with the southern response, make it quite clear that
after Appomattox there was no stillness in the bowels of the
nation. The issues over which the war was fought were
still there clamoring for decision and action--or so Methodists believed.

Wars are not discarded as easily as battle-torn uni-
forms. No one knew this better than those nineteenth-century
Methodists for whom the fiery trial of mortal combat was
more than a contention over constitutional interpretations.
Curry stated it tersely.

> The rebellion from which the nation has just now
> emerged was no accidental or hasty outbreak. It
> was concocted and promoted with perverse energy
> and persistent purpose through a long series of
> years. . . .
> . . . .
> Earnest and active men seldom suddenly reverse
> the objects for which they labor; aggregate bodies
> of men, never. [8]

The war was understood as a providential means of national
redemption. They, themselves, had felt the scorch of divine
chastisement. And in their repentance, northern Methodists
had pledged themselves to remove every vestige of the can-
cerous sin of which they and the whole nation had been
guilty. Victory on the battlefield had wrought a new birth of
the nation and the abolition of slavery only theoretically.
Because the cause of the war seemed to remain in the
hearts of the enemy and because the concrete fruits of victory had not yet been secured, Reconstruction came to be
understood as a new phase of the same operation. Two
years after Lee's surrender the Central Ohio Conference
defined Reconstruction in this way--as a prolongation of the
war. The Conference adopted the following resolution:

> We believe it the duty of every friend of his coun-
> try to keep in remembrance the issues of the late
> terrible war, and that as armed rebellion was put
> down by the bayonet, so disarmed rebellion must
> be by the ballot, if the American people would
> secure the union of these States and perpetuate
> liberty to all. ... We believe that the belligerent
> States should be reconstructed by the plan proposed
> by Congress, and we look forward with hope to the
> time when this reconstruction shall be consummated
> and every loyal citizen enjoy equality before the
> law and the right of suffrage. ... [9]

Just before the end of the war the Zion's Herald warned that

> The dangers of this struggle will not be over when
> the last hostile gun has been fired, and the last
> armed rebel has surrendered. The political arena
> will then be cleared away for the moral fight.
> There will remain the work of giving supremacy
> to the right moral and political ideas, in the forms
> of law, and in the sentiments of the people. ...
> The fear is that a disgraceful and dangerous com-
> promise may be effected; that the old leaven which
> begat this rebellion may not be thoroughly purged
> away from the body politic and out of the social
> system. [10]

In no place is an understanding of northern Methodist
involvement in the Civil War more clearly perceived than in
the Reconstruction story. Here the themes and issues of the
war were most keenly felt. Here the moral dimensions of
the war surfaced. And here the tenacious moral integrity of
northern Methodists was most visible. Donald Mathews, in
his study of the Methodist Episcopal Church and anti-slavery
movements, said that

> Methodism was not merely a mode of organization;
> it was also an ideology of moral responsibility. [11]

Remembering that this large denomination played a central
role in translating the fight for the Union into a moral con-
test against slavery, it should not be surprising that at the
close of the war they linked the Reconstruction struggle to
a continuance of this moral crusade. If the Mathews' assertion that Methodism was an "ideology of moral responsibility"
could be true regarding the period preceding the war, it is

equally an apt description of Methodism after the war--if
not more so. Any estimate of the motivation impelling northern Methodists along the various directions of their Reconstruction programs that does not take seriously the deep
moral commitment to the plight of the freedman and the
manifest destiny of the nation will be faulty. In short, the
sense of social responsibility of the Methodist Episcopal
Church between the years 1865 and 1877 ought to be viewed
as part of its basic commitment to the aims of the war and
understood in the context of its identification with and mission
to the nation or, in other words, its Protestant and civil religion. Much of the discussion in preceding chapters has
been devoted to an articulation of this background and is
therefore presupposed in the following analysis.

It is not the purpose of this chapter to examine in
any detail the relations between the two Methodist Churches,
North and South, nor to discuss the ecclesiastical relations
between the Methodist Episcopal Church and the Black
Churches. It is also not within the scope of this study to
describe the missionary efforts to uplift and aid the freedmen in the South. Much has already been written on these
aspects of northern Methodism during the reconstruction
period. In keeping with the general theme of this study,
the intention will be to explore the social and political attitudes of the Methodist Church North as related to two areas
of social concern: first, the meaning that was ascribed to
Reconstruction in general; second, the attitudes and teachings about race as related to the northern Methodist quest
for racial justice.

The Meaning of Reconstruction

The issues of Reconstruction were the issues of the
Civil War. They were two: the plight of blacks and the
vocation of the nation. While both concerns were intimately
related in the thought and action of Methodist clergymen,
they may be treated in order.

During the war concern for freedmen was expressed
in efforts to change the rule of the Church touching membership so as to make slaveholding a bar to membership in the
Methodist Episcopal Church. This was finally done in the
General Conference of 1864. Politically, this concern was
expressed in efforts to persuade Lincoln to emancipate the
slaves. In both cases slavery was the fundamental issue.

It might be assumed that with the change in the general rule
of the Church and with emancipation and the northern victory,
slavery as an issue would be dead. Such was not the case.
The New York Christian Advocate noted in March of 1865
that while the "system of slavery was at an end, " its "memory was still on trial. "[12] The Wisconsin Annual Conference
of 1865 said, "Thank God the nation is saved. Slavery is
dead--almost. "[13] Ministers from the East Genesee Conference acknowledged that "slavery as an institution ... has
been abolished. "[14] But they went on to warn,

> ... there is mournful evidence that its virus is
> by no means eliminated from the Southern mind
> and heart, and we are admonished by terrible
> events that multiplied securities are required to
> prevent speedy relapse into a condition of things
> which may be even worse than that which preceded
> the war. [15]

An Ohio preacher sermonized on the same problem. "American slavery, as an institution, is no more. "[16] He declared
that "the convulsions of the war have brought forth a new
race--a race of freedmen. " "Yet, " he continued, "we must
not be blind to the fact that the spirit of the rebellion still
lives. "[17]

The triumph at Charleston, the fall of Richmond and
Lee's surrender sent most northerners into ecstatic jubila-
tion. But Methodist leaders were fearful that this mood
could lead to forfeiting the intended gains of the war. Hence,
they cautioned against too much exultation before the fruits of
victory were actually secured. In a characteristically cautionary mood the clergyman from Ohio exclaimed,

> While the future of the Nation looks hopeful, even
> bright, yet we must not ignore existing facts, that
> have a calamitous tendency. There is still dan-
> ger, in the very important but critical work of
> reconstruction. The maniac is in chains, but not
> restored to his right mind. True the contest of
> arms is over, but now comes the fearful conflict
> of principle, righteousness and justice. The same
> proud, rebellious spirit, that was conquered on the
> battle-field, and beaten at the ballot box, is strug-
> gling to-day, by means of political chicanery and
> strategy, for the chief places of power and con-
> trol. [18]

Methodists were convinced that "the negro question" was at the base of the rift between Congress and the president. In the Spring of 1866, when Johnson turned back the Civil Rights Bill, the Christian Advocate stated that the crux of the problem was still slavery.

> The declaration so often made that slavery is dead, is true only as to the exterior of that abuse; the spirit of slavery, which so deeply affects the American character, is still not only alive, but powerfully active. It received a terrible blow during the war; but it survived, and, under the treatment awarded it, it is again rampant and aggressive. [19]

The temper of the Church regarding the task of reconstruction is seen in the following full quotation from the "Report on Slavery" adopted by the New York East Conference:

> Resolved, That we render thanks to Almighty God, that by the emancipation of almost the entire body of slaves in our country, we have pronounced ourselves an anti-slavery nation, and by an almost unanimous concurrence of Bishops, General Conference and annual Conferences, we are declaring ourselves to be an anti-slavery Church; and we trust that the work so far accomplished will be rendered complete by the adoption of the amendment of our National Constitution totally prohibiting slavery in our land.

> Resolved, Nevertheless, that, inasmuch as an aggravating part of the system of slavery consisted in the withholding all the means of education from the oppressed race, and the depriving them of all civil and political rights, therefore, we hold that the work of emancipation is not complete until the privileges of education, and the rights of citizenship and suffrage cease to depend upon complexional peculiarities. [20]

In all of the various resolutions and sermons during the early post-war period one cannot help but notice a central theme. It is stated above: "... the work of emancipation is not complete...."[21] As late as 1867 the New England Conference still had a committee on slavery. In their report that year the notion of a new and glorious national "work and destiny" was tied to the work of reconstruction which was to "consummate" the work of the war. [22] The task was set before the Church.

> ... the annihilation of caste, till the full intent of the fathers and the birth-right of man--equality before the law, and impartiality at the ballot-box-- shall be enjoyed by every American citizen, without distinction of race, color, or previous condition. [23]

The clergy had seen the war as a providential process of national purification. War "was God's amputating knife to cut out the cancer that was destroying the life of the nation, "[24] said one preacher. Another declared that through the war the distinctive cultural character of the South had to be extirpated "root and branch, stem and flower. "[25] The exact same sentiment was expressed by one New Englander with regard to Reconstruction. In an article for the Zion's Herald he cried out,

> If a single root of the Upas tree of slavery remains, it will sprout again. The last and smallest fibre must be grubbed out of the ground. If a single living seed is left uncrushed in the soil, it will again spring up and bear its deadly fruit. In the reconstruction of states, the last hope of its resurrection should be destroyed. [26]

Cautioning against a soft policy towards the South, the writer admonished his Methodist readers to "let not the nation's hurt be healed too lightly. "[27] The majority of northern Methodist ministers agreed with the implications of this injunction. To allow the wound on the national escutcheon to heal too quickly by indiscriminate expressions of forgiveness and mercy would only ensconce the deep-seated "prejudices against color and race" ever more deeply in the body politic. [28] The portent of easy pardon and healing was to end up with a land where the freedmen could not "grow up to the enjoyment of equal rights and privileges before the law...."[29] The task of the Church, then, was indicated by the meaning given to the purpose of reconstruction. That meaning was termed "political regeneration. "[30] The redeemer nation had itself to redeem. If this was the central meaning given the period following the war, what was the reasoning and motivation behind Methodist policy and activity? What about the alleged lack of charity toward the South?

How dominated Methodists were by the mood of malice and a spirit of vengefulness is still a debatable question. Some Methodists were more and some were less vindictive. But it would seem, after a close reading of the materials, that those arguing that the primary motivation was this spirit of vengefulness greatly overstate the case.[31] It is true that most of the leadership in the Methodist Episcopal Church warned against capitulating to the demands for easy treatment of the leaders of rebellion. But for the most part the rhetoric and the demands were conciliatory as applied to the general populace in the South. The most radical of the Methodist journals, the Zion's Herald, came out with a series of militant articles on Reconstruction in the winter and spring of 1865. One article in the series, discussing "Pardon for the Rebels," was written just before Lincoln's Second Inaugural Address in response to the president's expressed disposition to pardon the leaders of the Confederacy. The author of the article, like most Methodists, was uneasy about Lincoln's pragmatic approach to statecraft. The offer to pardon rebel leaders on condition that they lay down their arms and return allegiance to the government did not set well. The writer asked whether the nation had "nothing to do but to regain its revolted territory, and re-establish its repudiated territory?"[32] For someone who had given a profound religious and moral meaning to the war, the suggestion was unthinkable. He queried:

> Does it [the nation] owe nothing to future generations, nothing to the God of nations, but to fight for its own material interests? Has it nothing to do in the higher work of fixing at their proper standard, the great moral precedents of this rebellion, and of establishing them in the interests of humanity and national justice?[33]

His own response to the questions was to assert that it would be "wrong morally and politically to extend the blessing of pardon to leaders of this rebellion."[34] Important to note is that it was the leadership of the Confederacy that was deserving of punishment, according to this Methodist. Indeed, he pleaded amnesty for all ordinary soldiers and the common people of the South who, he believed, had been victimized by real perpetrators of the national crime. After making the distinction between the people and "criminals," as he called the rebel leaders, he sternly insisted that unless they were punished "according to the demands of political and moral justice," divine retribution could well be turned on the North.

"God will be displeased with us, " he said, "and ultimately turn his wrath and judgments against us. "[35]

A firm belief in the providential judgments and ordering of God and an intense commitment to the Pauline principle of civil obedience undergirded most of the Methodist reaction to the South after the war. Another lengthy quotation from the article cited above is offered as a typical expression of the way northern Methodists reasoned about the terms of peace.

> We should inflict upon them their merited punishment, not in anger nor in the spirit of revenge, but under the higher sense of moral obligation and the duty with which we owe to God. ... The Apostle teaches us that the Civil Government, as a minister of God, 'Beareth not the sword in vain. ' By its just and impartial administration it is appointed of God to be a 'terror to evil doers. ' What terror will it inspire to pardon the worst criminals? ... Will it not rather inspire contempt for the weakness of the government that will do it under such circumstances? While we long for the return of peace to our land, we do not think it wise for the Chief Magistrate to offer such terms in advance. Unconditional surrender to our aims, amnesty for the people, due punishment for all the leaders, are, as we believe, the only terms on which a righteous and an honorable peace can be concluded. [36]

Methodists took their religion very seriously in those days. When they talked about what was owed to God it must be assumed that this was no religious cloak covering up merely a vengeful spirit and a self-righteous attitude. In fact, a good case can be made for the thesis that the moral sternness represented by the northern attitude can be accounted for in terms of a strong sense of guilt. It has already been mentioned that guilt on the part of northern Methodists was a self-acknowledged motive for pursuing a vigorous war policy, and that the task of reconstruction was interpreted as works of penance.

The pleas for rooting out the spirit of caste in society and efforts in behalf of political justice were not sponsored only by the malice of hypocritical northern Methodists, as many southern people thought. Though it is

understandable why they might have thought that. A sense
of guilt is clearly manifested in a resolution offered by Wisconsin ministers.

> Resolved, That it is the sense of the Conference
> that intelligent loyalty, irrespective of color or
> nationality, is the only indispensible test to the
> political rights of freemen. The universal principle
> is as applicable to Wisconsin as South Carolina. It
> is a burning shame to Wisconsin that a loyal black
> soldier, who represented the State on the field of
> battle, when he returns to his home is not allowed
> to vote. He may suffer or die, but shall not vote.
> A loyal black man is a better citizen than a disloyal white man. [37]

Clergymen of New England, in a similar vein, saw that after
the war the old national iniquities were still rising up to confront the nation. This was interpreted as the way Providence
tested the sincerity of their repentance.

> In this way we are tried to-day. The great problem of the political, social, and ecclesiastical
> standing of the late slaves is thrust upon the notice
> of the American people, in this hour of political
> transformation, that it may be now resolved in harmony with justice and truth. [38]

The writers of this platform could not exempt the northern
Church from the readings of providential judgment. "The
mistake of the American Church, in its various branches, "
they noted, "has been in obeying, rather than creating, a
righteous public sentiment.... "[39] The Church of Christ,
they thought, could illustrate its repentance by "recognizing
the brotherhood of man"; by "recognizing the Christian rights
of every man and every class of men"; "by contending for
the rights of the oppressed"; and by laboring "to break up
and destroy the prevalent spirit of caste. "[40] Such a recognition of judgment upon their own Church and the solemn
call to new duties can hardly be adjudged as northern selfrighteousness. The story of the Methodist Episcopal Church
during Reconstruction is misread unless the statements of its
own leaders are taken with some seriousness. The doctrine
of Providence was the central doctrine by which they viewed
their role in American history. And while to the nineteenth
century world slavery was a "peculiar institution, " to the
providential Lord--so they were firmly convinced--slavery was

an unmitigated evil. This point is emphasized because of
the tendency on the part of twentieth-century theologians and
historians not to take the theology of the nineteenth-century
churchmen with sufficient seriousness. The following quotation from the Zion's Herald appearing in May of 1865
illustrates the point.

> ... slavery, or injustice to the enslaved race, is
> the real cause of all our woes arising from this
> war. In all these hearts the conviction is legiti-
> mate and strong that God will not cease to chastise
> this nation with his whip of scorpions until we let
> the oppressed go free and remove all the unright-
> eous disabilities which have been so unjustly
> heaped upon him; in other words, until we make
> him a citizen, in equal rights and privileges be-
> fore the law. While that feeling exists, there will
> be agitation; and to the wicked demagogues who
> oppose God in this, there will be no peace, day
> or night. [41]

Judgment and guilt were clearly operative motifs in the
thought of Daniel Curry as he reflected on the sins of the
northern Church:

> We believe that a great guilt rests upon our Church
> for its disregard of the claims of the colored
> people of the free states, before the rebellion. ...
> Nor are we as a Church doing much better now
> than formerly, and there is great force in the
> retort given by the South to our expressions of
> interest in the Freedmen, telling us to look at
> home, and take care of our own negro popula-
> tion. ... [42]

S. G. Arnold, in discussing the suffrage question for the
Methodist Quarterly Review, pleaded with northerners to
recognize the Negro problem in their own states. He noted
that in some northern states Negroes are not allowed to
vote at all; in others they may vote if they can prove they
are half white; and in nearly all the northern states they
are hampered by disabling laws "which were made in times
past in the interest of slavery."[43] He then remarked,

> And the fact of such negro proscription in the
> North is quoted by the opposers of negro suffrage
> as so shameful an inconsistency as ought to si-

lence all the advocates for that measure, living in
the free states; and yet those very opposers know
that the advocates of southern negro suffrage are
its advocates for the North. [44]

The most persistent advocates for a strong policy of
civil rights and social equality in the South were the persons
who consistently brought judgment to bear on color caste in
the North. Gilbert Haven never ceased reminding his own
brethren of the special forms of caste in the northern civil,
social and ecclesiastical life. [45] Nor did he fail to show the
error of the Methodist fathers who allowed slavery to creep
into the Church. "Those great men, Bishops Coke and
Asbury, " he lamented, "knew that the sin was great, and
said so, yet they did not exclude it. "[46] For eighty years
after that, Haven reminded his fellow Methodists, the Church
had not the strength to protest the iniquity of slavery. In
1860 the Methodist Episcopal Church finally gained strength
to issue a protest, but even then, according to Haven, it
was but "an affectionate admonition. "[47] This champion of
racial justice did not enter the South with illusions about the
moral purity of his own Church. His zeal was conditioned
by the knowledge that,

> The M. E. Church not only failed to abolish slav-
> ery in its limits, it introduced it. [48]

Bishop Thompson, in like manner, told the Freedmen's Aid Society they must not forget their own implication
in slavery. "Our Fathers covenanted to protect it, " he
said. [49] Using this background as a basis for his appeal, he
then declared,

> It is not right, therefore, that we should leave to
> the South the entire burden of supplying and educat-
> ing the Freedmen. If from complicity with slave-
> holders Providence will excuse us with charity to
> the emancipated, we should be thankful. [50]

In the report of the Board of Directors of the Freedmen's Aid Society in 1871 the appeal to work and labor in
behalf of the Freedmen was yet the same. The sense of the
statement was that because they--churchmen in the North--
had participated in the flagrant crimes of slavery, the freedmen had a special claim on them. "We are involved in this
terrible guilt, " the report said. The advice was as follows:

Let us atone for our sins, as much as possible,

>by furnishing schools and the means of improve-
>ment for the children, upon whose parents we
>have inflicted such fearful evils. Let us lend a
>helping hand in their escape from degradation into
>which we have forced them by our complicity with
>oppressors. Justice, stern justice, demands this
>at our hands. Let us pay the debt we owe this
>race before we complain of weariness in the tri-
>fling sums we have given for schools and churches.
>We may longer evade this claim, and turn a deaf
>ear to their cry for help, but who holds the scales
>of justice weighs our guilt, rejects our hypocriti-
>cal apologies, and demands that justice be ren-
>dered to this race before we congratulate our-
>selves in the mere pittance contributed to this
>cause. [51]

More than anything else, a genuine sense of guilt for
their complicity in the evils of slavery motivated northern
Methodists in their attempts to help the Negro after the war.
It was a firm belief in the judging and renewing activity of
a providential God and an historical memory sensitized by
the experience of the war that kept alive the slavery issue
after it was legally dead.

Another more immediate and practical reason which
kept the question of slavery alive was the reaction and the
recalcitrance of the South as touching the treatment of Negroes. One of the great sources of distress in the northern
camp was the increasing oppression of the freedmen in the
South. "We should have preferred universal amnesty," declared a northern Methodist, "and nothing but a sense of
unsafety prevented its adoption."[52] The bloody riot in Mem-
phis, the massacre of blacks in New Orleans, and frequent
announcements by southern politicians and churchmen that
the freedmen were destined to extermination, confirmed
Methodists in their suspicion that the "spirit of blood and in-
surrection was rife in the old dominant class" of the
South.[53] Bishop Thompson supported the strong measures
of Congress in carrying out its radical Reconstruction policy
because of the "Black Codes" which emerged in 1865 and
the news that southern whites were

>subjecting the Freedmen to disabilities, and mak-
>ing odious distinctions in the penalties attached to
>crime.... [54]

The Carl Schurz reports on conditions in the South were

carried in most of the Methodist periodicals, the result of which was to engender genuine fears that slavery would be established again unless the North took responsibility for the freedmen. [55] In the light of such reports--some from northern Methodist clergymen who had been in the South since before the close of the war--there was even fear that unless something was done soon to make the freedmen full citizens there would be another war. [56]

Two additional factors made the reports from the South all the more ominous. First was the growing awareness that full civil rights for freedmen was by no means popular among the masses of the people in the North, so that Johnson's reconstruction--or, what he liked to call "restoration"--policy was gaining favor among northerners. Second was what to Methodists was an incredible announcement by Johnson, in his annual Congressional message in December of 1865, that full restoration of the civil governments in the South was soon to take place and that the process of reconstruction would then be completed. [57] A Methodist editor saw in the presidential message evidence of the "President's anti-slaveryism," but no sign of "his antagonism to caste."[58] He went on, "he as yet fails to recognize the negro as quite a man."[59] As nearly every northern Methodist periodical, official body and major spokesman saw it, the future for the black man boded ill. The combination of southern intractability, Johnson's softness, and northern indifference to the plight of the freedman had the effect of increasing their support of the radicals in Congress and of prompting a more socially and politically oriented mission to the South.

The aggressiveness of the northern Methodist mission in the South during the post-war period resulted in the organization by 1869 of ten new annual conferences. [60] Firmly entrenched in an inhospitable land, clergymen--both black and white--of the Methodist Episcopal Church became, themselves, victims of harsh treatment at the hands of southerners. By this time the Ku Klux had entered the scene to protect and defend the southern way. Reports of Ku Klux outrages were heard in the northern Churches as urgent calls for more aggressive and uncompromising action in the South. In 1871 the New England Annual Conference listened to the reading of long lists of crimes committed by the Ku Klux. "Some of these crimes," the report stated, "are altogether too horrible and fiendish to be even named in this paper."[61] Here is an example of some cases that were adjudged fit for the ears of New England clerics:

Rev. Moses Sullivan, a white member of the Alabama Conference, was beaten with hickory whips by disguised Ku-Klux. His skull was fractured by a blow upon the head with the butt of the hickory. Strokes across the breast were so severe as to cause injury from which he will never recover.

Rev. A. S. Laken, presiding elder of Huntsville district, has been threatened, followed repeatedly, his house surrounded by Ku-Klux in disguise, and shots fired through his rooms.

Hon. Malcolm Claibourn (colored), a member of the House of representatives, Georgia, an influential and valuable member of our Church, was shot dead on the steps of the Capitol.

Uncle Peter (colored), an exhorter, was shot, and his throat cut, and his body thrown into a ditch in Grantville, Georgia, because he was loyal to the government, and a Northern Methodist.

Rev. Mr. Varnel, received on probation in the Alabama Conference at its last session, was shot dead by the Ku-Klux. His body was pierced by forty balls. His own son was also murdered.

And thus the list of sufferers and of martyrs goes on, until the sense sickens at the horrible narration. The 'voice of blood' cries 'from the ground. '62

The voice became as a summons for a thorough "reconstruction of Southern society. " "We have before us the sternest and most uncompromising conflict of our entire history, " the statement continued, "and we trust, under God, our most decisive and overwhelming victory. "63 As an indication of how Reconstruction for Methodists in New England was interpreted six years after the close of the war, the following statement is included:

When the Roman army, under Atilius Regulus, had slain with war-engines the serpent encountered on the banks of the Bagrada, all danger was not past; for the river was dyed with its blood, and the stench of its decaying body infected the air so fearfully as to drive the army before it. So slavery

is dead, --war-engines certainly killed it. Of this
the taint upon every Southern breeze is unanswer-
able proof; but, like the serpent of Livy, it may
prove to be by far the greatest trouble after death.
The malaria of slavery and secession hangs in
noxious vapors over nearly all the South. To be
a member of the Methodist Episcopal Church is to
be a Unionist, and an abolitionist, and hence ob-
noxious to unrepentant rebels. Our brethren are
suffering the most fearful indignities and cruelties,
and are sealing their devotion to Christ and human
rights with their blood. God bless these brave,
true men. 64

The churchmen vowed to exert all influence upon the government in the interest of the "instant and utter suppression of
this post-mortem rebellion. "65 For,

Having abolished slavery, the work of reconstruction cannot be completed until every thing born of
it, shares its fate. Its laws and maxims must be
displaced by those of the gospel. Emancipation
from the chain and the lash makes irresistible the
claim to emancipation from the thraldom of caste. 66

Methodists of the North played a major role in keeping the national wound open during the post-war period. Indeed, by keeping alive the slavery question; by supporting
radical Reconstruction; and by vigorously pursuing an ecclesiastical reconstruction policy of their own, they played a
crucial part in deepening the sectional gash and leaving an
angry scar. No attempt will be made to assess the rightness or wrongness of their activity and thought regarding Reconstruction. It is enough to conclude that Reconstruction
for northern Methodists was no political experiment and was
not simply a ground for denominational advancement--though
it was that to a great extent--; rather, it was fundamentally
an extension of the Civil War and, under God, an event of
political, social and religious regeneration. The central
issue was seen as the status of free blacks in the Church
and American society.

Reconstruction, however, had another important overarching meaning. Out of the war experience and the re-
capitulation of Methodist history in centennial celebrations
came a grand vision of American manifest destiny. Because Methodists had identified the mission of the Church

with the destiny of the nation, they believed that "the flag of
the republic and the flag of Methodism must go forward over
the revolted territory side by side. "[67] The task was to
first achieve "unity in the nation" and then "unity in the
Church, " declared the Christian Advocate. [68] This being the
goal, one might then wonder why Methodists kept agitating
over the slavery question, which most assuredly could not
contribute to binding the wounds of the nation. The question
is answered when it is seen that it was a "moral unity" that
was sought. [69] If America was to fulfill her destiny in the
moral renovation of the world, then the Methodist Episcopal
Church, as the self-appointed guardians of the nation's
morals, had a special responsibility to the country.

"In reorganizing southern society, and restoring civil
order, " observed the Christian Advocate, "moral and religious influences must largely be depended upon. "[70] Moreover, it was stated that though not formally political bodies,
Churches "are most powerfully effective in political affairs."[71]
Conscious of their own political power, Episcopal Methodists
of the North believed they were uniquely fitted "to help cement the Union, " to restore "moral and social unity" to an
America that had not been fully redeemed by the war. [72]
Methodists expressed the opinion that because they were the
largest denomination and because of their connectional system, they could wield the most political power and exert the
most moral and religious influence of any of the churches.
The northern bishops, thinking back to the 1844 schism in
Methodism and how that augured the national breach, exclaimed that since the Church had "been productive of evil
their union could be productive of good. "[73] Reunion, of
course, meant absorption of the southern branch into the
truly national Church. To most of the ministers in the northern connection, the sectional scope of the Church was a
matter of reproach and as long as it remained, the nation
would be imperiled.

The Methodist came out with a series of articles
calling for the reunion of the churches. In the final article
the main argument was summed up in this fashion:

> The religious ties of a people are indeed its chief
> ligaments, and it will hardly be questioned that
> the unity of American Methodism would be one of
> the best bonds of the National Union and peace;
> for Methodism is in fact the popular, in a sense,
> the national religion of the country.... We doubt,

indeed, whether any reflecting statesman would
hesitate to say that any means of consolidating the
two political or geographical sections can surpass
in real power and permanence the identification of
the two great Methodist bodies. [74]

But northern Methodist hopes for reunion were not to be fulfilled. Deeply engrained on the southern mind was the war-
time rhetoric of their Yankee foe who had labeled their
Church apostate and treasonous. Every suggestion from the
northern Methodists of reform and re-civilizing the South
was resented and combated. Hunter Farish put it well when
he said,

> The Southerners saw in the plans for their re-
> generation sponsored by the Northern Methodists
> only the malice of a hypocritical foe. [75]

The response of southern Methodism to overtures of
reunion was, needless to say, less than enthusiastic. They
could recognize the obvious accomplishments of the war, the
restoration of the Union and the emancipation of slaves, but
they showed no evidence of casting off their own visions of
what southern society and Methodism should be. The Rev.
Dr. Myers of the Southern Christian Advocate called on
fellow churchmen to lay aside the "antiquated garb brought
over from England a century ago, and work out for itself a
new destiny ... adapted to a new order of things."[76] To
northern Methodists who thought of themselves as representing true Methodism, such talk of a special destiny for the
southern Church was appalling beyond belief. Especially
was this true when they recalled that this was the Church
that claimed divine sanctions for the institution of slavery.
To Curry, all talk of a special destiny on the part of
southerners meant that the Methodist Episcopal Church must
enter the South with plans of "disintegration and reconstruction," beginning with southern Methodism. [77]

It is not hard to imagine the disappointment and
anguish of men who truly thought theirs was a national
Church to which most Methodists, including the masses in
the South, owed allegiance, and for whom the bonds of na-
tional unity were dependent on a unified Methodism. The
Rev. T. H. Pearne bitterly rejected the notion that the
Methodist Episcopal Church was a "Northern Church" or a
"Yankee Church," as southerners called it. He said, "the
Methodist Episcopal Church is a non-sectional Church--

national, instead of sectional. "[78] He genuinely believed that
great numbers of people in the South embraced this idea.
Objecting to having his Church referred to as being "Exotic"
and Methodist missionaries called "Northern raiders," he
responded:

> Large numbers of the members, and some of the
> ministers, belonged to the Methodist Episcopal
> Church before the Southern Church seceded from
> us.   They were conscripted into that Church by a
> legislation and usurpation in which they had no
> voice, more than twenty years ago. ... [79]

The assumption proved fallacious as it became clear that
dislike of Yankees increased and devotion to southern principles intensified on the part of southern Methodists.

It became apparent to most northern Methodists eventually that in order to achieve a true moral and social unity,
that the nation might fulfill its divine calling, they could not
assume a common understanding of what America was, and
was to be.   During the war it was well known that at the
heart of the struggle there was a conflict of societies.   But
it was believed that only the southern aristocrats, the politicians, and the military leaders had this alien vision of a
special destiny for a separate southern nation.   It was only
after the war and during their attempts at reconstruction
that Methodists of the North fully realized the great chasm
between the two sections at the grass roots level.   The
Advocates of southern Methodism constantly reminded their
people that they were different, declaring that "the civilization of the two sections, and the customs and character of
the people are in many things diverse. "[80]   The southern religious papers also gave warning that "the mission and objective point of the Northern mind and purpose" was that
"the South must be reconstructed and recast in the moulds
of Northern thought and opinion. "[81]   Thus, to unite with
northern churches would mean a surrender to the dominance
of Yankee manners, ideas, and religion--"a disaster to
Christendom. "[82]   In drawing distinctions between the sections,
the New Orleans Christian Advocate stated:

> One broad distinction is that the Southerner as a
> matter of honor and principle, minds his own
> business, while the inborn nature of the North is
> to meddle.   The South is tolerant, courteous and
> refined in its contact with people in the ordinary

associations of life. The North has a prying, in-
quisitive disposition, and is bent on bringing every
one to its way of thinking and doing. [83]

The southern religious press also claimed that there was a
south-side and a north-side to matters of religion. The difference was seen not so much in matters of polity, creeds
or doctrines; but rather, in "the type of piety that prevails."

The political meddling of the Northern Churches is,
of course, one difference.... There is a secular-
ity about them, and a style that brings them into
near fellowship with worldly enterprises and organizations. They run things up there--Churches as
well as factories and railroads. The style of
their preaching is in contrast with ours, and is
largely of the politico-sensational order. [84]

The above quotations, while coming from just one
article, could be duplicated many times over to support the
"two nations" theory, and the view that the fundamental conflict was a clash of two cultures. A most telling document,
produced and signed by most of the outstanding denominational leaders of the Confederacy in 1863, tends to confirm
without much doubt that the war was understood by southern
churchmen as a conflict of civilizations. It was signed by
seventeen leading Methodists, including bishops and the
editors of the southern Advocates. With reference to the
early splits between major denominations, the southern clergy
remarked that the split was only nominal, for the churches had
in fact already been divided. Hence, the summons for reunion on the part of the North met with this response:

We are actually divided, our nominal union is only
a platform of strife. [85]

A major thesis of the document was that

The separation of the Southern States is universally
regarded by our people as final, and the formation
of the Confederate States' Government as a fixed
fact, promising in no respect, a restoration of
the former Union. [86]

The commentary on this thesis gives one a clue as to the
role of the churches during the war as the ideological in-
structors and bearers of the cause. It also indicates the

irrepressible character of not only the war, but especially of Reconstruction.

> Politically and ecclesiastically, the line has been drawn between North and South. It has been done distinctly, deliberately, finally, and in most solemn form. The Confederacy claims to possess all the conditions and essential characteristics of an independent Government. Our institutions, habits, tastes, pursuits, and religion, suggest no wish for reconstruction of the Union. We regard the Confederacy, in the wise providence of the Almighty, as the result of causes which render its independent existence a moral and political necessity, and its final and future independence of the United States not a matter that admits of the slightest doubt. [87]

The document later noted that the only change of material importance to occur among the southern people during the war had been

> the change from all lingering attachment to the former Union, to a more sacred and reliable devotion to the Confederate Government. [88]

The background that gives special significance to this official declaration of southern clergymen is, of course, the official declaration in 1861 that the South constituted a separate nation and that southern people were ready to die for their way of life and distinctive institutions. Concerning this brand of civil religion, Merle Curti has made the following perceptive point:

> The argument was advanced that in geography, in climate, in common traditions, in its pure "Anglo-Saxon" and "Cavalier" stock, in its economic life and its glorious future the South constituted a nation, and that this nation had a Manifest Destiny to dominate the western plains and the shores and islands of the Caribbean. [89]

Albion Tourgée, a layman of the Methodist Episcopal Church who was a lay-delegate to the General Conference of 1872, settled in North Carolina after the war and became a chronicler of Reconstruction activity. By 1880 he had published his book, A Fool's Errand, in which he observed,

The North and the South had been two households
in one house--two nations under one name. The
intellectual, moral, and social life of each had
been utterly distinct and separate from that of the
other. They no more understood or appreciated
each other's feelings or development than John
Chinaman comprehends the civilization of John
Bull. It is true they spoke the same language,
used the same governmental forms, and, most unfortunately, thought they comprehended each other's
ideas. ... The Northern man despised his Southern
fellow-citizen in bulk, as a good-natured bragga-
docio, mindful of his own ease, fond of power and
display, and with animating principle which could
in any manner interfere with his interest. The
Southern man despised his Northern compeer as
cold-blooded, selfish, hypocritical, cowardly, and
envious. [90]

Tourgée emphasized that the basic issue about which the two
sections were at cross-purposes was the status of freed
Negroes:

THE NORTHERN IDEA OF THE SITUATION	THE SOUTHERN IDEA OF THE SITUATION
The negroes are free now, and must have a fair chance to make themselves some-thing. ... they have a right to equality before the law. That is what the war meant. ...	We have lost our slaves, our bank stock, everything, by the war. ... The slave is now free, but he is not white. We have no ill will towards the colored man in his place; but he is not our equal. ... [91]

Here the central dilemma of Reconstruction stands out clearly.
Just as slavery and the preservation of the Union came to be
intimately related in the mind of northern churchmen during
the war, so the status of the freedman and national destiny
became the two basic and related issues in the post-bellum
period. For Haven, the mission of America was to embody
"the utmost liberty and equality of all men...."[92] In America God "has built an ark for humanity," he said. The bold
declaration of the Apostle Paul, that "God made of one blood
all the nations of men," set the vocation of the nation.

America seems to be the spot where this divine
purpose is to be first accomplished. [93]

Given this vision of America, the place of the black man in
American society was not a simple matter of humanitarian
concern. Its dimensions were no less than eschatological,
while also touching the historical destiny of the nation.
Haven saw the world as approaching "its ultimate paradisi-
acal estate" which will reflect "... the solidarity of the human race. "[94] With this vision, he posed the issue as a
fateful choice.

> ... we must welcome them as brothers or die.
> There is no alternative. God, our Creator and
> theirs, has brought us to this shore, foreign to
> both of us, that He may here develop the fullness
> of that Gospel scheme He is seeking to establish
> in the earth. [95]

The appeals by the Freedmen's Aid Society of the
Methodist Episcopal Church frequently referred to freedmen
as a crucial factor in the final destiny of the nation. The
corresponding secretary, R. S. Rust, told the 1873 conference that four million freed slaves in American society
indicated,

> ... that their destiny is intertwined with ours,
> affecting us more for weal or woe than any other
> four millions on the face of the earth.... Four
> millions of ignorant citizens in a national crisis
> may wreck the Republic![96]

The same forewarning was sounded forth by the principal
speaker, Dr. Townsend, at the 1875 meeting of the Society.
"How much like a providence of God it would be, if those
black men, " he exclaimed, "In some impending crisis, would
be left to wreck the Republic which has so brutally wronged
them. "[97] His warning was placed in the context of the political struggles between Catholic Democrats and northern
Protestant Republicans. The final blow to the country would
be a coalition between an embittered black people and foreign
Democrats. The means of preventing such a possible crisis,
he thought was for Republican Congressmen to insist on
Negro suffrage.

> ... if the Congress of the United States continues
> recreant, God will not ... delay, but will lash
> this nation with the rod of his wrath. Unless
> there is a change of policy, the romanist, in the
> form of a black man, shall be the ordained instru-
> ment of infliction. [98]

A sense of impending doom provided strong motivation for the social and religious mission of northern Methodists to the freedmen. But it wasn't just fear of God's wrath and the possibility of national destruction that drove them to take seriously this social and political problem. There was a positive side to their platform. "This land is the battleground of freedom ... the asylum of the world," read one report. 99 To be effective in the battle for Christ around the world, Methodists believed "especial care must be devoted to our own country," for upon the achievement of a true humanity on their own shores "hangs the destiny of the world."100 Another report said,

> we must render this service to the freedmen if we would accomplish the grand work assigned to us as a nation, in molding the development of humanity. The Almighty has given the American people what Archimedes in vain desired, a place upon which to stand in order to move the world. 101

The concern of northern Methodists for racial justice can also be viewed as part of the massive effort upon which they were embarked to evangelize the world. Who better could evangelize Africa than Africans? Bishop Thompson instructed:

> Providence has two modes of evangelizing--sending Christians into pagandom, and sending pagans into Christendom. Behold our providential, domestic, African mission. 102

Dr. Townsend noted that "the salvation of Africa has been a most difficult problem in missionary calculation and effort."103 He then suggested that,

> if we mistake not, this difficult problem is in process of self-solution. Africa is to be redeemed by her own sons. 104

The depth of the conflict between the two sections during Reconstruction as relates to the role of northern Churches cannot be properly estimated apart from the knowledge of the radical distinction in points of view concerning the freedmen. To the northern Methodist the freedman was not only a subject for regeneration, he was a means of regeneration. 105 Whereas, the typical southerner was convinced that the Negro would only be in the way and prevent

progress in his section. Speaking of this southern view a
northern Methodist stated the sharp conflict of views in these
words:

> When we reflect that God is training this people to
> do a missionary work of the greatest magnitude,
> we tremble for those who dare thus afflict them.
> The speaker before one of the Southern colleges,
> at a late commencement, must have thought other-
> wise, and must have imagined that the universe is
> really orphaned, when saying that the negro is in
> the way, significantly asking, 'Why cumbereth he
> the ground?'

> Why cumbereth he the ground! Is that the Southern
> man's inquiry? The impertinent question deserves
> but one answer: The colored man has earned his
> right to that soil, and God is not dead. 106

Despite the bitter confrontations and disillusionments
in the early years of Reconstruction, the vision of chosen
people called to redeem the world kept a hold on the deepest
motivations of northern Methodists as they sought to bring
religious and political regeneration to a torn land. It is one
of the ironies of American History that one of the major
achievements of northern Methodism in Reconstruction was an
"Angry Scar." It could not have been otherwise, for the
claim of the Freedman also kept hold of their conscience.
And however much they desired to cement the unity of the
nation and affect reunion with southern Methodism, northern
Methodists had to take the side of the black minority. New
England Methodists faced squarely the moral dilemma. On
the one hand they declared their commitment to "magnanimity and Christian charity," and on the other, they resolved not to recognize "distinctions based upon race, color,
or previous condition."107 Finally, the principle of unity
based on compromise was seen as a "surrendering of basis
[sic] principles, at the demand of a seeming and temporary
expediency."108 Confident that the principle of justice
would eventually be implanted in American life and that "no
power in earth or hell can stay or essentially hinder the onward march of that principle," they put the critical question
to the northern Church:

> Shall our church, though clothed as she is with a
> mighty power, make the attempt to stay that tri-
> umph? Or shall she consent, as alas she too

often has seemed to do, to be left to follow re-
luctantly the lead of statesmen in such great moral
questions.

> Nay, rather let us at once seize upon this right-
> eous watchword, and with it march in confidence,
> through difficulties, to certain and glorious vic-
> tory. Let us inscribe, upon every institution we
> plant or sustain, 'There is neither Greek nor
> Jew, circumcision nor uncircumcision, barbarian,
> Scythian, bond, nor free; but Christ is all and in
> all. ' 109

The General Conference of the Methodist Episcopal
Church during its 1868 session stated, in like manner, the
earnest hope for a genuine restoration of the southern states
to the Union, but only when "brotherly feeling and confidence
shall exist between all sections and classes.... "110 Thus,
the decision of the official body and the direction of its
social mission was stated in these words:

> ... we must enter our solemn protest against any
> system of reconstruction which does not secure
> hearty loyalty to the Federal Government and place
> all men equal before the law and in all the rights
> and eligibility of citizens without distinction of
> class or color. 111

In attempting to clarify the actual position taken by
northern Methodists on the various issues related to the
free Negro in America after the war, certain questions
arise: What was their teaching regarding race? What was
the position of the Church on social caste in both the North
and the South? Where did they stand on the suffrage question and other issues of political reconstruction? These
questions may now be taken up.

Racial Attitudes and Social Justice

Northern Methodists, who engaged in the struggle for
racial justice during the reconstruction period, became pain-
fully aware that one of the chief obstacles to the extension of
social and political equality was the existence of a deep
seated racial prejudice in the country, North and South. This
stubborn fact was candidly acknowledged by the Christian Advocate in a declaration that

The existence of an intense and inveterate prejudice among our white population against the
colored is a fact that cannot be ignored. We may
ridicule it as absurd, and denounce it as wicked,
(we do both,) but still the fact remains and must
be dealt with. Wherever this prejudice attempts
to override civil rights it should be restrained by
law. But civil law extends to much the less portion of the affairs of life. Social laws, unwritten,
·and often not consciously recognized, affect us
more intimately and powerfully, and these lie for
the most part beyond the scope of either civil or
ecclesiastical authority, and it is just here that
the white man's prejudice against the negro oper-
ates most effectively and injuriously. [112]

The Rev. J. C. Hartzell, later a bishop in the northern connection of Methodism, granted that there were
problems of ignorance, poverty and population concentrations
that hinder the assimilation of freedmen into society, but he
went on to say that "a yet more difficult factor remained,
and that is the factor of race antagonism. "[113] An article
titled "Nigger" in the Zion's Herald stated that the struggle
of the day was to get the ballot into the hands of any qualified person regardless of "whatever may be his color. "[114]
But while that warfare takes place in the political arena
there "is another phase of the struggle in the church, in
the parlor, in the workshop. "[115] The article enjoined
readers to take a hard look at the situation.

The colored man is everywhere elbowed from the
path. The word 'Nigger' says, 'Let him sit
apart, travel apart, work and worship apart. '
The laborer refuses to hoe in the field, to work
at the bench, by the side of his colored brother;
the girl in the factory declines to sit by the side
of her tinted sister. The real estate owner is
loth to admit a colored family into his tenements;
the master carpenter will not take a colored ap-
prentice; the storekeeper will not employ a colored
girl to sell ribbons across his counter ... there
is not a society in the New England Conference
that would employ a colored pastor, though he was
as devoted as the Apostle John and as eloquent as
Appolos. Most New England congregations would
be shocked at the mere suggestion. [116]

At the heart of an all-pervading racial prejudice in

the nation was the common assumption that Negroes were innately inferior. Northern Methodists were quite well aware that this assumption was one of the props for slavery in the ante-bellum days as well as one of the main ideological justifications for social and political exclusionary policies during Reconstruction. In this widespread popular belief in the natural inferiority of black people, Methodist clergymen of the North saw one of the major obstacles to the extension of social and political equality for Negroes. Hence, to argue for civil rights and against social caste they had to combat the concept of racial inequality.

To grasp the significance of the northern Methodist teaching on race, it ought to be clearly understood that most white Americans in the mid-nineteenth century believed that blacks were by nature relegated to a lower order of being than the Caucasian race. It was taken for granted that Negroes were naturally childlike, barbaric, shiftless and incapable of social assimilation into the white society. The distinguished editor of the Southern Review, Albert T. Bledsoe, in a review of Gobineau's The Moral and Intellectual Diversity of Race, said,

> The African is entitled to the protection of the laws as to life and liberty, and the acquisition of property; but he can claim no natural or moral right to equality in those personal matters which are the special and artificial product of the cultivation, social organization, skill, and energy of the white man. Nor can he expect the whites to forget, in a moment, his recent barbarism, and the steps of his progress from it, nor to ignore the fact that the highest point his race has yet arrived at is far below their own. [117]

Bledsoe did not deny progress for the Negroes, but did believe that in 1874 they were very low on "the scale of human life. "[118] But it is not necessary to quote southerners to document the pervasive belief in Negro inferiority. For most of his life, Lincoln shared the traditional attitude of his contemporaries that Negroes were, for biological reasons, incapable of living with white people "on terms of social and political equality. "[119] Andrew Johnson, in a speech in Nashville before the end of the war, said he would "not argue that the negro race is equal to the Anglo-Saxon--not at all. " "If the negro is better fitted for the inferior condition of society, " he continued, "the laws of nature will

assign him there. "[120]   Once earlier in the war he had
bluntly told an audience in Indiana:

> If, as the car of state moves along, the negroes
> get in the way, let them be crushed. [121]

Schuyler Colfax, soon to be nominated by the Republican
party for the Vice-Presidency, told an audience in Detroit
that

> I never believed in Negro equality.   I believe God
> made us, for his own wise purposes, a superior
> race. ...   But forgive me if while I think so I
> would endeavor to grind down lower this oppressed
> race.   Our principle is liberty to all. ...   But I
> think I can say without any impiety, I wish He had
> made all these races white, for had he done so,
> there would not be a Democrat today. [122]

That most white Americans in the North looked upon
Negroes as inferior and incapable of entering fully into the
social and political life of the nation may be fairly inferred
from the fact that black people continued to suffer from
legal, political, and economic disabilities in almost every
northern state.   In 1865 the question of Negro suffrage was
submitted to the voters in Connecticut.   After the smoke
had cleared from a bitterly fought campaign, a substantial
majority had decided against the Negro.   Elsewhere in the
North, Pennsylvania, New York, New Jersey, Ohio and Indiana ignored the issue altogether, while Wisconsin, Michigan and Minnesota turned down respective bills that would
have allowed impartial suffrage to Negroes.

While the notion of Negro inferiority was submerged
in the North during the war in favor of idealistic views promoted by clergymen and editors, the post-war period was
marked by a steady decline of this idealism.   In the Methodist Episcopal Church, for instance, laymen who had kept
quiet for the most part about the question of the Negro began to voice their own opinion.   One Pennsylvania Methodist
layman before the end of the war became angered over the
Philadelphia Annual Conference resolutions concerning emancipation and wrote "A Reply."   Addressing himself to "Fellow Sufferers of the M. E. Church," he said,

> ... God made the African race for servile labor,
> and that they never have been, nor ever will be

of any use on the face of the earth except as
slaves, and are a natural curse to society, just
in the ratio that they are freed. And that if they
should be all freed even by common consent of
their masters, it will ruin this whole nation. Yet,
as slaves they have proved one of God's greatest
natural blessings to this whole nation.... Doubtless, many voted for the above resolutions for
bunkum, others voted through latent fear, whilst
others voted with a clear design to make the negro
the white man's equal, when they know that both
the Old and New Testament Scriptures protest by
all their teachings against such ruin and degradation to his, God's people, and that everything in
the natural appearance, physical nature, natural
habits, and his whole history from Abraham to
our Lord Jesus Christ, and from our Lord to Abraham the first intended king of America, proves
beyond all successful contradiction that the African
negro was made for servile labor. [123]

Another very prominent Methodist layman, John A.
Wright, wrote a book advising the clergy of the "dangers
that threaten the pace, purity, and prosperity of the Methodist Episcopal Church. "[124] In one chapter he pointed out
the dangers posed by "the presence of colored representatives in the last General Conference. " He invoked the "law
of nature, of race, and of common sense, " to show that the
presence of black ministers, who were "ignorant" and "gross-
ly immoral, " could corrupt the life of the Church. [125]

Methodist clergy worked tirelessly but with little success not only to combat the views of the general populace,
North and South, but to deal with those within their own denomination. The depth and pervasiveness of the traditional
racial attitudes held by most Americans in the post-war
period must be regarded as a major factor contributing to
the failure of Reconstruction and of the northern Methodist
retreat from its own reconstruction program in the later
1870s. But, for a season, the leaders of the Church who
had guided their people through the struggles of the anti-
slavery movement and the tragic war years urged their
thesis of Negro fitness for social and political participation
with uncommon energy. They regarded it as one of the major aspects of their social ministry to teach a better theory
concerning the Negroes than the country had heretofore held.

What was their teaching? In answering that question,

caution must be used in making sweeping judgments. In the first place there was no complete and uniform theory of race represented by the teaching of the Methodist Episcopal Church, though there were striking commonalities. A further problem in dealing with racial attitudes a century ago is that patterns of thought, dominant ideas, and ideological perspectives were quite different from twentieth-century views. Hence, the interpreter must judge the previous generations in the light of their own standards. Another problem confronting one in the attempt to evaluate racial attitudes in the nineteenth century is the curious and imprecise way in which the term "race" is employed. Methodists could talk about the "Celtic" race with reference to Irish Catholics who "degraded our ballot-box and endanger our public order, " and at the same time believe that the Protestant Irish stock represented "sterling material for us."[126] Or, they could speak of emancipation producing a "new race of men" with reference to the freedmen.[127] Or again, one writer referred to American women as a "feeble race."[128] Daniel Curry could discuss the "Africo-American" race that is all "native-born" in contrast to immigrants of an "un-American character and tendencies" who are not native born, then suggest that it was the alien who challenged the native and genuine "American race, " to a great work.[129] When he uses the phrase, "American race, " in this context, to whom is he referring? It is difficult to know when there is such a variety of ways the term "race" functioned in the language of the day. All of the above mentioned limitations must be kept in mind in the following discussion.

Conservative and progressive Methodist clergy in the North, whatever their views on social or political equality for the free Negro, shared a firm belief in the basic humanity of Negroes. Articles in the Methodist Quarterly Review over a period of years demonstrated the unitary origin of the human race on philosophical, ethnological and theological grounds.[130] The clerics had to contend with the major ethnologists in the country. Men such as Josiah Nott, Louis Agassiz, Samuel G. Morton, and George Glidden, who constituted what was known as the "American School, " taught a "diversity of origins" theory of the human race. These polygenists taught that the various races of the world constituted separate species along a scale of being, with the Negroes at the bottom of the scale. They challenged the theory of Linnaeus that the test of species was the ability of two organisms to produce fertile offspring. Morton, however, argued that while mulattoes were fertile, their progeny

tended to be weak and would eventually die out. [131] Sometimes Methodists took up the cause on ethnological grounds,
arguing that the unity of species was

> ... indicated by the power of mutual and perman-
> ent reproduction, and is perfectly consistent with
> wide and tenacious varieties. [132]

Some disputants were more empirical in their approach,
noting that most of the blood in the Negro of the South represents a considerable racial mixture.   One article declared
that

> There are thousands of colored persons, scattered
> all over the once slaveholding States, who not only
> bear the names, but carry the features and ani-
> mate the blood of the so-called patrician race.
> The old Kaffir, Congo, Guinea blood has been
> mixed beyond all distinction and separation with
> that of every other nation that has had a foothold
> upon their shores. [133]

Abel Stevens disagreed with the theory that intermarriage between blacks and whites produced an inferior type.
He thought the Negro race was in a transition stage in an upward movement and that amalgamation could only have salutary consequences. Indeed, he thought that just as the
"British race" has risen from "its primitive inferiority ...
to the supreme place among nations, " so the Negro race,
through amalgamation will achieve "superior results. "[134]
His conclusion to a discussion on "The Problem of Our African Population" was that racial intermarriage was the final
solution to the American problem.   He wrote,

> But it is on scientific grounds that we chiefly
> assert, contrary to prevalent opinion, that 'amal-
> gamation, ' and nothing but amalgamation, in some
> way or other, must be the final solution of the
> problem. ...   England, France, Spain, modern
> Greece, have all homogeneous populations com-
> pounded of various races; ... is there any other
> historical or scientific solution to be offered us?
> If not, should it not be the aim of all thinkers,
> and of all good men among us, to diminish rather
> than fortify the prevalent prejudice against it?[135]

Lending Episcopal support to his thesis, Stevens recalled

that the "amalgamationist" Bishop, Gilbert Haven, constantly
preached that the Caucasian race would be improved and social caste would be solved through racial intermarriage.
Stevens wrote that after Gilbert Haven had studied the black
man all over the South,

> he could never criticize Moses's choice of an
> Ethiopian wife; and he believed it quite possible
> that, some day or other, an American leader of
> the people might not hesitate to introduce one into
> the presidential mansion. [136]

More comfortable ground than the scientific or pragmatic approaches was the Bible, as Methodists countered the
diversity of origins theory. Professor Agassiz had stated
that the Bible was "solely an account of the white race, and
makes no reference at all to ... the non-historical races."[137]
The respondent traversed much of the Old and New Testament
to show that this theory was fallacious, urging that the whole
of scriptural teaching pointed to the essential unity of the
races. Ending up with Paul's declaration that "God has
made of one blood all nations of men," he asked,

> Is not the entire Bible-teaching about sin, the
> moral government of God, the fall of man, and
> redemption in Christ, based on this assumption?
> If we exclude the non-historic races from all con-
> nection with Adam, must we not, by the express
> language of Paul, ('as in Adam all die, so in
> Christ shall all be made alive,') also exclude
> them from all connection with Christ? And if on
> the contrary they are expressly affirmed to be
> connected with Christ, does not this also affirm
> their connection with Adam? Must not a cause
> that requires such exegesis as this be pressed
> for support?[138]

The writer concluded that if one took the thesis of Agassiz
seriously, then all missionary efforts of the Church would
simply be "foolish and futile attempts to traverse the im-
mutable ordinations of the Creator."[139]

Though some Methodists did take up the pen against
the scientists on a theoretical level, they were primarily
concerned with the practical implications of their doctrines.
They firmly believed that theories of Negro inferiority
functioned as a justification for maintaining the system of

social caste existing throughout the country. Therefore, they combated the teaching that denied the essential humanity of Negroes, primarily to change the public mind, social patterns and certain political institutions.

The main locus of the debate was with southerners who "had been educated to believe that the negro is by nature an inferior being."[140] Northern writers were quite aware that in the South it was generally believed that Negroes innately lacked the qualities necessary to exercise the privileges of freedom on the level of the Caucasian population. The Rev. N. E. Cobleigh remarked that many in the South actually believed that the Negro "had descended not from Adam, but from some federal head of the monkey tribe, and therefore was incapable of cultivation and refinement...."[141] With this belief in their very souls, he said, they

> revolted at the idea of placing the white and colored races on the plane of either social or civil equality. While the North believed this to be right, and the solemn duty of the nation to make it an accomplished fact, to the South it really appeared all wrong, and that it was their religious duty and privilege to oppose it.[142]

Commenting on the honesty and the depth of their convictions, Cobleigh then chided northerners for "not giving them credit for sincerity in their beliefs."[143]

Gilbert Haven was one northerner who did not need to be educated to see that the character of the Negro was the underlying issue in the slavery controversy. Indeed, he exhorted,

> ... we cannot expect, we shall never see, the complete removal of this curse from our land until we stand boldly and heartily upon the divine foundation--the perfect unity of the human race.[144]

A writer for The Methodist stated his comprehension of the Confederate attitude in the following way:

> In no elevated sense was the negro a man; he was incapable of any rights except the lowest; his mental faculties were such as to barely establish humanity; it was generally conceded that he had a soul, though a book or two was even written on

the negative side of that question; but the southern
leaders would have soon as thought of addressing
the intellect of the turkeys or mules of the Confederacy as that of their negroes. [145]

Statements such as this appeared many times over in the northern Methodist press during the post-bellum period. [146]   Believing that the character of the Negro was the underlying
issue in the slavery controversy and in the questions concerning the destiny of the freedmen, northern representatives of
Methodism proclaimed "it as their mission to teach a better
theory concerning the Negro...."[147]   They used their pens
and their voices to attack the concept of Negro inferiority by
attempting to show that cultural disabilities and social vices
of black people were caused by environmental conditions.   A
few illustrations will be sufficient to show the line of thought.

One of the common reasons given for retaining a system of social separation was that there was a "natural antipathy" between "different races."[148]   Countering this "consciousness of kind" theory, a Methodist editor declared that
"No such 'natural antipathy' keeps us away from the hotel
where we have him ever at our elbow as we eat...."[149]
Turning to the South, he averred that

> No such 'natural antipathy' has prevented the lord-
> liest of the Southern aristocrats from being nursed
> at the breasts, and dandled on the knees of colored
> women.   In fine 'natural antipathy' does not prevent
> us from employing a colored man as porter, hack-
> man, barber, waiter, but it does prevent our em-
> ploying him in an occupation that we would follow
> ourselves.   It is not nature, it is caste. [150]

Illustrating how unreasonable and ludicrous it was to taunt
the black man as being "unfitted for social and political duties," the editor exclaimed,

> Tie his hands, and curse him that he does not
> work!   Fasten weights upon his limbs, and then
> scoff at him that he does not outstrip us in the
> race. [151]

Northerners, who presumed to tell southerners what
to do about the freedman, were usually met with the argument that they were meddling with matters beyond their
knowledge.   It was the white southerner who understood the

Negro. A writer for The Methodist thought it was a cardinal
error for northerners to believe this claim of southerners to
superior knowledge about Negroes. He believed that in fact
the southern white people were in error in estimating Negroes
on two counts: first, because they looked at a slave and
thought they saw a Negro, and secondly, because they studied
the Negro as a Negro, and not as a man.

> As to the first assumption, that the South had the
> slaves and therefore understood the negro, nothing
> could have been more unfair or misleading. They
> hobble the horse, and, without allowing him to be
> liberated for one hour, undertake infallibly to esti-
> mate his capacity for speed. They clip the wings
> of the carrier pigeon and carefully keep them
> clipped, and then learnedly discuss his powers of
> aerial travel. [152]

Making the obvious application, the northern Methodist lectured that it was unjust to draw conclusions about Negro fitness for social and political participation in the common life
of society when he was not permitted to enter society as a
man. Moreover, he asked, "was it just to infer the natural
inferiority of the negro from his degradation in slavery?"
As for the second southern assumption, the writer said that
because they studied the Negro as a Negro and not a man,
"the problem of negro humanity was separated from that of
general humanity. "

> The Yankee knew the negro better. He conceded
> his humanity, and studied him as simply a man.
> He saw a man under his black skin.... [153]

Most of the spokesmen for northern Methodism exhibited a dynamic view of social reality. They believed that
social institutions and cultural patterns had profound effects
on people. Indeed, some of the arguments put forth to
counter the belief in the Negro's basic inferiority sounded
like a thoroughgoing social determinism. Dr. J. P. Newman, one of northern Methodism's most aggressive advocates of social and political equality for freedmen, admitted
to deficiencies in the Negro race, but he claimed that adverse
social effects of slavery and prejudice were responsible.
The proof of this, he thought, could be seen in the substantial successes in the field of education. "It is no longer an
experiment whether the child of the freedmen can learn to
read and write, " he said. "They learn with the ease, accuracy, and rapidity of white children. " Hence, he exclaimed,

The question is being experimentally settled that
the African race is inferior only from oppression,
neglect, and deprivation. Nor is this intellectual
aptitude to learn confined to mulattoes and quad-
roons, for the genuine Congo, with receding fore-
head and prognathous jaws, evinces the same aptitude and equal delight.[154]

George Peck saw slavery as morally wrong because
in the slave system the Negro was regarded not "as a person, but as a thing." Consequently it was slavery that "de-
nudes the slave of all that constitutes him an intelligent,
moral, and responsible being."[155] The key to restoration
of essential manhood was freedom, for when they were
"free from the shackles of forced servitude ... they ceased
to be "things," they became "men."[156] A Methodist educator pressed the claim that it was not innate inferiority that
caused the mental disability of southern Negroes; rather it
was slavery that "came well-nigh [to] obliterating the Negro's native wit and genius."[157] To advance his contention
that just as social conditions can debilitate, they can also
elevate, he cited the testimony of Theodore Parker, who
told about a young Negro, Anthony Burns. Burns was first
taken to Oberlin "as a dull clod of stupidity," but, so the
story goes, "the change that came over him was the most
wonderful thing the Oberlin teachers had ever seen."[158]
Capping his argument, the writer said,

When it fairly dawned upon him that he could
learn to read, his zeal to improve has unbounded.
He was at his books the whole time, and his capacity for learning developed more and more.
The whole manner of the man was altered.[159]

The effects of prejudice and slavery on the character
of Negroes, according to Daniel Curry, were such that would
preclude "any tendency to 'negro worship.'" "The negro,
contemplated simply as he is," said Curry, "can hardly be
made a hero." In a candid comparison with "the average of
civilized Christian society," he saw Negroes as "low--weak,
ignorant, debased." The chief defects seen were: immor-
ality, lack of self-respect, idleness, lack of self-reliance
and ignorance. This pessimistic picture did not, however,
serve as a justification for a system of caste. Nor did he
conclude natural inferiority of Negroes. They are "crude ...
rather than vitiated," he declared.[160] S. G. Arnold was
equally forthright in and unsentimental in his estimate of the
freedmen's condition.

> Men just out of slavery, and especially cotton and
> sugar slavery, are not, it is true, of the very
> highest order of manhood. 161

He could not agree with the traditional southern notion that
slavery served to elevate the African; to Christianize and
civilize him. Rather, slavery produced a race "diseased
in body," "diseased in mind," "without self reliance," and
"without self government." What was the solution? For
both Curry and Arnold and most of the northern Methodist
clergy, the two immediate needs were enfranchisement and
education. Then they could

> confidently anticipate the complete deliverance of
> that long scourged but still enduring race from
> its present afflictions, and its not distant elevation
> among the peoples of the earth. 162

The attack on the notion of the inherent inferiority of
Negroes and the belief in natural antipathy between races
was never more forceful than when Gilbert Haven lifted his
voice. He believed that the very cornerstone of the social
caste system in America was "prejudice against color" and
that this prejudice arose not by "natural" aversions; rather,
it came from "American caste." Speaking of Negroes, he
said, "Their social status has wrought this prejudice in
us." Arguing that social conditions breed feelings that are
falsely articulated as "natural aversions," he made this
point:

> The English Norman would have felt unutterable
> disgust had his Saxon neighbor claimed social
> equality and intimacy. To this day the English
> noble, or even gentleman, would profess that he
> had a 'natural aversion' to the serf, though of one
> parentage a few generations back. 163

In nineteenth-century America, people tended to reason that
because the slave was black and the white man freed, therefore, it was "natural" for the "black man to be a slave."
However, if that is the case there was a fundamental theological issue at stake, as Haven saw it:

> ... then there is a vital natural and eternal dis-
> tinction between them 'the white man and the
> black man'--a great gulf fixed by God. 164

Haven's main argument against the view that racial

antagonism was natural was rooted in the Scriptures. "It finds no place in all Bible history, " he proclaimed.

> Solomon treated the Queen of Sheba, a negress of Abyssinia, with the utmost respect and cordiality; Philip ran reverently by the side of the chariot of a negro, and chief minister of the court of her successor; Moses married an Ethiopian; a negro was called of God and his brethren to be one of 'the prophets and teachers of the church at Antioch, ' with Barnabas. ... [165]

"More than this, " claimed Haven, "the Bible constantly proclaims the ... oneness of the race of man, in Adam, Noah and Christ. "[166] At another time he said the real question was simply whether the Biblical doctrine of "the absolute oneness of the human race" was true or not and "whether Christ is the elder brother of all humanity, or only of a proud and petty portion thereof. ... "[167]

Haven never once suggested that there might be basic differences between the races. This was not the case with some other leading clergymen of his Church. Some northern Methodists, although they contended for the essential unity of the races, nevertheless suggested that there were inherent differences. Daniel Whedon criticized southerners for their white supremacy attitudes, but then suggested that social separateness might not be all wrong. Stating his case very cautiously, he said,

> Beyond all reasonable question there is in each race, we will not say 'antipathy' to the other, but a spontaneous preference for its own color, which is a rightful basis not for slavery or inequality, but for a social separateness which is not justly or truthfully called caste. Each of the two colors, equally and alike, feels this natural self-preference. Were both colors in this country absolutely equal in numbers and in every point of power and respectability, and perfectly friendly to and on a level with each other, yet each would by spontaneous affinity gravitate to its own, and a perfectly Christian and amicable distinctness, without caste, would exist. [168]

Whedon thought it correct to use the term "natural" to signify racial differences

if we hold 'natural' to signify that aesthetic taste
super-induced upon our primitive nature by the
physiological variations of race. [169]

Daniel Curry, second only to Haven in urging social and political equality for Negroes, said,

Their extreme diversity, physically, from the rul-
ing type of our people seems to effectually forbid
their physical assimilation; and this, also, makes
their social union an impossibility. [170]

The editor of the Western Christian Advocate, John
Reid, wrote that both white and black men were subject to
"the inevitable tendency not to amalgamate, but to separate,
even in church relations."[171] The Pittsburgh Advocate expressed, editorially, the same sentiment and probably echoed
views of the vast majority of ordinary clergymen in northern
Methodism. Certainly the belief in a natural propensity for
social separation among the races provided a strong impetus
for making official a segregated structure within Methodism
at a later date. The Pittsburgh editor used this belief to
promote what he believed to be the wisest policy toward the
South; that was "to leave the freedmen to be harvested by
the African Methodist churches."[172] While his views did
not prevail during the early days of Reconstruction, by the
end of the 1870s white northern Methodist efforts to evangelize the freedmen had almost totally diminished. And in
the North, by the close of Reconstruction, social caste in
the Churches was the normal pattern. But this did not happen without a struggle. Most of the leadership in northern
Methodism, including those who thought "social separation"
was natural, denounced "social and ecclesiastical caste" as
a sin.

Before turning to a brief consideration of the actual
stand of the Church on matters of ecclesiastical caste; social
and political equality and Reconstruction policies, one observation is offered. It may be said that in the teaching about
race, which northern Methodists took to be a central aspect
of their social mission, one finds a standpoint strikingly
alien to commonly held views. The extraordinary thing about
these northern religionists was not that some of them accepted the view of racial differences and inferiority, but that at
a time when the overwhelming majority of people believed in
the Negro's absolute inferiority, there were prominent denominational leaders who boldly declared their faith in the
basic equality of all men, regardless of race.

But, these men, who sought to teach a more Christian
theory about race than was generally held, did so in the
interest of actually changing conditions. This social ministry focused on three main questions: What was the Church
to do about caste within its own common life? What was the
message of the Church regarding patterns of social inequality
in society in general? And, what was the position of Methodism on the question of suffrage?

Concerning caste in the Church, the 1866 New England
Annual Conference declared that of

> ... conferences, churches, or schools organized,
> designated, or designed for colored people, when
> based upon a supposed taint of blood, a spirit of
> caste or prejudice against race because of color
> or condition, we can but regard as a recognition
> of that foul spirit, and as being alike unreason-
> able, absurd, and wicked in the sight of heaven,
> a gross insult to the common Father and Saviour
> of us all. [173]

Wisconsin ministers in the same year rejected an ecclesiastical reconstruction policy that would make distinctions
between blacks and whites: "... let us not divide the body
of Christ, " they said, "nor make unscriptural discrimina-
tions. "[174] Having in mind a social witness to the broader
society, they said that by banishing the "spirit of caste from
the church, " they would be doing their "part towards its ex-
tirpation from civil society. "[175] Abel Stevens called on his
denomination to resolutely direct its "leaders to obliterate
the 'color' line 'from our Churches. '"[176] He judged that
the prejudice which lay back of the "color line" was

> an egregious social fallacy, against which every
> really high-minded citizen should protest as be-
> littling to our national good sense, our religion
> and our republicanism. We believe, further, that
> nearly all our apprehensions of social inconven-
> iences from the obliteration of that 'line, ' especial-
> ly in the Church, are utterly fallacious. [177]

The editorial policy of the Christian Advocate in New York
was unequivocal in stating that the Church must "regard
man as God does, as redeemed and called to the inheritance
of the saints" and so, "entitled ... to the common benefits
of the Gospel. "[178] Abolishing all caste in the structure and

life of the Church was not only morally and religiously ordained, but because "The negro is the coming man" and because his progress "will be relatively greater than that of
any other division in society, " that policy of inclusiveness
was considered as a very practical one. By doing away
with caste, and by securing "to itself the colored-population
of the country, " the Advocate thought Methodism would
"make sure of a great power in the future. "[179] . This commingling of religious motives and sectarian interests was
not at all untypical of the Methodist Episcopal Church.

For three years before the end of the war, northern
Methodists had been following the victorious Union soldiers
into the captive cities and territories of the South.   They
assumed control over many Methodist Churches that had been
vacated by Confederate clergymen, while pursuing a missionary policy designed to win both southern blacks and
whites.   They soon found that it was expedient to draw color
lines, especially as northern preachers attempted to minister to southern white Methodists.   When the war ended and
evaluations of the southern mission reached the northern
connection, it became apparent that the Methodist Episcopal
Church had failed to win the white people and had virtually
turned the mission to Negroes over to the African Methodist
Episcopal Church.

In two consecutive articles, Gilbert Haven addressed
the question as to "how the northern Church should go
South. " His assessment of the situation was expressed as
follows:

> We have had this field in our grasp for nearly
> three years, but have done comparatively nothing,
> and are still doing nothing.   Why is this?[180]

His answer was direct--and in his words, "in the fear of
God. " "We have not dared to do right. " The problem, as
he saw it, was that the Church persisted in recognizing the
spirit of caste in its attempts at organizing "colored Churches
after the old God-accursed and God-chastened pattern. " "We
have committed the great and deplorable blunder, nay sin, "
he cried, "of organizing conferences with this ignominious
prefix, and of saying to these brethren,

> 'If you would labor with us in the ministry you
> must do it in these Pariah bodies.   Though you
> preach in Charleston you must hold your relation

290 / The Sectional Crisis

in the Washington Conference; though we can re-
vive the conference of East Tennessee, we cannot
admit you if preaching at Knoxville into its ranks.'
Nay we go further and have made these missionary conferences, thus disfranchising all these brethren who still remain with us, and putting upon them
the brand which the state is hastening to remove.[181]

Haven thought that to embody the spirit of caste in the organization of the Church would be to say to the southern black
man that the white southerner was much superior, however
much Negroes "surpassed them in intelligence, virtue, in-
dustry and piety. " The answer to the problem was clear.
And that was

... to entirely ignore the idea of color in the organization of our Churches and conferences throughout the whole land.[182]

Haven's position may not have been popular with some
northern ministers and bishops, but it did prevail in the official policy of the Church during the reconstruction years.
The measure of his influence is indicated by the fact that he
was elected to the Episcopacy during the 1872 General Conference. And this happened in spite of efforts, on the part
of his enemies, to discredit him by printing and passing out
the "ultra passages" from his books and sermons on social
and political questions.[183] His views not only prevailed,
but he, himself, as the appointed Bishop of the George area,
carried them into the southern field where, according to his
biographer, "Mr. Haven practiced that doctrine of political
and social equality which he had so urgently taught as one
of the chief duties of the Church in our times."[184]

As has already been shown, Methodists of the North
were convinced that one of the chief roles of their denomination was in forming the conscience of society. Certainly
this was true when it came to the temperance question and
questions pertaining to loyalty and obedience to the United
States government. It was equally true concerning the
"Negro question. " Most northern Methodists could agree
with The Rev. J. C. Hartzell when he said,

The needed conscience toward the Negro as a
freeman the whole American Church must give.
Politics or commercial activity will not do this.
The Churches of the North must lead the way in

the development of this needed and new conscience,
and the Methodist Episcopal Church, to a great
extent responsible for freedom to the slave, is
therefore, largely responsible before God for the
conscience of the South and the nation toward the
Negro as a freeman. [185]

Northern Methodists were faithful enough to that charge
to earn the reputation, in some quarters, for being that
"negro equality Church. "[186] Whether that was meant pejora-
tively or as commendation is not necessary to know.   It
was probably both.   By 1867 the rumor got around in Alabama that the Methodist Episcopal Church was "Massa Link-
um's church. "[187]   The reputation was no doubt earned by
the massive presence of the northern Methodists all over
the South during Reconstruction; by their close identification
with the Republican party; and by the endless pronouncements,
sermons and articles stating in various ways that the Methodists mean "to stand up for exact, equal and Gospel-like
justice for the Negro. "[188]   The Methodist distinction for
standing by the Negro was noted by an arch denominational
rival.   The American Presbyterian remarked on how young
the denomination was, then said that "if they were a thousand
years old, they could not be better champions of Christian
justice and freedom. "[189]

A sampling of statements made by the official press
and official bodies of the Church leaves little doubt as to
where the Methodist Episcopal Church stood on the question
of social justice for Negroes.   As early as 1864 the General
Conference took a strong stand favoring equal rights for
Negroes and significantly elected three outspoken men for the
cause to edit the New York, Western and Central Advocates. [190]   The new editors, Daniel Curry, J. M. Reid and
B. F. Crary, consistently made appeals to their readers for
supporting the "right" side on the Negro question.   In 1868
the General Conference issued a

> solemn protest against any system of reconstruction
> which does not secure hearty loyalty to the Federal
> Government, and place all men equal before the
> law in all the rights and eligibility of citizens with-
> out distinction of class or color. [191]

The official body that year received a petition from the Rev.
Lucius Matlack requesting the General Conference to rescind
the resolutions passed by the Conference of 1836 censuring

abolitionist Methodist preachers. In an act of official repentance, such action was taken. [192] In 1872 the General
Conference refused to allow the word "colored" in designat-
ing Annual Conferences and rejected a petition offered by
black and white delegates from Alabama to authorize separate
Conferences. [193]

The Church press uniformly went on record favoring
civil justice for Negroes. Whedon, in an editorial statement
in the Methodist Quarterly Review, called for the "extension
of just and equal laws and impartial enfranchisement ...
under a policy of freedom and regulated justice."[194] The
editor of the Western Christian Advocate, discussing a resolution in the Ohio legislature to strike the word "white" from
the Constitution, said,

> It is right, as well as politic, to strike out this
> word.... It is a trespass upon manhood, a viola-
> tion of the rights of our neighbor, a wrong which
> we should hasten to redress. Religion cries out
> against it, and this sad discrepancy between the
> Constitution and the law of God should at once be
> effaced. [195]

The Zion's Herald admonished Christians to work for "all
the rights and privileges of citizenship to the freedmen and
to colored race within the national domain."[196] A writer
for the Northwestern Christian Advocate told his readers
that the Methodist pulpit was right when it "sounded the trump
[sic] of war," and when it led thousands of brave men "to
fight, bleed, to die, for liberty, for justice, for truth."
Urging a continuance of that struggle, he said the Church
could not "cancel those statements," nor could it "revoke
that action ... for, before God, we believe we were right."[197]

It is hardly necessary to cite examples of the numerous statements made by the Annual Conferences calling on
the Church and the nation to rise above the common prejudices of the land. The general position of nearly all the
Conferences is perhaps best exemplified by the statement
of the committee on the "State of the Country," chaired by
George L. Crooks of the New York East Conference. It
reads:

> The Bible, our text-book and standard, teaches
> the common origin and equality of the race. We
> should, therefore, as pastors and teachers, rising

above the prejudices of ignorance or education,
maintain the rights of all classes of people among
us, and claim the brotherhood of man. [198]

The generalities about equality and freedom reached
concretion in the political question of suffrage. Clergymen
from the Methodist Episcopal Church were on the front line
in efforts to pass the Civil Rights bill of 1866 and continu-
ously agitated for passage laws granting suffrage to Negroes.
Columns dealing with this issue filled the religious press, as
they later would concerning temperance and prohibition.

Most abolitionists called for universal suffrage, arguing that it was unfair to impose literacy qualifications on the
franchise when the freedman for generations had been denied
educational opportunities. [199] Universal suffrage was not,
however, the position of northern Methodists. Nearly all
came down on the side of impartial suffrage. But they were
adamant about that. Although they were true men of the
nineteenth century, deeply committed to the democratic creed,
they maintained a strain of eighteenth-century Wesleyan Tory-
ism. In addition to the well-honored heritage of Wesley there
was another factor that may have contributed to a more conservative approach than the run of the mill abolitionists. It
should be remembered that the bishops, educators, religious
journalists and other leaders of northern Methodism were a
very well educated group. In some respects, one gets the
impression that as clergymen they even thought of themselves
as constituting an elite company in society--which they no
doubt were. At any rate, there was a strong feeling that
you can only have good government by having a good class
of voters.

In one of the better articles on the question of suffrage
qualification, S. G. Arnold cited De Tocqueville's strictures
on the "tyranny of the majority," to support his contention
that so far as democratic government has been a success
"it has succeeded not because the people have ruled, but because the people who ruled were, in some sense, qualified
to rule...."[200] His conclusion, then, was that the good of
the state requires the "admission of those who are intellect-
ually and morally qualified to the suffrage."[201] As to the
Negro, he thought there was only one course of action "if
he is to be treated in the spirit of that 'democratic principle.'"[202] The course advocated in the article was this:

By action of the general government and a large

> majority of the states he is made a free man, and
> must be in the eye of the Constitution and before
> the law a citizen on the same footing as any other
> citizen. All laws which relate to color or descent
> must be blotted from the statute-book. He must
> be able to hold property, to give his testimony in
> courts of justice, to prosecute before all judicial
> tribunals, and to vote at elections on precisely the
> same terms as any other citizen. Nay, he must
> have the right to be elected to office, if he can
> secure a majority, with no disability which does
> not attach to other men. The negro, if we treat
> him wisely, or even fairly, must henceforth be
> a man, no more or less. [203]

Jesse T. Peck, soon to be elected bishop, wrote that it was
by the "order of Providence" that partiality based on color
was wiped away in the "Great Revolution."[204] And that with
the war over,

> It may be that the American people will be able to
> find some standard of intelligence which belongs
> to true responsible civil manhood, and that the
> right of the ballot will be as broad as this ascer-
> tained legal manhood. But whatever may be its
> basis, when the new nation is completed, the as-
> serted, conceded right of suffrage will be impar-
> tial. [205]

From his editor's chair in Chicago, T. M. Eddy exclaimed
that

> Universal suffrage is quite clearly postponed. The
> moral convictions of the country are against partial
> suffrage, or caste suffrage; against disfranchising
> any man on account of his nationality or color, but
> they are gravitating towards an impartial, intelli-
> gent suffrage--toward some test by which the capa-
> city of men to exercise the prerogative of suffrage
> shall be decided. [206]

    The rationale given for enfranchising Negroes was
varied. One northern Methodist, after giving a scriptural
justification for equal suffrage, quite candidly admitted that
"the time is coming when we may need not merely the negro
labor but the negro Vote."[207] He had in mind, of course,
the Catholic immigrant who would most assuredly be voting

as a Democrat and whose vote would be neutralized by masses
of Negro Republicans. [208]   But there was a further reason for
supporting equal suffrage, as indicated in this unabashed remark:

> And we may add, by the way, that in moral influ-
> ence over our political destinies Methodism would
> have nothing to lose by an enfranchisement that
> might double the Methodist vote in the nation. [209]

In looking for underlying reasons for the enthusiastic
support of Methodists for suffrage, it is important to remem-
ber that the social ideals of clergymen in the mid-nineteenth
century were to a very large extent shaped by the pervasive
belief in democratic ideals. Of those ideals, Ralph Gabriel
has noted, one of the most important for the mass of Americans was that of "the free and responsible individual. "[210]
The social thinking of the time focused on the doctrine of
liberty, and Methodists, no less than any other group, were
captive to this credo. The exaltation of the free individual
lay back of their sentiments on women's suffrage; of their
drive to give laymen the voting privilege in official bodies
of the Church; as well as their interest in enfranchising Negroes. Whedon spoke for most Methodists when he said,

> A belief in the right of every competent human in-
> dividual to have a due share in controlling the so-
> cial system controlling that individual's destinies,
> lies at the bottom of our advocacy of negro eman-
> cipation, of lay representation, and of female suf-
> frage in State and Church. [211]

Beyond pragmatism and democratic ideology was the
Christian faith. Haven placed the matter of "civil equality
and fraternity" right at the heart of the Gospel. In answer
to the question, "What must be done?" he answered,

> This and this only: to abolish from the national
> action and the national heart all distinctions aris-
> ing from color or origin; all thought and feeling
> that such distinctions are divinely intended to sep-
> arate members of the same human family, who
> are and must ever be one in blood and in destiny,
> in sin and in salvation, in Adam and in Christ. [212]

This work, he believed, should be carried forward in the
Church.

> She should proclaim the great doctrine of the
> cross, the unity, the fraternity of man, and should
> declare that what God hath put together man shall
> not put asunder. [213]

It should be mentioned that while most Methodists did
proclaim political and social justice, not all were as enthusiastic about fraternity as was the intrepid Bishop Haven.
A Methodist writer mentioned above with regard to increasing the Methodist vote--assured his readers that "the two
things, political rights and social equality, do not belong to
the same sphere of thought. Political rights are a matter
of public law and constitution;" he continued, "social intercourse belongs to individual taste and choice. "[214] To Haven
such a view evaded the basic problem with which Americans
had to deal. He claimed that equality at the polls was not
the only work laid upon the nation. He spoke of a "leprosy"
that "lies deep within. It dwells in our churches, in our
souls, in our education, in society. "[215] That prejudice he
exclaimed,

> still leads us to erect barriers between us and
> our kindred, and to make us and them talk of
> 'our race' as if they and we had a different parent-
> age, Savior, and eternity. It must come to an
> end. It is coming to end. [216]

Not stopping with fraternity in the shop, the parlor or the
sanctuary, he yearned for the hour

> 'not far off' when the white hued husband shall
> boast of the dusky beauty of his wife, and the
> Caucasian wife shall admire the sun-kissed coun-
> tenance of her husband. [217]

It would be the day when

> The Song of Songs will have a more literal fulfill-
> ment than it has ever confessedly had in America;
> and the long existing, divinely-implanted admira-
> tion of Caucasians for black but comely maidens,
> be the proudly acknowledged and honorably grati-
> fied life of Northern and Southern gentlemen. [218]

"Amalgamation is God's Word, " proclaimed Haven before a
Medford, Massachusetts congregation, "Who art thou that
fightest against God. "[319] While Abel Stevens openly declared

his sympathy for Haven's amalgamation ideas, it may be
fairly estimated that he was one of the few northern Methodists who did. Indeed, many of his colleagues were to
lament the fact that his proposition for "mixing and inter-
mingling all colors" was converted into a weapon with which
enemies tried to beat back the Methodist challenge in the
South. [220] Haven's endorsement of amalgamation gave him
"the reputation as one of the most radical equalitarians in
the country, " as William Gravely quite rightly points out. [221]

The story of the northern Methodist challenge has been
well told by Ralph Morrow, Hunter D. Farish, William Warren Sweet and others, as has the story of their final retreat
from an inhospitable land. The efforts to break down social
and religious caste in the North met with the same fate. By
1876 the General Conference was forced to designate "colored"
conferences in the structure of ecclesiastical boundaries.
The same year northern and southern Methodists took their
first step in establishing official fraternal relations along
the long road to a unified denomination which would culminate
at the Uniting Conference of 1939. Just as the schism in 1844
anticipated the sectional conflict, so that Cape May Conference
in 1876 anticipated by a year the compromise designated by
the name of the newly elected president, Rutherford B. Hayes.

It has not been the intent of this chapter to either vilify
or vindicate northern Methodists in their approach to social
issues. Rather, the purposes have been to show that leading figures of the Methodist Episcopal Church did have an
approach to social issues and to investigate that approach in
terms of the meaning they ascribed to Reconstruction and in
terms of their social and religious thought regarding questions
posed by free blacks in the post-war period. In light of the
historical evidence presented in this chapter and in the book
as a whole, it may be fairly concluded that Methodists in the
North were not at all complacent about social problems and
that, for all their limitations in systematizing a social ethic,
they were able to state fundamental national problems in
such a way as to do reasonable justice to both the moral and
the political dimensions of those perplexing issues. Because this has not usually been acknowledged, some concluding observations may be in order. They will be made by
way of a brief response to certain allegations already noted
in various parts of the study and specifically to the following
statement by Professor Robert Moats Miller:

Hopkins, May, and the other historians of the rise

of social Christianity devote isolated sentences, not chapters or books, to Protestantism's fight for racial justice. The story does not deserve much fuller treatment. Assuredly, the churches contributed alms to the freedmen in the South. They established schools, hospitals, and charitable institutions to succor the untrained blacks, but few were the clerical voices to challenge the racial status quo or to question the divine right superiority of the white man. 222

It may be fair to suggest that had southern Methodist clerics or northern Methodist laymen or any number of other groups living between the years 1864 and 1876 heard such a statement, they would have been dumbfounded. This volume stands as a sharp dissent to such conventional wisdom.

In response to the above statement by Miller and in conclusion, the following brief observations are offered. First, historians of the "social Christianity" have generally overlooked or at least underestimated the activities of the Churches during the reconstruction period. With reference to the Methodist Episcopal Church, it was quite generally held throughout the country that this denomination was too involved in the political questions of Reconstruction and, specifically, too taken up with the racial question. It has not been the purpose here to assess the actual effects of the social mission of the Church. Nevertheless, it can be said that the unstinting efforts to elevate former black slaves from ignorance, poverty, disease, and environmental debasement resulted in the establishment of schools, colleges, and seminaries which to this day stand as a tribute to northern Methodist concern for the freedmen. The results of these charitable acts ought not be underestimated.

In the realm of politics it may be said without hesitancy that the political influence of the Methodist Episcopal Church was greater in this period than any time before or since. Under no other explanation can the inclusion of the "Methodist church" in the following telegram be accounted for. On May 16, 1868, four hours before the vote in the Senate on the removal of President Johnson took place, this telegram was sent out over the wires:

Charley to Hon. Geo. H. Pendeleton, Cincinnati:
We have beaten the Methodist Episcopal Church
North, hell, Ben Butler, John Logan [,] Geo.

Wilkes, and Impeachment. President Johnson will
be acquitted if a vote is had today. Tell my
wife. [223]

When the Methodist Church is placed first--ahead of hell and
Ben Butler--in the list of Johnson's opponents, Methodism's
influence in Reconstruction politics cannot be forgotten in
explanations of the period. Also not to be forgotten is that
during this period of considerable Methodist political influence, the Thirteenth, Fourteenth, and Fifteenth Amendments
were adopted with the enthusiastic and concrete support of
northern Methodism. And whatever may be said about the
final results of their social ministry, they did have a hand
in the passage of the Civil Rights laws of 1866 and 1875.
This was one time, however brief, in the history of Methodism in America when the followers of Wesley did not com-
prise the rearguard in the struggle for racial justice and for
the greater destiny of America; rather, they were at the van.

As to the substantive social and religious analysis of
the racial problem, in America Methodists challenged status
quo views and ways on the levels of individual and cultural
prejudice, social and ecclesiastical caste, and political inequality. One of the central themes running through Freedmen's Aid Society reports, editorials, sermons and official
pronouncements was that the future of American blacks was
intimately related to the historical destiny of the nation.
Many honestly believed that mere survival as a nation depended on equal suffrage. Many arguments in favor of enfranchising the freedman were just that pragmatic. A more
common elaboration of this theme was to tie the mission of
America to the requirements of justice for the Negro. Motivation here can be assessed in terms of an intense nationalistic civil religion as well as evangelical fervor. Northern
Methodists were firmly convinced that for America to be
the chief missionary agent for the redemption of the world,
it must embody democratic ideals and be faithful to biblical
injunctions. Social historians who emphasize the individualism, revivalism, and pietism of mid-nineteenth-century
Protestantism ignore the effects and full implications of this
religious nationalism.

Because of a deep commitment to the goals of the
Civil War and a faith lodged in a conservative biblical
Christianity, northern Methodists were led to acts of social
repentance; to interpret the meaning of the war and Reconstruction as social and political regeneration; and to enter-

tain visions of a theocratic society. Indeed, something remained of the Puritan dream of a practical world built under the ordering of a providential God. As has already been shown, Methodists understood themselves as rooted in the Puritan tradition. To what extent that is actually the case is beside the point. That they did justify "meddling in politics" and supporting the war effort by reference to both the English and American Puritan tradition is in itself the point.

In reviewing the debates around the issue of racial differences, the alleged inferiority of the African Americans, and relative racial capacities, one may conclude tartly that at no other time in the history of Methodism was the discussion of race undertaken with quite the same boldness and candor. And that includes the period of civil rights activism in the 1950s and 1960s. Methodists freely discussed the substantive question and the implications of the belief in the inherent inferiority of the black race in the nineteenth century. They debated the question of cultural and natural determinism with a degree of sophistication not common among clergymen of any time or place. And in drawing the moral and social implications from their conclusions, they did not fail to challenge the various collective forms of evil.

It would be foolhardy to look at revivalists and evangelists of the twentieth century and draw conclusions about the social thought of northern Methodists during the sectional crisis. The ecclesiastical figures treated in this study were highly individualistic and lacked respect for ecclesiastical authority when it came to matters of belief. In this respect they stood clearly in the pietist and revivalistic tradition. However, when it came to ecclesiastical discipline, to questions of civil authority, to a sense of corporate mission to society it was a different matter. They were eminently Churchmen and not sectarian revivalists. To focus on figures such as Peter Cartwright and the frontier experience, on the other hand, is to miss the fact that Methodism in the North was a highly organized denominational structure which had made its greatest advances in the urban centers just prior to the Civil War. Timothy L. Smith has noted that the Philadelphia, Pittsburgh, East Baltimore, New York, and New York East conferences outnumbered in that order the largest Western conferences of the Church. [224] The sociological significance of this fact must be considered in any estimate of Methodist social ideas, goals and approaches.

The period under discussion here was a time of transition for the Methodist Episcopal Church. It was still dominated by revivalistic impulses, but those impulses were channeled into a denominational missionary movement that included a profound sense of responsibility for the social order. Northern Methodism during Reconstruction had not yet settled down to conventional culture-Protestantism, though the years between 1864 and 1876 may be regarded as a prelude to that eventuality.

We may conclude that for a brief period in the history of American Methodism, leaders in that denomination saw that in the Civil War and during Reconstruction, moral, religious and social ideals were at stake that imperiled both the Church and the nation. Grappling with the question of slavery, the causes of the war, the origin and authority of civil government, political and ecclesiastical Reconstruction gave content and shape to a social ethic that compares well with future attempts of Methodists to articulate a theology of social responsibility. And we should not forget that the increasing improvement in the quality of social justice in the nineteenth century was in large part because of actions and ideas of these and other evangelicals who affirmed the credo of American civil religion.

Finally, it is poignant and telling to recall that the night before Gilbert Haven's name was to come before the 1872 General Conference for election as bishop, his enemies had printed and distributed his most epigrammatic declaration of the right and propriety of marriage between white and black people. And it is to the credit of the Methodist Episcopal Church that the majority of its clerical members elected him as their episcopal leader. Could that have happened at any time since? Perhaps, perhaps, but certainly not between 1876 and 1956.

The full effects of northern Methodist social thought and activity during the nineteenth century sectional crisis are yet to be examined. This book should be considered as prolegomena to the task. Hence, a comment from an editor of The Methodist in 1867 is at once an invitation to further inquiry and an appeal to do justice to those stouthearted religious forebearers of the American tradition

> We must be content to leave [it] to future generations ... to appreciate the value of the work done by us today. [225]

Notes

1. The phrase, "destiny of the nation," is used in the same sense as it is used in Chapter 6, i. e. , Methodists assumed that the "future," the "welfare," or the "vocation" of the nation was a special object of concern on the part of the Church.

2. This view is represented in varying degrees--sometimes directly and sometimes in the general tone of the writing--in the following works: Paul Buck. The Road to Reunion, Chapters I and II; Hodding Carter. The Angry Scar. Garden City, New York: Doubleday and Co. , 1959, Chapter V; Walter Flemming. The Sequel of Appomattox. New Haven: Yale University Press, 1919, Chapter IX; Richard Cameron. Methodism and Society in Historical Perspective, Vol. I, pp. 196-205; Edward Jervey, "Motives and Methods of the Methodist Episcopal Church in the Period of Reconstruction," Methodist History, IV, (July 1966), pp. 17-25; Ralph Morrow. Northern Methodism and Reconstruction, Chapter II and IX.

3. For a good discussion of this problem, see Paul Buck, Road to Reunion, Chapter I.

4. Daniel Whedon, "The New York East Conference and the Southern General Conference," Methodist Quarterly Review, XLVIII, (July 1866), p. 461.

5. Ibid.

6. Daniel Curry, "As We Supposed," Christian Advocate (New York), XL, (May 18, 1865), p. 156.

7. For a brief sketch of the northern debate, see Hunter D. Farish. The Circuit Rider Dismounts. Richmond: The Dietz Press, 1938, pp. 40-50. Also, for a good contrast of northern views, see articles by Daniel Curry, Gilbert Haven and Abel Stevens on the editorial page of the Christian Advocate (New York), XL, p. 164.

8. Daniel Curry, "The Nation's Peril," Christian Advocate (New York), XLI, (September 6, 1866), p. 284.

9. Minutes of Central Ohio Conference, 1867. Cincinnati: Methodist Book Concern, 1867, pp. 29-30.

10. "Prospects of Peace, " Zion's Herald, XXXVI, (April 19, 1865), p. 62.

11. Donald G. Mathews, "The Methodist Episcopal Church and the Antislavery Movements, " p. 6.

12. "Baltimore Conference, " Christian Advocate (New York), XL, (March 23, 1865), p. 92.

13. Minutes of the Wisconsin Conference, 1865. Milwaukee: Jermain & Brightman, Book & Job Printers, 1865, p. 25.

14. Annual Register of East Genesee Conference, 1865. Rochester: Curtis, Morely & Co. 1865, p. 16.

15. Ibid.

16. S. L. Yourtee. "A Thanksgiving Sermon on the Day of National Thanksgiving, " December 7, 1865. Springfield: Printed at News and Republic Office, 1865, p. 9.

17. Ibid.

18. Ibid. See also, "Communication--Methodist Episcopal Re-Union, " Northwestern Christian Advocate, XV, (November 20, 1867), p. 374.

19. "Public Affairs, " Christian Advocate (New York), XLI, p. 68.

20. New York East Conference Minutes, 1865, p. 41.

21. Ibid.

22. Minutes of the New England Annual Conference, 1867, p. 33.

23. Ibid.

24. Ralph Morrow, Northern Methodism and Reconstruction, p. 19.

25. Ibid.

26. "Prospects of Peace, " Zion's Herald, XXXVI, p. 62.

27. Ibid.

28. Ibid.

29. Ibid.

30. Ibid. Clergymen in Illinois saw Reconstruction as a prelude to peace. As such it was a time of "public regeneration." See Minutes of the Rock River Conference, 1864, p. 25.

31. Wm. A. Russ has contended that after the assassination of Lincoln the Methodist press swung over "to the most extreme radicalism.... Instead of the Church's power being used in a conservative policy toward the South," he said, "it would be employed to produce one of vengefulness." See William A. Russ, Jr. "The Influence of the Methodist Press Upon Radical Reconstruction," Susquehanna University Studies, I (January 1937), p. 52. It is true that immediately after the assassination many northerners clamored for swift punishment of rebel leaders, but there was considerable debate as to the policy toward the South for nearly two years. It was with the emergence of "Black Codes" and the disappointment over Andrew Johnson's policy that produced unanimity for a vigorous reconstruction policy.

32. "Pardon for the Rebels," Zion's Herald, XXXVI, (February 22, 1865), p. 30.

33. Ibid.

34. Ibid.

35. Ibid.

36. Ibid.

37. Minutes of the Wisconsin Conference, p. 26.

38. Minutes of the New England Annual Conference, p. 34.

39. Ibid.

40. Ibid.

41. "Citizenship to the Freedmen," Zion's Herald, XXXVI, (May 31, 1865), p. 86.

42. "The Church and the Freedmen," Christian Advocate (New York), XLI, (November 8, 1866), p. 356.

43. S. G. Arnold, "The Suffrage Qualification," Methodist Quarterly Review, XLVII, (October 1865), p. 591.

44. Ibid.

45. Gilbert Haven, "The More Excellent Way," Christian Advocate (New York), XLI, (February 22, 1866), p. 58.

46. Ibid.

47. Ibid.

48. Ibid.

49. Reports of the Freedmen's Aid Society, 1869, p. 14.

50. Ibid.

51. Reports of the Freedmen's Aid ..., 1871, p. 15.

52. "The Charleston Advocate," Methodist Quarterly Review, XLIX, (April 1867), p. 322.

53. Ibid.; see also "President Johnson--The New Orleans Riot," Christian Advocate (New York), XLI, (August 30, 1866), p. 276.

54. Reports of the Freedmen's Aid ... 1869, p. 14.

55. "Negro Suffrage," Christian Advocate (New York), XL, (December 1865), p. 386.

56. "Citizenship to the Freedmen," Zion's Herald, XXXVI, p. 86.

57. Most of the presidential address was printed and then commented upon in "The President's Message," Christian Advocate (New York), XL, (December 14, 1865), p. 393.

58. Ibid.

59. Ibid.

60. For a listing of the Conferences and a discussion of the influence of the Church on parties and individuals during Reconstruction see William Warren Sweet, "The Methodist Episcopal Church and Reconstruction," Illinois Historical Society Review, VII/3, pp. 152-65.

61. Minutes of the New England Annual Conference, 1871, p. 33.

62. Ibid.

63. Ibid., p. 32.

64. Ibid., p. 34.

65. Ibid.

66. Ibid. See also S. G. Arnold, "The Ku-Klux Conspiracy," Methodist Quarterly Review, LV, (January 1873), pp. 89-111.

67. "Methodist Reconstruction in the South," Christian Advocate (New York), XL (March 16, 1865), p. 84.

68. Ibid.

69. Ibid.

70. "Methodism in the South," Christian Advocate (New York), XL, (May 11, 1865), p. 148.

71. Ibid.

72. Ralph Morrow, Northern Methodism and Reconstruction, p. 20.

73. "To the Reverends the Bishops of the Methodist Episcopal Church, South," Christian Advocate (New York), XLIV, (May 20, 1869), p. 156.

74. "Ecclesiastical Reconstruction," The Methodist, VI, (May 20, 1865), p. 156.

75. Hunter D. Farish, The Circuit Rider Dismounts, p. 111.

76. Quoted in Daniel Curry, "Future of Southern Methodism,"

Christian Advocate (New York), XLI, (February 22, 1866), p. 60.

77. Ibid.

78. Thomas H. Pearne. "An Address on the Two Churches." Knoxville, Tennessee: Brownlow & Haws, 1867, p. 25.

79. Ibid.

80. New Orleans Christian Advocate, January 29, 1880, cited by Hunter D. Farish, The Circuit Rider Dismounts, p. 148.

81. Ibid.

82. Ibid.

83. Ibid.

84. Ibid., p. 149.

85. Edward M. McPherson. The Political History of the United States of America During the Rebellion. "Address of the 'Confederate' Clergy, 1863. Address to Christians Throughout the World by the Clergy of the Confederate States of America." Washington, D. C.: Philip & Solomans, 1865, p. 518.

86. Ibid.

87. Ibid.

88. Ibid., p. 519.

89. Merle Curti. The Growth of American Thought. 3rd ed. New York: Harper & Row Publisher, 1964, p. 440.

90. Albion W. Tourgée. A Fool's Errand, by One of the Fools. New York: Fords, Howard & Hulbert, 1880, pp. 120-21.

91. Ibid., pp. 121-22.

92. Gilbert Haven, Sermons..., pp. 345-46.

93. Ibid., p. 346.

94. Ibid., p. 344.

95. Ibid., pp. 344-45.

96. Reports of the Freedmen's Aid Society, 1873, p. 40.

97. Ibid., 1875, p. 82.

98. Ibid.

99. Ibid., 1871, p. 14.

100. Ibid., p. 15.

101. Ibid., 1873, p. 45.

102. Ibid., 1874, p. 33.

103. Ibid., 1875, p. 67.

104. Ibid.

105. Bishop Thompson, while believing that Negroes would serve a central role in the evangelization of the world, also said the freedmen would be the cause of a "regenerated South." See Freedmen's Aid Society Reports, 1869, p. 37.

106. Ibid., 1875, p. 88.

107. Minutes of the New England Annual Conference, 1866, p. 42.

108. Ibid.

109. Ibid., p. 44.

110. Journal of the General Conference, 1868, p. 629.

111. Ibid.

112. "The Church and the Negro," Christian Advocate (New York), XLI, (March 22, 1866), p. 92.

113. J. C. Hartzell, "A Plea for Schools in the South," Reports of the Freedmen's Aid Society, 1867, p. 6.

114. Neos, "Nigger," Zion's Herald, XXXVII, (February 7, 1866), p. 21.

115. Ibid.

116. Ibid.

117. Albert T. Bledsoe, "The African in the United States, "
A Review of The Moral and Intellectual Diversity of
the Races, by Count A. De Gobineau, Southern Review, XXXIX, (January 1874), p. 128.

118. Ibid., p. 127.

119. Speech at Charleston, Illinois, September 18, 1858.
The Collected Works..., Roy P. Basler, III, pp.
145-46. See Leon F. Litwack. North of Slavery--
The Negro in the Free States, 1790-1860. Chicago:
University of Chicago Press, 1961, pp. 276-79; Ben-
jamin Quarles. Lincoln and the Negro. New York:
Oxford Press, 1962, Chapter II.

120. "Incompatibility of Slavery with the Preservation of
the Union, " Western Christian Advocate, XXXI,
(February 3, 1864), p. 36.

121. David Donald. The Politics of Reconstruction. Baton
Rouge: Louisiana State University Press, 1965, p.
22.

122. Leslie H. Fishel, Jr., "Northern Prejudice and Negro
Suffrage, 1865-1870, " Journal of Negro History,
XXXIX, (January 1954), p. 18.

123. John Bell Robinson. "A Reply to the Resolutions
Passed by the Late Philadelphia Annual Conference."
Philadelphia: James Challen & Son, 1864, p. 24.

124. John A. Wright. People and Preachers in the Methodist Episcopal Church. Philadelphia: Lippincott
Co., 1886, p. 15.

125. Ibid., pp. 265-66.

126. Abel Stevens, "Teutonic America, " The Methodist,
XII, (May 13, 1871), from "Clippings" by Abel
Stevens, Drew University Library.

127. "Our Freedmen, " Zion's Herald, XXXV, (June 15,
1864), p. 93.

128. "American Women: Their Health and Education," review article, Methodist Quarterly Review, LVII, (January 1875), p. 123.

129. Daniel Curry, Platform Papers, pp. 126-27.

130. T. V. Moore, "Unity of the Human Race," Methodist Quarterly Review, XXXIII, (July 1851), pp. 345-77; "Classical and Miscellaneous," A Review of The Collected Works of Dugald Stewart, Methodist Quarterly Review, XXXVII, (January 1855), pp. 166-67; Edward Blyden, "The Negro in Ancient History," Methodist Quarterly Review, LI, (January 1869), pp. 71-93.

131. Thomas Gossett, Race--The History of an Idea in America. Dallas: Southern Methodist University Press, 1963, pp. 54-70.

132. T. V. Moore, "Unity of the Human Race," Methodist Quarterly Review, XXXIII, p. 364.

133. Henry J. Fox, "The Negro," Methodist Quarterly Review, LVII, (January 1875), p. 92.

134. Abel Stevens, "The Problem of Our African Population," Methodist Quarterly Review, LXVI, (January 1884), pp. 114-15.

135. Ibid., p. 114.

136. Ibid., p. 118.

137. T. V. Moore, "Unity of the Human Race," Methodist Quarterly Review, XXXIII, p. 374.

138. Ibid., pp. 374-75.

139. Ibid., p. 375.

140. N. E. Cobleigh, "Southern Reconstruction," Methodist Quarterly Review, LII, (July 1870), p. 883.

141. Ibid.

142. Ibid.

143. Ibid.

144. Gilbert Haven, Sermons..., p. 150.

145. "Martial Alchemy, " The Methodist, VI (April 1, 1865), p. 100.

146. For a good review of the discussion between northern and southern Methodists see Hunter Farish, The Circuit Rider Dismounts, Chapter VI.

147. Ibid., p. 231.

148. Neos, "Nigger, " Zion's Herald, XXXVII, p. 21.

149. Ibid.

150. Ibid.

151. Ibid.

152. "Who Understand the Negro?" The Methodist, VI, (August 12, 1865), p. 252.

153. Ibid.

154. J. P. Newman, "Colored Methodists of the South, " Christian Advocate (New York), XL (June 29, 1865), p. 202.

155. George Peck, Our Country ..., pp. 141-42.

156. "Our Freedmen, " Zion's Herald, XXXV, (June 15, 1864), p. 93.

157. Henry J. Fox, "The Negro, " Methodist Quarterly Review, LVII, (January 1875), p. 93.

158. Ibid.

159. Ibid. See also, Freedmen's Aid Society Reports, 1873, pp. 12-13: "... as the educational successes increase, the view of inferiority of the race is being abandoned. "

160. Daniel Curry, "The Freedmen, " Christian Advocate (New York), XLI, (January 11, 1866), p. 12.

161. S. G. Arnold, "The Suffrage Qualification, " Methodist Quarterly Review, XLVII, (October 1865), p. 587.

162. Curry, "The Freedmen, " Christian Advocate (New York), XLI, p. 12.

163. Haven, Sermons ..., p. 123-135.

164. Ibid. , p. 135.

165. Ibid. , p. 137.

166. Ibid.

167. George Prentice, Life of Bishop Gilbert Haven, p. 420.

168. John Caldwell, "Relations of the Colored People to the Methodist Episcopal Church South, " Methodist Quarterly Review, XLVII, (July 1866), p. 442. (Comment by editor Whedon at the close of the article.)

169. Ibid.

170. Curry, Platform Papers, p. 126.

171. John Reid, "Colored Methodists and Their Future, " Western Christian Advocate, XXXII, (July 12, 1865), p. 220.

172. Pittsburgh Advocate, (March 12, 1864), cited by Ralph Morrow, Northern Methodism and Reconstruction, p. 126.

173. Minutes of the New England Annual Conference, 1866, p. 43.

174. Minutes of the Wisconsin Annual Conference, 1866, p. 29.

175. Ibid.

176. Abel Stevens, "The Problem of Our African Population, " Methodist Quarterly Review, LXVI, p. 124.

177. Ibid. , p. 125.

178. "The Church and the Negro, " Christian Advocate (New York), XLI, p. 92.

179. Ibid.

180. Gilbert Haven, "How Shall Our Church Go South?" Christian Advocate (New York), XL, (May 25, 1865), p. 164.

181. Ibid.

182. Ibid.

183. George Prentice, The Life of Bishop Haven, p. 377. The 1872 General Conference declined to authorize separate conferences though in 1876 they did draw a "color" line.

184. Ibid. , p. 428.

185. J. C. Hartzell, "A Plea for Our Schools in the South," Freedmen's Aid Society Pamphlet, 1867, p. 8.

186. Thomas Pearne, "An Address on the Two Churches ...," (Pamphlet, 1867), p. 27.

187. Morrow, Northern Methodism and Reconstruction, p. 129.

188. Pittsburgh Advocate (June 17, 1865), cited by Ralph Morrow, Northern Methodism and Reconstruction, p. 204. See also, William W. Sweet, "The Methodist Episcopal Church and Reconstruction, " Illinois Historical Society Review, VI/3, p. 163: "The Methodist Episcopal Church was practically a unit in favor of the radical or congressional reconstruction policies. "

189. Quoted in "The Churches and the Freedmen, " Christian Advocate New York, XLI, (May 31, 1866), p. 169.

190. James Buckley, A History of Methodism, II, pp. 173-95.

191. General Conference Journal, 1868, p. 629.

192. Ibid. , pp. 561-62.

193. Marian Elias Lazenby. History of Methodism in Alabama and West Florida. Parthenon, 1960, pp. 410-11.

194. Daniel Whedon, "The Southern General Conference, "

Methodist Quarterly Review, XLVIII, (July 1866), p. 461.

195. "White," Western Christian Advocate, XXXIV, (October 16, 1867), p. 332.

196. "Citizenship to Freedmen," Zion's Herald, XXXVI, (May 31, 1865), p. 86.

197. "Methodist Episcopal Re-Union," Northwestern Christian Advocate, XV, (November 20, 1867), p. 374.

198. Minutes of the New York East Conference, 1866, p. 24.

199. James McPherson. The Struggle for Equality. Princeton: Princeton University Press, 1964, p. 328.

200. S. G. Arnold, "The Suffrage Qualification," Methodist Quarterly Review, XLVII (October 1865), pp. 583, 585.

201. Ibid., p. 588.

202. Ibid., p. 586.

203. Ibid.

204. Jesse T. Peck, The Great Republic, pp. 689, 690.

205. Ibid., p. 690.

206. T. M. Eddy, Northwestern Christian Advocate, XVI, (January 1, 1868), p. 4.

207. The Negro Problem Solved by Hollis Read. A review in the Methodist Quarterly Review, XLVII, (January 1865), p. 154.

208. Ibid., p. 155.

209. Ibid.

210. Ralph Gabriel, The Course of American Democratic Thought, p. 19.

211. Daniel Whedon, "Education," a review of The College, The Market, and the Court, by Caroline H. Dall,

Methodist Quarterly Review, XLIX, (October 1867), p. 632.

212. Gilbert Haven, "The Great Election," Methodist Quarterly Review, XVII, (April 1865), p. 268.

213. Ibid.

214. "The Negro Problem Solved," a review in the Methodist Quarterly Review, XLVII, p. 155. See also, "The Suffrage Qualification," Methodist Quarterly Review, XLVII, p. 586: "It does not follow that when we maintain the right of suffrage, irrespective of color, that we maintain the negro's right to marry our daughter."

215. Haven, Sermons ..., p. 622.

216. Ibid.

217. Ibid., p. 626.

218. Ibid., p. 624.

219. Ibid., p. 626.

220. Ralph Morrow, Northern Methodism and Reconstruction, pp. 184-85.

221. William Gravely. Gilbert Haven Methodist Abolitionist: A Study in Race, Religion, and Reform. Nashville and New York: Abingdon Press, 1973, p. 180.

222. Robert Moats Miller. American Protestantism and Social Issues, 1919-1939. Chapel Hill: University of North Carolina Press, 1959, p. 10.

223. "Raising of Money to Be Used in Impeachment," House Report 75, 40th Cong., 2nd sess., II, cited by William A. Russ, "The Influence of the Methodist Press Upon Radical Reconstruction," Susquehanna University Studies, I, p. 62.

224. Timothy L. Smith. Revivalism and Social Reform. New York: Harper and Row, 1957, p. 22.

225. "North and South," The Methodist, VIII, (January 5, 1867), p. 4.

BIBLIOGRAPHY

I. Official Documents: Journals, Reports, Minutes, etc.

Annual Conferences. Minutes of the Annual Conferences of the Methodist Episcopal Church, 1864-1876.

Church Extension Society. Annual Reports of the Church Extension Society of the Methodist Episcopal Church. Philadelphia: Methodist Episcopal Book Room, 1865-1876.

Debates and Addresses of the New England Methodist Centenary Convention. Boston: B. B. Russell and Co., 1866.

Formal Fraternity, Proceedings of the General Conferences of the Methodist Episcopal Church and of the Methodist Episcopal Church, South, in 1872, 1874, and 1876. and of the Joint Commission of the Two Churches on Fraternal Relations, at Cape May, New Jersey, August 16-23, 1876. New York: Nelson and Phillips, n. d.

Freedmen's Aid Society. Reports of the Freedmen's Aid Society of the Methodist Episcopal Church. Cincinnati: Western Methodist Book Concern, 1866-1875.

General Conference. Journal of the General Conference of the Methodist Episcopal Church, 1864.

_____. Journal of the General Conference of the Methodist Episcopal Church, 1868. New York: Carlton & Lanahan, 1868.

_____. Journal of the General Conference of the Methodist Episcopal Church, 1872. New York: Nelson & Phillips, 1872.

_____. Journal of the General Conference of the Methodist Episcopal Church, 1876. New York: Nelson & Phillips, 1876.

New Jersey Methodist Convention. Minutes of the New Jersey Methodist State Convention. Held in Trenton, New Jersey, September 27-29, 1870. Trenton, New Jersey, 1870.

New York State Methodist Convention. Methodism in The State of

317

New York, as Represented in State Convention, Held in Syracuse, N. Y., February 22-24, 1870. New York: Carlton & Lanahan, 1870.

_____. Second New York State Methodist Convention, Held in Syracuse, N. Y., December 5-8, 1871. New York: Carlton & Lanahan, 1872.

II. Periodical Literature

A.   The Northern Methodist Press

Central Christian Advocate, St. Louis.

Christian Advocate, New York. Published as the Christian Advocate and Journal, became The Christian Advocate in 1866. Here referred to as the Christian Advocate (New York).

Daily Christian Advocate, 1864, 1868, 1872, 1876. Published quadrennially at the site of the General Conference of the Methodist Episcopal Church.

Ladies Home Repository, Cincinnati.

Methodist Quarterly Review, New York.

Northern Christian Advocate, Auburn and Syracuse, New York.

Northwestern Christian Advocate, Chicago.

Pittsburgh Christian Advocate, Pittsburgh.

Southwestern Christian Advocate, New Orleans.

Western Christian Advocate, Cincinnati.

Zion's Herald, Boston.

B.   Non-Methodist Periodicals

Atlantic Monthly. Vols. I-X.

Harper's Weekly. Vols. VIII-XV.

Independent. Vols. XX-XXIV.

Nation. Vols. XXV-XXXIX.

Southern Review. Vols. IV-XVI.

III. Works of Northern Methodist Authorship
in the Nineteenth Century

Crane, J. T. Methodism and Its Methods. New York: Nelson &
Phillips, 1876.

Crooks, George R. Life and Letters of the Rev. John M'Clintock.
New York: Nelson & Phillips, 1876.

_____. The Life of Bishop Matthew Simpson. New York: Har-
per & Brothers, 1890.

_____, ed. Sermons by Bishop Matthew Simpson. New York:
Harper & Brothers, 1885.

Curry, Daniel. Life-Story of Rev. Davis Wasgatt Clark. New York:
Nelson & Phillips, 1874.

_____. New York: A Historical Sketch of the Rise and Pro-
gress of the Metropolitan City of America, By a New
Yorker (pseud.). New York: Carlton & Phillips, 1853.

_____. Platform Papers: Addresses, Discussions, and Essays
on Social, Moral, and Religious Subjects. Cincinnati:
Hitchcock and Walden, 1880.

Daniels, W. H. , ed. Memorials of Gilbert Haven, Bishop of the
Methodist Episcopal Church. Boston: B. B. Russell &
Co. , 1880.

Dorchester, Daniel. The Problem of Religious Progress. New
York: Phillips & Hunt, 1881.

_____. The Why of Methodism. New York: Phillips & Hunt,
1888.

Elliot, Charles. A History of the Methodist Episcopal Church in
the South-West from 1844 to 1864. New York: Carlton &
Porter, 1868.

_____. Sinfulness of American Slavery. 2 Vols. Cincinnati:
Poe and Hitchcock, 1863.

Foster, Randolph S. Centenary Thoughts for the Pew and Pulpit of
Methodism. New York: Phillips & Hunt, 1884.

Fuller, Erasmus Q. An Appeal to the Records: A Vindication of
the Methodist Episcopal Church, in Its Policy and Proceedings Toward the South. New York: Nelson & Phillips, 1876.

Hartzell, J. C. Methodism and the Negro in the United States.
New York: Hunt & Eaton, 1894.

Haven, Gilbert. Sermons, Speeches and Letters on Slavery and Its

War: From the Passage of the Fugitive Slave Will to the Election of President Grant. New York: Carlton and Lanahan, 1869.

Hopkins, Alphonso A. The Life of Clinton Bowen Fisk. New York: Funk & Wagnalls, 1890.

Hosmer, William. The Higher Law in Its Relation to Civil Government. New York: Carlton and Phillips, 1852.

Matlack, Lucius C. The Antislavery Struggle and Triumph in the Methodist Episcopal Church. New York: Phillips & Hunt, 1881.

Mattison, Hiram. The Impending Crisis of 1860. New York: Mason Brothers, 1859.

Moore, H. H. The Republic, To Methodism, Dr. (Debtor). New York: Hunt & Eaton, 1891.

Peck, George. Our Country: Its Trial and Its Triumph. A Series of Discourses Suggested by the Varying Events of the War for the Union. New York: Carlton & Porter, 1865.

_____. Slavery and the Episcopacy: Being an Examination of Dr. Bascom's Review. New York: Lane and Tippett, 1845.

Peck, Jesse T. The History of the Great Republic Considered From a Christian Stand-Point. New York: Broughten and Wyman, 1868.

Phillips, George. The American Republic and Human Liberty Foreshadowed in Scripture. Cincinnati: Poe & Hitchcock, 1864.

Prentice, George. The Life of Gilbert Haven, Bishop of the Methodist Episcopal Church. New York: Phillips & Hunt, 1883.

Simpson, Matthew. Lectures on Preaching, Delivered Before the Theological Department of Yale College. Lyman-Beecher Lectureship. New York: Phillips & Hunt, 1879.

Sims, Charles. The Life of Rev. Thomas M. Eddy. New York: Nelson & Phillips, 1879.

Stevens, Abel. The Centenary of American Methodism: A Sketch of Its History, Theology, Practical System, and Success. New York: Carlton & Porter, 1865.

_____. A Compendious History of American Methodism. New York: Carlton & Porter, 1868.

_____. Supplementary History of American Methodism. New York: Eaton & Mains, 1899.

Tefft, B. F. Methodism Successful, and the Internal Causes of Its Success. New York: Derby & Jackson, 1860.

Tourgée, Albion. A Fool's Errand. By One of the Fools. New York: Fords, Howard & Hulbert, 1880.

Whedon, Daniel D. Public Addresses, Collegiate and Popular. Cleveland, Ohio: Jewett, Proctor & Worthington, 1852.

_____ . Statements: Theological and Critical. New York: Phillips & Hunt, 1887.

Wright, John A. People and Preachers in the Methodist Episcopal Church. Philadelphia: J. B. Lippincott Company, 1886.

Wood, Ezra M. Methodism and the Centennial of American Independence; or, The Loyal and Liberal Services of the Methodist Episcopal Church During the First Century of the History of the United States. New York: Nelson & Phillips, 1876.

IV. Pamphlets, Sermons and Addresses (Selected from Rose Memorial Library, Drew University)

Brown, S. D. Our Recent National Struggle-Its Triumphs and Its Blessings: A Sermon Preached in Bedford St. M. E. Church, New York, December 7, 1865. New York: C. A. Alvord, 1866.

Caldwell, John H. Reminiscences of the Reconstruction of Church and State in Georgia. Wilmington, Delaware: J. Miller Thomas, 1895.

Cleveland, J. J. The Lost Tribes Are the Teutonic Race. Their Model City of God is in America. San Francisco: C. W. Gordon, Printer, 1887.

De Puy, William H. Statistics of the Methodist Episcopal Church of the United States. New York: Nelson & Phillips, 1878.

Fancher, Enoch L. Methodist Fraternity. New York: Samuel Hamilton's Son, Printer, 1876.

Hartzell, J. C. Education in the South. Cincinnati: Western Methodist Book Concern Press, 1882.

_____ . The Negro Exodus. (Special printing from Methodist Quarterly Review, LXI, October, 1879).

Haygood, Atticus G. The New South: Thanksgiving Sermon, 1880. ed. , Judson C. Ward. Atlanta, Georgia: The Library, Emory University, 1950.

Hubbard, G. W. A History of the Colored Schools of Nashville, Tennessee. Nashville Tenn. : Wheeler, Marshall & Bruce, Printers and Stationers, 1874.

Marvin, Enoch M. (Bishop). The Duty and Destiny of the Methodist Episcopal Church, South. Introduction by Warren A. Candler, n. p. , n. d. (Published in 1920 a few weeks after adjournment of the General Conference of the Methodist Church at Des Moines, Iowa).

Merrick, Frederick. Religion and the State, A Centennial Sermon. Cincinnati: Hitchcock & Walden, 1875.

Miscegenation: The Theory of the Blending of the Races, Applied to the American White Man and Negro. n. a. New York: H. Dexter, Hamilton & Co. , 1864.

Newman, John P. Christianity Triumphant. New York: Funk & Wagnalls, 1884.

Pearne, Thomas H. An Address on the Two Churches: or the Methodist Episcopal Church, and the Methodist Episcopal Church, South. Delivered in the M. E. Church, Knoxville, Tenn. , March 27th, 1867. Knoxville, Tennessee: Brownlow & Haws, 1867.

_____ . Color-Caste. (Pastor of Grace M. E. Church, Dayton, Ohio. Written sometime around 1876). n. p. , n. d.

Peck, Jesse T. Methodism and the Only True Catholic Church: Fifth Lecture of the First Addisonian Course, 1865. San Francisco: Towne & Bacon, Book, Card, and Job Printers, 1866.

Phelps, Elisha Payne. An Appeal to the People. Staunton, Va. : n. p. , 1868.

Robinson, John Bell. A Reply to the Resolutions Passed by the Late Philadelphia Annual Conference of the Methodist Episcopal Church in March, 1864. With a Slight Notice of the Acts of the Late General Conference of Said Church in the Following May. Philadelphia: James Challen & Sons, 1864.

Rust, R. S. The Freedmen's Aid Society of the Methodist Episcopal Church. Society Series, No. Six. New York: Tract Department Methodist Book Concern.

Sunderland, B. Liberia's Next Friend. The Annual Discourse Delivered at the Sixty-Ninth Annual Meeting of the American Colonization Society, Held in Foundry M. E. Church, Washington, D. C. Sunday Evening, Jan'y 17, 1886. Washington City, Colonization Building, 1886.

Thompson, Edward (Bishop). Address Before the Educational Convention, Held in Delaware, Ohio, June 27, 1865. Cincinnati: Printed at the Methodist Book Concern, 1865.

Tourgée, Albion. Is Liberty Worth Preserving? Chicago, Illinois: The Inter Ocean, 1892.

Walden, J. M. The Methodist Episcopal Church in the South. Cincinnati: Western Methodist Book Concern Press, 1884.

Warren, Henry W. The Ideas and Feelings Necessary to National Greatness, A Sermon Delivered Before the Executive and Legislative Departments of the Government of Massachusetts, at the Annual Election, Wednesday, January 2d, 1867. Boston: Wright & Potter, State Printers, 1867.

_____. Past Successes--Future Possibilities: A Centennial Sermon, Delivered Before The New York East Conference of the Methodist Episcopal Church, April 6, 1876. New York: Nelson & Phillips, 1876.

Wentworth, E. Gilbert Haven: A Monograph. New York: Phillips & Hunt, 1880.

Yourtee, S. L. A Thanksgiving Sermon, Delivered in the Central M. E. Church, Springfield, Ohio, on the Day of National Thanksgiving, December 7th, 1865. Springfield: Printed at News and Republic Office, 1865.

V. Articles from Periodical Literature in the Nineteenth Century (Arranged according to category and journal--selected).

A. Church and Politics

"Respect for Government." Christian Advocate (New York), XXXVIII (March 5, 1863), 76.

"Divine Law above Human." Christian Advocate (New York), XXXVIII (March 12, 1863), 84.

"The Late Election--Its Lessons." Christian Advocate (New York), XLI (November 24, 1864), 372.

"The Suffrage Question." Christian Advocate (New York), XLI (February 1, 1866), 36.

"Public Affairs." Christian Advocate (New York), XLI (March 1, 1866), 68.

"Political Tests." Christian Advocate (New York), XLI (May 17, 1866), 156.

Stevens, Abel. "Centenary Discourse." Christian Advocate (New York), XLI (May 24, 1866), 162.

"The Fenians and the Politicians. " Christian Advocate (New York), XLI (July 12, 1866), 220.

"Religion and Secular Life. " Christian Advocate (New York), XLIV (October 7, 1869), 318.

Stevens, Abel. "G. Haven's Sermons--Liberty of the Pulpit. " Christian Advocate (New York), XLI (December 30, 1869), 410.

"Temperance and Politics. " Christian Advocate (New York), XLIV (1869), 292.

"The Puritans. " The Methodist, IV (January 24, 1863), 20.

"Religion and Benevolence in N. Y. C. " The Methodist, XI (January 29, 1870), 36.

"Political Reform. " The Methodist, XI (October 22, 1870), 340.

Haven, Gilbert. "The Great Election. " Methodist Quarterly Review, XLVII (April 1865), 272.

Horner, Joseph. "Christianity and the War Power. " Methodist Quarterly Review, XLVII (April 1865), 180.

McCauley, J. A. "Religion and the Reign of Terror. " Methodist Quarterly Review, XXI (October 1869), 569.

Pullman, J. "Methodism and Heresy. " Methodist Quarterly Review, LXI (April 1879), 334-35.

Hawley, Bostwick. "Relations of Politics and Christianity. " Methodist Quarterly Review, LXI (July 1879), 468-69, 472.

Haddock, George C. "Politics and the Church. " Northwestern Christian Advocate, XVI (February 19, 1868), 62.

Fallows, Samuel. "Politics and Religion. " Northwestern Christian Advocate, XVI (March 11, 1868), 86.

Linebarger, Rev. J. "Religion and Politics of Luthardt. " Northwestern Christian Advocate, XVI (August 12, 1868), 262.

Stevens, Abel. "Criticism of the American Pulpit. " Northwestern Christian Advocate, XVIII (November 23, 1870), 372.

"How Shall We Vote?" Western Christian Advocate, XXXI (October 12, 1864), 324.

"The Pulpit and Politics. " Western Christian Advocate, XXXL (November 9, 1864), 356.

"True Americanism: or, Our Duties to Our Govn't. " Zion's Herald, XXXV (May 11, 1864), 73.

"Our Freedmen. " Zion's Herald, XXXV (June 8, 1864), 89.

"Puritanism in Politics. " Zion's Herald, XXXV (September 14, 1864), 146.

B. Church and the Negro

"Methodism in the South. " Christian Advocate (New York), XL (May 11, 1865), 148.

Curry, Daniel. "As We Supposed. " Christian Advocate (New York), XL (May 18, 1865), 156.

Haven, Gilbert. "How Shall Our Church Go South. " Christian Advocate (New York), XL (May 25, 1865), 164.

Newman, J. P. "Colored Methodists of the South. " Christian Advocate (New York), XL (June 29, 1865), 202.

"Negro Suffrage. " Christian Advocate (New York), XL (December 1865), 386.

Curry, Daniel. "The Freedmen. " Christian Advocate (New York), XLI (January 11, 1866), 12.

Haven, Gilbert. "The More Excellent Way. " Christian Advocate (New York), XLI (February 22, 1866), 58.

"The Church and the Negro. " Christian Advocate (New York) XLI (March 22, 1866), 92.

Curry, Daniel. "The Nation's Peril. " Christian Advocate (New York), XLI (September 6, 1866), 284.

"The Church and the Freedmen. " Christian Advocate (New York), XLI (November 8, 1866), 356.

"To the Reverends the Bishops of the Methodist Episcopal Church, South. " Christian Advocate (New York), XLIV (May 20, 1869), 156.

"Martial Alchemy. " The Methodist, VI (April 1, 1865), 100.

"Who Understands the Negro?" The Methodist, VI (August 12, 1865).

Moore, T. V. "Unity of the Human Race. " Methodist Quarterly Review, XXXIII (July 1851), 345-77.

Haven, Gilbert. "The Great Election. " Methodist Quarterly Review, XLVII (April 1865), 268.

Arnold, S. G. "The Suffrage Qualification. " Methodist Quarterly Review, XLVII (October 1865), 591.

Caldwell, John. "Relations of the Colored People to the Methodist Episcopal Church South. " Methodist Quarterly Review, XLVIII (July 1866), 442.

Whedon, Daniel. "The New York East Conference and the Southern General Conference. " Methodist Quarterly Review, XLVIII (July 1866), 461.

"The Charleston Advocate. " Methodist Quarterly Review, XLIX (April 1867), 322.

Fox, Henry J. "The Negro. " Methodist Quarterly Review, LVII (January 1875), 92.

Stevens, Abel. "The Problem of Our African Population. " Methodist Quarterly Review, LXVI (January 1884), 114-15.

Eddy, T. M. "1867-8. " Northwestern Christian Advocate, XVI (January 1, 1868), 4.

"Incompatibility of Slavery with the Preservation of the Union. " Western Christian Advocate, XXXI (February 3, 1864), 36.

Reid, John. "Colored Methodists and Their Future. " Western Christian Advocate, XXXII (July 12, 1865), 220.

"White. " Western Christian Advocate, XXXIV (October 16, 1867), 332.

"Our Freedmen. " Zion's Herald, XXXV (June 15, 1864), 93.

"Pardon for the Rebels. " Zion's Herald, XXXVI (February 22, 1865), 30.

"Prospects of Peace. " Zion's Herald, XXXVI (April 19, 1865), 62.

"Citizenship to the Freedmen. " Zion's Herald, XXXVI (May 31, 1865), 86.

Neos. "Nigger. " Zion's Herald, XXXVII (February 7, 1866), 21.

"No Caste in the Church of God. " Zion's Herald, XXXVIII (April 10, 1867), 57.

C.   Interpretation of the Civil War and Reconstruction

"Cause of Our Conflict. " Christian Advocate (New York), XXXVI
(June 6, 1861), 180.

"Victories. " Christian Advocate (New York), XXXVIII (December 3,
1863), 388.

"Methodist Reconstruction in the South. " Christian Advocate (New
York), XL (March 16, 1865), 84.

"Our Next Duty. " Christian Advocate (New York), XL (April 13,
1865), 116.

"The Philosophy of Political Progress. " Christian Advocate (New
York), XLI (November 1, 1866), 348.

"The Church and the Freedmen. " Christian Advocate (New York),
XLI (November 8, 1866), 356.

"Sentiments Appropriate to the Times. " The Methodist, III (March
1, 1862), 60.

"Dangers of the Times. " The Methodist, VI (January 14, 1865),
12.

"Passing the Amendment. " The Methodist, VI (February 11, 1865),
44.

"Ecclesiastical Reconstruction. " The Methodist, VI (May 20, 1865),
156.

Stevens, Abel. "Methodism After Wesley's Death. " Methodist
Quarterly Review, (January 1861), 5, 6.

Rusling, James F.   "The War for the Union. " Methodist Quarterly
Review, XLVI (April 1864), 310.

Wilson, n. i.   "Our Historical Position as Indicated by Nature and
Philosophy. " Methodist Quarterly Review, XLVIII (January
1866), 19, 20.

Foote, H. S.   "Review of War of the Rebellion. " Methodist Quarterly Review, XLVIII (April 1866), 306-07.

Cobleigh, N. E.   "Southern Reconstruction. " Methodist Quarterly
Review, LII (July 1870), 883.

"Punishment. " Western Christian Advocate, XXXI (March 2, 1864),
68.

"The Providence in the War. " Western Christian Advocate, XXXI
(December 14, 1864), 393.

"Another Theory of Ecclesiastical Reconstruction." Western Christian Advocate, XXXII (June 7, 1865), 180.

Haven, Gilbert. "The Church and the Negro." Zion's Herald, XXXIV (June 10, 1863), 89.

"Our National Thanksgiving." Zion's Herald, XXXIV (November 25, 1863), 186.

D. National Destiny and the Church

"The N. Y. Tribune and the M. E. Church." Christian Advocate (New York), XLI (January 4, 1866), 4.

De Hass, F. S. "Metropolitan M. E. Church, Washington." Christian Advocate (New York), XLI (September 20, 1866), 298.

Foss, Cyrus D. "The Mission of Our Country." Christian Advocate (New York), LI (July 6, 1876), 210.

Haven, Gilbert. "God's Purpose for America." Ladies Home Repository (December 1876), 522-33.

"Indiana Conference." The Methodist, II (October 12, 1861), 313.

"American Methodism, Its Position in American Civilization." The Methodist, V (July 9, 1864), 212.

"Methodism--A Church." The Methodist, VI (December 9, 1865), 338.

"The New York East Conference and the Southern General Conference." Methodist Quarterly Review, XLVIII (July 1866), 456.

Hillman, S. D. "The United States and Methodism." Methodist Quarterly Review, XLIX (January 1867), 31, 40-43, 49.

"Position and Prospects of the American Union." Methodist Quarterly Review, LVI (1874), 49, 59.

"Our Land and Its Religion." Northwestern Christian Advocate, XV (December 11, 1867), 396.

"The Situation Yet Again." Western Christian Advocate, XXXI (March 22, 1864), 92.

"Central Ohio Conference." Western Christian Advocate, XXXI (October 3, 1864), 313.

Stevens, Abel. "The National Christianity." Western Christian Advocate, XXXVII (July 6, 1870), 210.

"Freedman and Freeman. " Zion's Herald, XXXVII (January 3, 1866), 1.

"The Plan of God in Regard to the American People. " Zion's Herald, XXXVII (May 2, 1866), 69.

Simpson, Matthew. "Speech at Boston Centenary Festival. " Zion's Herald, XXXVII (June 20, 1866), 97.

VI. General Books

Abell, Aaron Ignatius. The Urban Impact on American Protestantism 1865-1900. London: Archon, 1962.

Barclay, Wade C. Widening Horizons, 1845-95. Vol. III of the History of Methodist Missions. New York: The Board of Missions of the Methodist Church, 1957.

Basler, Roy P., ed. The Collected Works of Abraham Lincoln. 9 vols. New Brunswick: Rutgers University Press, 1955.

Bellah, Robert. The Broken Covenant. New York: Seabury Press, 1975.

Boles, Donald E. The Bible, Religion, and the Public Schools. Ames, Iowa: Iowa State University Press, 1961.

Boorstin, Daniel. The Genius of American Politics. Chicago: University of Chicago Press, 1953.

Brauer, Jerald C. Protestantism in America. Philadelphia: Westminster Press, 1953.

Brock, W. R. An American Crisis--Congress and Reconstruction. New York: Harper Torchbooks, Harper & Row, 1966.

Bryce, James. The American Commonwealth. London: Macmillan and Co., 1891.

Buck, Paul H. The Road to Reunion, 1865-1900. New York: Vintage Books, Inc., 1959.

Bucke, Emory Stevens. (gen. ed.). The History of American Methodism. Vol. II. New York: Abingdon Press, 1964.

Buckley, James M. A History of Methodism in the United States. 2 vols. New York: Christian Literature Co., 1897.

Burns, Edwar McNall. The American Idea of Mission. New Brunswick: Rutgers University Press, 1957.

Bushnell, Horace. Building Eras in Religion. New York: Scribner's Sons, 1881.

_____. Work and Play. New York: Scribner & Co., 1866.

Butts, Freeman R., and Lawrence A. Cremin. A History of Education in American Culture. New York: Henry Holt & Co., 1953.

Cameron, Richard M. Methodism and Society in Historical Perspective. Vol. I of the series Methodism and Society. Alfred Dudley Ward (gen. ed.). New York: Abingdon Press, 1961.

Cash, W. J. The Mind of the South. New York: Vintage Books, 1941.

Clark, Robert D. The Life of Matthew Simpson. New York: Macmillan Co., 1956.

Clebsch, William A. From Sacred to Profane America: The Role of Religion in American History. New York: Harper & Row, 1968.

Cole, Charles C., Jr. The Social Ideas of the Northern Evangelists, 1826-1860. New York: Columbia University Press, 1954.

Coulter, E. Merton. The South During Reconstruction, 1865-1877. Baton Rouge: Louisiana State University Press, 1947.

Crum, Mason. The Negro in the Methodist Church. n. p., n. d.

Culver, Dwight W. Negro Segregation in the Methodist Church. New Haven: Yale University Press, 1953.

Cummings, Anson W. The Early Schools of Methodism. New York: Phillips & Hunt, 1886.

Current, Richard N. Reconstruction, 1865-77. Englewood Cliffs, New Jersey: Prentice-Hall, Inc., 1965.

Curti, Merle. The Growth of American Thought. New York: Harper & Row, 1943.

Davis, David Brion. The Problem of Slavery in Western Culture. Ithaca, New York: Cornell University Press, 1966.

Donald, David. Lincoln Reconsidered. New York: Vintage Books, 1956.

_____. The Politics of Reconstruction, 1863-1867. Baton Rouge: Louisiana State University Press, 1967.

Duberman, Martin, ed. The Antislavery Vanguard: New Essays on the Abolitionists. Princeton, New Jersey: Princeton University Press, 1965.

Dumond, Dwight Lowell. Antislavery Origins of the Civil War in the United States. 3d. printing. Ann Arbor, Michigan: University of Michigan Press, 1963.

Elkins, Stanley M. Slavery, A Problem in American Institutional and Intellectual Life. New York: The Universal Library, Grosset & Dunlap, 1963.

Encyclopedia Americana. New York: Grolier, Inc., 1967.

Ezell, John Samuel. The South Since 1865. New York: The Macmillan Co., 1963.

Farish, Hunter Dickinson. The Circuit Rider Dismounts, A Social History of Southern Methodism, 1865-1900. Richmond, Va.: The Dietz Press, 1938.

Fishel, Leslie H., Jr., and Quarles, Benjamin. The Negro American, A Documentary History. Glenview, Illinois: Scott, Foresman and Company & William Morrow and Company, 1967.

Fleming, Walter L. Civil War and Reconstruction in Alabama. New York: Columbia University Press, 1905.

_____. Documentary History of Reconstruction, Political, Military, Social, Religious, Educational & Industrial 1865 to the Present Time. New York: Peter Smith, 1950.

Franklin, John H. The Emancipation Proclamation. Garden City, New York: Anchor Books, Doubleday & Co., 1965.

_____. From Slavery to Freedom: A History of American Negroes. New York: Alfred Knopf, 1947.

_____. Reconstruction: After the Civil War. Chicago: University of Chicago Press, 1961.

Gabriel, Ralph Henry. The Course of American Democratic Thought. 2d ed. New York: The Ronald Press, 1956.

Garrison, Winfred Ernest. The March of Faith, The Story of Religion in America Since 1865. New York: Harper & Brothers Publishers, 1933.

Gaustad, Edwin Scott, ed. Religious Issues in American History. New York: Harper & Row, 1968.

Gossett, Thomas F. Race, The History of an Idea in America. Dallas: Southern Methodist University Press, 1963.

Graebner, Norman A., ed. Manifest Destiny. Indianapolis: The Bobbs-Merrill Co., 1968.

Graham, John H. Mississippi Circuit Riders, 1865-1965. Nashville,
    Tennessee: The Parthenon Press, 1967.

Gravely, William B. Gilbert Haven Methodist Abolitionist. Nash-
    ville, Tennessee, Abingdon, 1973.

Handy, Robert T. The Protestant Quest for A Christian America.
    1830-1930. Philadelphia: Fortress Press, 1967.

_____. We Witness Together. New York: Friendship Press,
    1956.

_____, ed. The Social Gospel in America. New York: Ox-
    ford University Press, 1966.

Harkness, Georgia. The Methodist Church in Social Thought and
    Action. New York: Abingdon Press, 1964.

Haygood, Atticus G. Our Brother in Black: His Freedom and His
    Future. New York: Phillips & Hunt, 1881.

Herberg, Will. Protestant--Catholic--Jew, An Essay in American
    Religious Sociology. Rev. ed. Garden City, New York:
    Anchor Books, Doubleday & Co. , 1960.

Higham, John. The Reconstruction of American History. New York:
    Harper Torchbooks, Harper & Row, Publishers, 1962.

Hirshop, Stanley P. Farewell to the Bloody Shirt, Northern Re-
    publicans & the Southern Negro, 1877-1893. Bloomington:
    Indiana University Press, 1962.

Hofstadter, Richard, ed. Great Issues in American History, A
    Documentary Record. New York: Vintage Books, 1958.

Hopkins, Charles Howard. The Rise of the Social Gospel in Ameri-
    can Protestantism, 1865-1915. New Haven: Yale University
    Press, 1940.

Hudson, Winthrop S. American Protestantism. Chicago: Univer-
    sity of Chicago Press, 1961.

_____. Religion in America. New York: Charles Scribner's
    Sons, 1965.

Huntingdon, William Reed. The Church-Idea, an Essay Towards
    Unity. New York: Charles Scribner's Sons, 1899.

Hyman, Harold M. The Radical Republicans and Reconstruction,
    1861-1870. Indianapolis: The Bobbs-Merrill Co. , 1967.

Katz, William Loren. Eyewitness, The Negro in American History.
    New York: Pitman Publishing Corporation, 1967.

Kelsey, George D. Racism and the Christian Understanding of Man. New York: Charles Scribner's Sons, 1965.

_____. Social Ethics Among Southern Baptists, 1917-1969, Metuchen, N. J.: Scarecrow Press, 1973.

Kohn, Hans. American Nationalism. New York: Macmillan Co., 1957.

Lazenby, Marion Elias. History of Methodism in Alabama and West Florida. Nashville: Parthenon Press, 1960.

Littell, Franklin Hamlin. From State Church to Pluralism: A Protestant Interpretation of Religion in American History. Garden City, New York: Anchor Books, Doubleday & Co., 1962.

Litwack, Leon F. North of Slavery, The Negro in the Free States, 1790-1960. Chicago: University of Chicago Press, 1961.

Luccock, Halford E.; Hutchinson, Paul; and Goodlee, Robert W. The Story of Methodism. New York: Abingdon-Cokesbury Press, 1949.

Lynd, Saughton, ed. Reconstruction. New York: Harper & Row, Publishers, 1967.

MacKenzie, Kenneth M. The Robe and the Sword, The Methodist Church and the Rise of American Imperialism. Washington, D. C.: Public Affairs Press, 1961.

McLouglin, William G., Jr. Modern Revivalism. New York: The Ronald Press, 1959.

McPherson, James M. The Negro's Civil War. New York: Pantheon Books, 1965.

_____. The Struggle for Equality, Abolitionists and the Negro in the Civil War and Reconstruction. Princeton, New Jersey: Princeton University Press, 1964.

Marty, Martin. Righteous Empire. New York: Dial Press, 1970.

Mathews, Donald G. Slavery and Methodism, A Chapter in American Morality, 1780-1845. Princeton, New Jersey: Princeton University Press, 1965.

May, Henry F. Protestant Churches of Industrial America. 2d ed. New York: Harper Torchbooks, Harper & Row, Publishers.

Mead, Sidney E. The Lively Experiment. New York: Harper Torchbooks, Harper & Row, Publishers, 1963.

Merk, Frederick. Manifest Destiny and Mission in American History, A Reinterpretation. New York: Vintage Books, 1966.

Miller, Perry, ed. American Thought, Civil War to World War I. 10th ed. New York: Holt, Rinehart and Winston, 1967.

Miller, Robert Moats. American Protestantism and Social Issues. Chapel Hill: University of North Carolina Press, 1958.

Miyakawa, T. Scott. Protestants and Pioneers, Individualism and Conformity on the American Frontier. Chicago: University of Chicago Press, 1964.

Moellering, Ralph L. Christian Conscience and Negro Emancipation. Philadelphia: Fortress Press, 1965.

Morrow, Ralph E. Northern Methodism and Reconstruction. East Lansing, Michigan: Michigan State University Press, 1956.

Mott, Frank Luther. American Journalism: A History: 1690-1960. 3d. ed. New York: Macmillan Co., 1962.

Murray, Andrew E. Presbyterians and the Negro--A History. Philadelphia: Presbyterian Historical Society, 1966.

Nagel, Paul. This Sacred Trust: American Nationality 1798-1898. New York: Oxford U. Press, 1971.

Niebuhr, H. Richard. The Kingdon of God in America. New York: Harper Torchbooks, Harper & Row Publishers, 1959.

_____, and Williams, Daniel D., eds. The Ministry in Historical Perspective. New York: Harper & Brothers, 1956.

Niebuhr, Reinhold. The Irony of American History. New York: Charles Scribner's Sons, 1952.

Nolen, Claude H. The Negro's Image in the South. Lexington: University of Kentucky Press, 1967.

Norwood, Frederick A. The Story of American Methodism. Nashville, Tenn., Abingdon Press, 1974.

Nye, Russel B. This Almost Chosen People. East Lansing, Michigan: Michigan State University Press, 1966.

Paludan, Philip S. A Covenant with Death. Urbana, Ill.: University of Illinois Press, 1975.

Pressly, Thomas J. Americans Interpret Their Civil War. New York: The Free Press, 1962.

Quarles, Benjamin. Lincoln and the Negro. New York: Oxford University Press, 1962.

Richey, Russel E. Denominationalism. Nashville Tenn.: Abingdon Press, 1977.

_____, and Donald G. Jones, eds. American Civil Religion. New York: Harper and Row, 1974.

Schaff, Philip. America, A Sketch of Its Political, Social, and Religious Character. Edited with an introduction by Perry Miller. Cambridge, Massachusetts: The Belknap Press of Harvard University Press, 1961.

Schlesinger, Arthur Meier. The American as Reformer. Cambridge, Massachusetts: Harvard University Press, 1951.

Schmidt, George P. The Old Time College President. New York: Columbia University Press, 1930.

Sellers, Charles Grier, Jr., ed. The Southerner as American. New York: E. P. Dutton & Co., 1966.

Silbey, Joel H. The Transformation of American Politics, 1840-1860. Englewood Cliffs, New Jersey: Prentice-Hall, 1967.

Simkins, Francis Butler. The Everlasting South. Baton Rouge: Louisiana State University Press, 1963.

_____, and Woody, Robert Hilliard. South Carolina During Reconstruction. Gloucester, Massachusetts: Peter Smith, 1966.

Smeltzer, Wallace Guy. Methodism on the Headwaters of the Ohio. Nashville, Tennessee: Parthenon Press, 1951.

Smith, H. Shelton; Handy, Robert T; and Loetscher, Lefferts A. American Christianity. Vol. II, 1820-1960. New York: Charles Scribner's Sons, 1963.

Smith, James Ward, and Jamison, Leland, eds. Religion in American Life. Vol. I. The Shaping of American Religion. Vol. II. Religious Perspectives in American Culture. Princeton, New Jersey: Princeton University Press, 1961.

Smith, Timothy L. Revivalism and Social Reform. New York: Harper Torchbooks, Harper & Row Publishers, 1965.

Snyder, Louis L. The Idea of Racialism, Its Meaning and History. Princeton, New Jersey: D. Van Nostrand Company, 1962.

Spain, Rufus B. At Ease in Zion, Social History of Southern Baptists, 1865-1900. Nashville, Tennessee: Vanderbilt University Press, 1961.

Stampp, Kenneth M. The Era of Reconstruction, 1865-1877. New York: Alfred A Knopf, 1965.

Strout, Cushing. The New Heavens and New Earth. New York: Harper & Row, 1974.

Swaney, Charles Baumer. Episcopal Methodism and Slavery. Boston: The Gorham Press, 1926.

Swartz, Barbara Meyers. The Lord's Carpetbagger: A Biography of Joseph Crane Hartzell. Dissertation, State University of New York, Stony Brook, 1972.

_____. The Methodist Episcopal Church and the Civil War. Cincinnati: The Methodist Book Concern, 1912.

_____. Religion in the Development of American Culture. New York: Charles Scribner's Sons, 1952.

_____. Revivalism in America. New York: Abingdon Press, 1944.

Sweet, William Warren. Methodism in American History. Rev. ed. New York: Abingdon Press, 1953.

Swint, Henry Lee. The Northern Teacher in the South, 1862-1870. 2d ed. New York: Octagon Books, 1967.

Taylor, William R. Cavalier and Yankee, The Old South and American National Character. Garden City, New York: Anchor Books, Doubleday & Co., 1963.

Tuveson, Ernest Lee. Redeemer Nation, The Idea of America's Millennial Role. Chicago: University of Chicago Press, 1968.

Velde, Lewis G. Vander. The Presbyterian Churches and the Federal Union, 1861-1869. Cambridge: Harvard University Press, 1932.

Weatherford, W. D. American Churches and the Negro. Boston: The Christopher Publishing House, 1957.

White, Bouck. The Book of Daniel Drew. New York: Doubleday, Page & Co., 1913.

Williamson, Joel. After Slavery, The Negro in South Carolina During Reconstruction, 1861-1877. Chapel Hill: University of North Carolina Press, 1965.

Wolf, William J. The Religion of Abraham Lincoln. New York: The Seabury Press, 1963.

Woodward, C. Vann. The Burden of Southern History. New York: Vintage Books, 1960.

_____ . Reunion and .Reaction, The Compromise of 1877 and the End of Reconstruction. Boston: Little, Brown and Co., 1951.

_____ . The Strange Career of Jim Crow. 2d rev. ed. New York: Oxford University Press, 1966.

INDEX

Adams, John 163
Agassiz, Louis 278, 280
Alger, Horatio 64
Ames, Edward R. 39-40, 44
Arnold, S. G. 258, 284-285, 293
Asbury, Francis 149, 151

Bacon, Francis, Lord 132
Baker, Osmon C. 126
Bangs, Nathan 115
Barclay, Wade 110
Barnhart, Kenneth Edwin 6
Beecher, Henry Ward 38, 63, 163
Beecher, Lyman 163
Bidwell, Ira G. 130
Blaine, James G. 15
Bledsoe, Albert T. 49, 275
Boniface VIII 211
Boorstin, Daniel 124
Booth, W. A. 31
Brownson, Orestes Augustus 213
Bryce, James 17, 21
Bucke, Emory Steven 5
Burke, Edmund 132
Burns, Anthony 284
Bushnell, Horace 88-89, 163
Butler, Ben 298-299

Calhoun, John C. 32
Cameron, Richard 108, 221
Cameron, Simon 92
Carter, Hodding 1
Cartwright, Peter 300
Chase, Salmon Portland 150
Clark, D. W. 20
Clark, Robert 156
Clay, Henry 30-32
Clebsch, William 162
Cobleigh, N. E. 281

Coke, Thomas 149, 151
Colfax, Schuyler 276
Crane, Jonathon T. 136, 150
Crooks, George 10, 121, 123, 127, 212-213, 292
Cross, Whitney R. 20-21
Cummings, Joseph 80
Curti, Merle 268
Curry, Daniel 47-48, 82, 87, 117, 121, 126-127, 133-134, 159, 162, 167, 170, 173, 199, 213, 221, 226, 248, 258, 265, 284-285, 287, 291

Davis, Jefferson 125, 220
de Tocqueville, Alexis 145, 293
Diderot, Denis 132
Dorchester, Daniel 111, 115
Drew, Daniel 1, 10, 233
Dunham, Chester F. 88

Eddy, Thomas Mears 1, 11-12, 71, 159, 294
Ehrenstrom, Nils 108
Eliot, Charles W. 15-16, 18
Evans, John 15, 42

Farish, Hunter 265, 297
Fisk, Clinton B. 9, 44-46
Flack, Alonzo 201, 224-225
Foster, Randolph S. 59, 115, 149, 233
Franklin, Benjamin 73, 163
Furfey, Paul Hanley 127

Gibbons, William 233
Glidden, George 278
Godkin, Edwin Lawrence 15-16, 18

339